REINVENTING JUSTICE

PRINCETON STUDIES IN CULTURAL SOCIOLOGY

EDITORS

Paul DiMaggio
Michèle Lamont
Robert Wuthnow
Viviana Zelizer

REINVENTING JUSTICE

THE AMERICAN
DRUG COURT MOVEMENT

James L. Nolan, Jr.

PRINCETON UNIVERSITY PRESS   PRINCETON AND OXFORD

Published by Princeton University Press, 41 William Street,
Princeton, New Jersey 08540
In the United Kingdom: Princeton University Press,
3 Market Place, Woodstock, Oxfordshire OX20 1SY

Second printing, and first paperback printing, 2003
Paperback ISBN 0-691-11475-7

*The Library of Congress has cataloged the cloth edition of this book as
follows*

Nolan, James L., Jr.
Reinventing justice : the American drug court movement /
James L. Nolan, Jr.
    p. cm.—(Princeton studies in cultural sociology)
Includes bibliographical references and index.
ISBN 0-691-07452-6 (CL : alk. paper)
1. Drug courts—United States. 2. Drug abuse—Treatment—
Law and legislation—United States. I. Title. II. Series.
KF3890.N65   2001
364.1′77—dc21   00-051677

British Library Cataloging-in-Publication Data is available

This book has been composed in Sabon

Printed on acid-free paper. ∞

www.pupress.princeton.edu

Printed in the United States of America

10 9 8 7 6 5 4 3 2

To My Parents

Contents

Acknowledgments _____

THIS INVESTIGATION of the American drug court movement benefited from the support of several resources and the help of a number of individuals. The work was significantly aided by the financial assistance of two National Endowment for the Humanities fellowships—one in the summer of 1997 and a second to complete the project during the 1999–2000 academic year. Williams College and then Dean of Faculty, David L. Smith, also supplied useful research support at more than one stage of the project. Several Williams College students provided valuable research assistance, including Meg Davis, Jon Francis, and Joan Walling, while others offered thoughtful contributions in the context of my "Drugs and Society" and "Law and Modern Society" courses. I have several to thank for reading and commenting on all or part of the book manuscript, including Philip Bean, Mary Ann Glendon, Jonathan Imber, Russell Muirhead, and Chuck Slater. Once again, I profited from the support of my colleagues in the Anthropology and Sociology Department at Williams College. Robert Jackall, in particular, offered timely advice at several points in the process.

I'm grateful, too, to Ian Malcolm for his helpful editorial guidance; to the series editors, Paul DiMaggio, Michèle Lamont, Robert Wuthnow, and Viviana Zelizer, for supporting the book as part of the Princeton Studies in Cultural Sociology series; to Jeff Tatum for providing materials from ongoing investigations at one local drug court site; and to Shirley Bushika and Donna Chenail for transcribing and proof-reading numerous interviews (and always with admirable care and good humor). Inestimable credit goes to my wife, Cathy, for her tireless patience, wise counsel, and clear insights. Finally, for welcomed input on this project and so much more, I owe a great deal to my parents—to whom this book is justly dedicated.

Revised portions of chapter 5 appeared in *Stories of Change: Narrative and Social Movements* (Albany: SUNY Press, 2001), edited by Joseph E. Davis. Permission to use this material is gratefully acknowledged.

REINVENTING JUSTICE

Introduction ⸻⸺⸻⸺⸻⸺⸻

> The history of punishment can serve as a lens to
> illuminate major cultural changes in a society.
> —Myra C. Glenn

ONE OF THE MORE interesting and too often overlooked figures in American maritime history is Uriah P. Levy, an enigmatic nineteenth-century Jewish naval officer. Variously described by historians as "pugnacious," "controversial," and "flamboyant," Levy was an anomaly for his time. Few Jews in the early nineteenth century were naval officers. Fewer still rose to the rank of Captain. Uriah Levy's colorful career as a sailor included fighting in the War of 1812, chasing pirates in the Caribbean, surviving a shipwreck off the coast of Honduras, challenging and killing a man in a duel, and saving the life of a fellow U.S. sailor in a Rio de Janiero street brawl. For his heroism in the latter episode and his overall reputation as an exceptional seaman, the Emperor of Brazil offered Levy command of a new sixty-gun Brazilian frigate. Ever the uncompromising American loyalist, Levy turned down the offer claiming that he would "rather serve in the American Navy as a cabin boy than as a captain in any other service in the world."[1] A great admirer of Thomas Jefferson, not only did Levy procure and donate to the U.S. government a statue of the nation's third president, but he purchased Monticello from the debt ridden descendants of Jefferson in 1836 and sought thereafter to restore the beleaguered two hundred-acre estate.[2] His mother, Rachel Levy, is buried on the site, which remained in the Levy family until it was purchased by the Jefferson Memorial Foundation in 1923.

But Levy is perhaps most famous neither for his devotion to Jefferson and curatorial care of Monticello nor for his successes in American maritime, but for the unusual forms of discipline he employed on the ships he commanded. In fact, Levy viewed as among his greatest accomplishments his role in ridding the U.S. Navy of corporal punishment. On his tombstone it is recorded, as directed by his will, "Father of the law for the abolition of the barbarous practice of corporal punishment in the United States Navy."[3] During his life, Levy was known for his opposition to corporal punishment, but he was even better known for the alternative forms of punishment that he imposed. Curiously, in his attempts to stamp out corporal punishment, Commodore Levy reverted to forms of discipline more typical of the colonial period.

Instead of flogging drunken sailors, the usual practice of the time, Levy made each violator wear a black wooden bottle inscribed with the words "punishment for drunkenness" around his neck. Petty thieves would be made to wear a wooden collar or some other badge proclaiming their crime. Those who engaged in fighting would be made to drink a pot of sea water to "cool the blood and clean the stomach."[4] Levy's most notorious act of punishment occurred on 7 July 1839. At the time Levy was the Commander of the *U.S.S. Vandalia*. A mess boy named John Thompson had mimicked a junior officer. For his infraction Thompson was strapped to a gun in front of a crowd of sailors, his pants were then removed, and tar and parrot feathers were applied to his buttocks.[5]

Levy's actions angered many of his fellow officers who eventually had him court martialed. George Hooe, Levy's first lieutenant on the *Vandalia*, formally charged his commanding officer with "scandalous and cruel conduct." The punishment was particularly abhorrent to Hooe because it "humiliated and degraded a sailor in front of his peers." The court reviewing the case upheld Hooe's charges and decried Levy's actions as not only "unusual but wholly unlawful and at the same time exceedingly cruel." And this, because its aim was to "dishonor and degrade" Mr. Thompson.[6] For this incident Levy was stripped of his command and ultimately dismissed from the Navy.[7]

Punishment and Culture

This extraordinary anecdote in the annals of U.S. military history raises several important questions as it concerns the larger issue of the meaning and practice of punishment. Why were Levy's actions viewed as so draconian? More generally, why are some forms of punishment considered acceptable in one period and regarded as scandalous in another? How are we to understand the social acceptance or the implausibility of particular types of social control at different historical moments?

Central to answering these questions is understanding the cultural context within which particular types of punishment are practiced. As sociologists have long held (albeit from varying theoretical vantage points), the moral codes and symbols pervading a particular culture at a particular time greatly influence which behaviors will be regarded as deviant and what types of punishment will be used to sanction them. Today Americans clearly reject the shame-based disciplinary practices of Puritan New England as well as the types of corporal punishment used during the antebellum period. Changing cultural codes of moral understanding have played no small part in effecting departures from these previous practices.[8] But what new disciplinary practices have emerged in the criminal justice system at the turn of the twenty-first century, and how has culture shaped these new forms of social control?

For Uriah Levy to have sent someone to court monitored treatment for drunkenness would have been regarded as just as unacceptable in 1839 as making someone wear a scarlet letter for adultery or disciplining another through some form of corporal punishment would be today. Why would employing Levy's disciplinary practices as well as those he was trying to abolish be regarded as entirely unacceptable in the contemporary United States? Relatedly, what does the current acceptance of alternative forms of social control tell us about contemporary American culture? And how do culturally inspired new forms of legal social control, in turn, shape public understandings of justice, guilt, and crime? A comprehensive examination of the American drug court movement promises to offer insights into these questions.

The burgeoning drug court movement first developed in response to the growing number of drug cases overcrowding America's criminal court calendars. The drug court offers mostly drug offenders the choice of participating in an intensive court-monitored treatment program as an alternative to the normal adjudication process. The innovative adjudicative model draws heavily on the American therapeutic idiom to give direction and meaning to its philosophy, forms, and procedures.[9] Since the first drug court was launched in Dade County, Florida, in 1989, more than eight hundred similar courts have been initiated or are in the planning stages.[10] The model has received almost uniformly positive media coverage and overwhelming public support at both the national and local levels. Judges celebrate the drug court as an exciting movement, a new way of justice, even a revolution in American jurisprudence. Before considering a detailed account of the historical developments that led to the emergence and proliferation of drug courts, we first make some initial forays into several of America's local drug courts, where we find a form of criminal adjudication as dissimilar as one could imagine to the types of punishment practiced by Commodore Levy.

Snapshots of America's Drug Courts

On a summer afternoon in 1998 several dozen drug offenders sat in the Hayward County Criminal Court, situated about forty miles outside of San Francisco. These defendants were participants in Hayward's drug treatment court, presided over by Judge Peggy Hora. After an introduction by the court clerk, Judge Hora entered the courtroom and seated herself behind the bench. Before starting into the court calendar the judge made several special announcements. A drug court participant who had recently passed his GED test was called forward and presented with a graduation balloon. The judge explained that graduation balloons are hard to find in August and that she had trudged through several stores before finally locating one.

The judge then orchestrated a raffle of sorts, where the names from a pool of successful drug court "clients" (as they are commonly referred in the drug court setting) were selected to receive special prizes. One client received four tickets to a Giants baseball game; another, a mug; and another, a hat. After each name was drawn and announced the whole court applauded. The judge then made another special announcement. This day was the last for the drug court defense attorney, who after being with the court since its inception was getting a new assignment. For her service to the court the defense lawyer was awarded a balloon, a cook book, and a certificate. Taken aback, the defense attorney began to cry. She stood up to receive her gifts, then turned to address the audience of drug court participants. "You guys make everything worthwhile," she said. "I want so bad for you all to succeed. We all want you to do what you need to do to get through this. I am going to miss you. This is the hardest part of my reassignment." Appearing touched by the sentiments conveyed, the judge invited participants to come forward and share their thoughts. One participant presented the departing defense attorney with a large cup of cappuccino coffee he had purchased especially for her. Another came forward, hugged the lawyer, and tearfully thanked her for all the help she had been to her and to everyone else in the program.

The judge then began the court calendar. She started with successful drug court clients. Among them was the recent GED graduate, who although he had not used drugs for several months had come up positive for marijuana on his most recent urinalysis test. The judge and this client talked at length about the incident trying to make sense of what triggered the use. According to the client, he had been given a bag of marijuana from a friend for his birthday. The judge mused, "Funny, my friends don't give me marijuana for my birthday." She discussed with the client the problem with having friends who do such things.

Later during the proceedings, another client came before the bench. "Hi dear," he said to the judge. Visibly irritated with the greeting, Judge Hora retorted, "That will be 'judge dear' for you, or how about just 'judge.'" Later another client who had been doing well in the program said, "I'm proud of myself." "You should be proud of yourself" the judge responded. "We are proud of you. You are doing well." To others Judge Hora said things like, "You can get what you want, you deserve it." To others, "I want you to become NORPs—normal, ordinary, responsible people." Throughout the afternoon Judge Hora offered similar admonishments, compliments, and entreaties in her unusual judicial role of directly helping clients in their recovery efforts.

On the other side of the country, in Washington, D.C., a similar court operates under the judicial watch of Judge Stephanie Duncan-Peters. Unlike Judge Hora, who in traditional style sits behind the bench, Judge Duncan-Peters with microphone in hand roams the courtroom like a daytime talk show host. At one drug court session held in the winter of 1996, Judge Duncan-Peters initiated the proceedings with a discussion of two movies the drug court clients had recently seen as part of the drug court treatment program. Of the two movies, the one of greatest interest to the participants was *White Man's Birth*. The mostly African American participants reflected on some of the racial issues raised by the movie; they discussed the problems with racism and the importance of justice and equality. One client talked about the foolishness of acting on impulse. Another discussed the impressionability of children and recognized that using drugs in front of children problematically communicates to them that such behavior is somehow acceptable.

Judge Duncan-Peters customarily conducts talks like this at the beginning of her drug court sessions. She has found movies to be a useful tool in the treatment process. "So I think that's kind of good," she later explained to me of the practice. "It gets them thinking and discussing other things. Obviously they need to talk about their own problems and what leads to them, but I also think it's good to have distractions in life. I've found that if there are periods of your life when you are unhappy, sometimes going out to see an interesting movie or going out with a friend and talking about something else, or going to the gym to work out, these kinds of things can help you through a bad day." This judge, therefore, does not want to focus only on individual problems and strategies for solving them; in addition, she wants to give clients, through watching movies and other activities, the "ability to see something else that might challenge their minds and distract them in a positive way from their problems."

After discussing the movies, Judge Duncan-Peters then called up individual clients who were on the drug court calendar. One client summoned, a Mr. Taylor, was moving to a higher level in the treatment program that day. Drug court programs typically have several levels of treatment through which clients progress as they successfully comply with the treatment regimen. The following exchange transpired between Judge Duncan-Peters and this advancing client.

> DUNCAN-PETERS: How are you doing today Mr. Taylor?
> TAYLOR: All right.

DUNCAN-PETERS:	And you are moving up to level three, having survived level two. So, how are you feeling?
TAYLOR:	Feeling good.
DUNCAN-PETERS:	Feeling good? How come?
TAYLOR:	I'm moving.
DUNCAN-PETERS:	You're moving up. Moving up in the world. Moving up and out of the program. Keep on going. And that gives you a good feeling, right? Well, you got some words of advice for these other folks that are trying to move up to where you are?
TAYLOR:	Stay focused.
DUNCAN-PETERS:	Stay focused. Yep. How long have you had a problem with drugs?
TAYLOR:	Not long.
DUNCAN-PETERS:	Not too long. Not too long. Think you are going to be able to make it a permanent good-bye to these drugs?
TAYLOR:	Yeah, as long as I got these court dates. [Laughter in audience]
DUNCAN-PETERS:	Even if you don't have them, do you think you are going to be able to stay off of them even if you don't have the court building, and you don't have to come back to court except for good reasons?
TAYLOR:	I ain't coming back.
DUNCAN-PETERS:	No way, huh. Well, here is your mug, and here is your certificate. Congratulations.

At this point everyone in the courtroom applauded. These kind of exchanges with clients are typical in Judge Duncan-Peters's drug court. Later in the session another client, a Mr. Stevens, was called forward and had the following discussion with the judge.

DUNCAN-PETERS:	Where is Mr. Stevens? Mr. Stevens is moving right along too. Right?
STEVENS:	Yep.
DUNCAN-PETERS:	How come? How come it is going so great?
STEVENS:	I made a choice.
DUNCAN-PETERS:	You made a choice. Why did you do that? Why did you make that choice? What helped you to make up your mind to do it?
STEVENS:	There had to be a better way than the way I was doing it.
DUNCAN-PETERS:	What was wrong with the way you were living? What didn't you like about it?
STEVENS:	It was wild.

DUNCAN-PETERS:	It was wild, like too dangerous? Is that what you mean by wild?
STEVENS:	Dangerous.
DUNCAN-PETERS:	Too dangerous, for you personally, like a bad roller coaster ride. So, what do you think? Is this new life boring?
STEVENS:	No, not at all.
DUNCAN-PETERS:	Not at all. What do you like about the new life?
STEVENS:	I like it better than the old.
DUNCAN-PETERS:	Even though the old one was wild, the wild was kind of not a good wild. You like this way.
STEVENS:	I love it.
DUNCAN-PETERS:	You love it. Well, we're glad that you love it. We're very proud of you. In addition to your certificate, you're getting your pen which says, "I made it to level four, almost out the door." How about that? Anybody in the program that you are helping out a little bit, do you think?
STEVENS:	Trying to help everybody if I can.
DUNCAN-PETERS:	Trying to help everybody if you can. Well, hopefully you are helping them, because I think that it is interesting for them to hear what you feel about having given up this old style, and starting a new one.

Mr. Stevens was also applauded by everyone in the crowded courtroom for his efforts. The judge proceeded through the court calendar and had similar exchanges with other clients. To those who were doing well and graduating to higher levels of treatment, she offered certificates, mugs, pens, and words of encouragement.

Judge Stanley Goldstein presided over the Miami, Florida, drug court from its inception in 1989 until his retirement in 1999. A crusty exprosecutor and street cop, Goldstein would mix tough talk with words of encouragement in discussions with his clients. Between exchanges, he offered commentary, even short sermons, about the harms of drug use, the efficacy and basic focus of the drug court program, and his personal concern for the clients' success in drug court. During a January 1995 court session, for example, he explained: "This is a two part program. First is to get you off drugs. Second is to teach you how to live in this world. The first lesson you learn is you follow the rules." Later during the same session he offered the following.

Let me tell you guys something. I told almost everyone of you when you came in here, there ain't no other way. Any other way out of here and you lose. You stay being a junky: you lose, I win. You die: I win, you lose. You burn your brain out: you lose, I win. Forget about it. You hate me, want to get even with me? Quit using drugs, and get yourself a good job. Then you get even with me. I love you. I want everyone here to beat me into the ground with goodness.

A female defendant stood before Judge Goldstein. "You looked in the mirror lately?" he asked her. "Yeah," the client responded with a smile. "Nice, huh?" Goldstein continued. Again, the client smiled and answered, "Yeah." "Keep it up baby," Goldstein offered before calling up another client. To another participant who had not been doing so well he implored, "When are you going to stop using cocaine? I can't stop it for you. Nobody can stop it for you. You have worked hard enough to get yourself into Phase III. You're getting pretty close to graduation, and you got to go out and use cocaine. Are you a little baby? Do I have to treat you like a little baby. Huh? Say no more. I will see you back here in sixty days." To another who had also had a recent failure in the program, Goldstein exhorted, "Any problem you got, you come to me. I'm your Daddy. . . . You're a little baby. Hey little baby boy. There is only one way to stop and that is to stop. And it is going to hurt. It is going to hurt a lot of ways. You got three options: You can die. You can go insane. You can quit. Knock it off. Knock it off."

To a client holding a young child Goldstein instructed, "Stop thinking about yourself all the time. You're going to make that kid a junky by going out and having a good time for a couple hours. You're dirty every day and you're killing your baby." Another client who stood before Goldstein was accompanied by her mother and asked the judge if she could graduate from the program early. Goldstein explained, "The deal was one year. The statute says one year. . . . Okay? You look beautiful. You looked like hell when I first saw you. Your gorgeous." Then to the mother standing beside the client, "What did I tell you? Didn't I tell you I'd give you a new daughter? Right out of the factory." To another client who unexpectedly came into contact with drugs, Goldstein warned, "What do you do at a party and someone lights up? Get the hell out of there. If you're in a car and someone lights up? Get the hell out of there."

During the court session Goldstein reflected on his experience in the drug court program and on his previous experience in a regular criminal court. "I used to sit up here and try cases. And I had big jury trials, with murderers, and with robbers, and all of this crap. And I put people away for seventy years and seventy-five years." During those years in a regular criminal court, Goldstein explained, he found his work profoundly unsatisfying. "It never made me feel like I did anything. . . . I was taking one jackass off the street, that was all." With the drug court, contrastingly, "I walk out of this program almost everyday and feel like I have accomplished something. If I save one guy a day I'm happy. It took me awhile to realize that you can't save everybody. Some of them just ain't got it. . . . Some people I praise. Some people I try to insult. Some people, I'll try anything, anything that might work."

These examples provide just a glimpse into the unique character of the American drug court model. The chapters that follow consider in more detail the various qualities and consequences of this new form of criminal adjudication. Such an examination aims not only to explicate the defining features of the drug court movement and the reasons behind its widespread proliferation but to make sense of its effects, both practical and theoretical, on legal and public understandings of justice.

A Note on Method

The findings reported in this book are based upon ethnographic observation of drug courts throughout the United States. In the four-year period between August 1994 and August 1998, I visited twenty-one different drug courts in a total of eleven different states and the District of Columbia. The drug courts I visited varied by region. Seven were in the Northeast, six on the West Coast, five in the Mid Atlantic region (i.e., Maryland, Delaware, Virginia, and the District of Columbia), and three in the South. The courts also varied with respect to the size of the locations in which they were situated. Twelve of the courts were in large urban areas; five were in rural regions; three were in midsize cities of around 100,000 residents; and one was in an outlying suburban area of a Northeastern city. The courts also varied with respect to how long they had been in existence, varying from first generation drug courts to courts that were still in the planning stages. Eleven of the courts I visited had been in existence for more than one year; eight had been in existence for less than a year; and two were still in the planning stages.

At each of the drug courts, I conducted a face-to-face open-ended interview with the judge. I also had occasion to interview three other judges whose drug courts I did not visit. In all, I formally interviewed twenty-four different drug court judges. At the drug court locations, national drug court conferences, and mentoring court programs I attended, I also formally interviewed or had informal discussions with dozens of other drug court officials, including district attorneys, public defenders, treatment counselors, private attorneys, program coordinators, evaluators, and acupuncturists. I also, on occasion, had informal conversations with drug court clients.

At each court I visited, in addition to interviewing the judge, I talked with other drug court officials, and if allowed, visited one of the outside-of-the-court treatment sites serving the drug court. The treatment modalities that I observed included acupuncture sessions, Alcoholics/Narcotics Anonymous meetings, group counseling sessions, and a probationary/treatment introductory meeting. At five of the courts I was invited to sit in on the preliminary meetings preceding the drug court session. At these meetings the judge and other drug court officials discussed each of the clients who would be appearing in the drug court that day.

In addition to visiting individual courts I also attended three national drug court conferences; one in Portland, Oregon, in December 1995; one in Washington, D.C., in May 1996; and another in Washington, D.C., in June 1998.[11] At the conferences, I attended lectures and panel discussions featuring key players in the drug court movement; I interviewed drug court officials; and collected valuable written materials from drug courts throughout the country. I also attended two training or mentoring court programs. Mentoring courts are drug courts that have been in operation for several years and have been designated as locations where emerging courts can visit and receive training in the operation of a drug court. I attended a training session in Louisville, Kentucky, in April 1996, and another in Rochester, New York, in June 1997. There were representatives from five courts at the Louisville program, and representatives from twelve courts at Rochester.

Finally I participated in the planning stages of a local drug court (near where I lived at the time) over a period of approximately four months. Officials had heard about my research from another court in the state and invited me to be on their planning board. We made a deal of sorts. They would allow me to sit in on their planning meetings, some of which I was allowed to tape-record, and they could draw upon the "expertise" I had acquired from having visited other courts around the country. My contribution was limited basically to a short presentation at one meeting, where I briefly described the features and structure of four other courts I had recently visited. On occasion they would ask me a question about how other courts operated, but for the most part I remained a very quiet observer.

With the exception of drug court client/defendants, all drug court officials and drug court sites identified in the book are actual names and places. I provide pseudonyms for any drug court client whose behavior is discussed or whose words are quoted in this book, the only exception being names cited in already public sources (e.g., justice department reports or newspaper descriptions of individual drug courts).[12]

I should note that, by in large, I found the people in this movement to be courteous, welcoming, and accessible. I also found drug court movement activists to be earnest, committed, and sacrificially generous in the amount of time and energy they devoted to the drug courts. I imagine that some may be disappointed by what they find in this book. It is not a celebration of the movement, but neither is it a policy oriented debunking of the movement. Rather it seeks to place the phenomenon in a broader socio-historical context, and it attempts to bring to the surface what might be some of the unintended consequences of the drug court move- ment as it relates to practical and theoretical understandings of justice. In any respect, I am very grateful for the level of access I was afforded by a group of hardworking and dedicated people, and hope that, even if not satisfied with the sociological focus of the analysis, drug court officials will find my treatment of their words and of the broader movement to be fair and even handed.

Forecast

Again, the book is not a policy statement, though it may have certain policy implications. Any program alternative to the drug court, however, is not given specific articulation. Furthermore, while the book touches upon issues of efficacy in certain contexts, the project is not an analysis of the utility of the drug courts, which has been the focus of most academic investigations of the drug court movement to date. A question about whether the drug courts work is certainly a valid question in its rightful place, but it is not the inquiry pursued here, nor is it, I would argue, the more important question to ask of the movement.

Rather, the book seeks to understand the movement against the back- drop of the history of the social control of drugs in the United States and to understand the consequences of this judicial innovation on the pro- cesses of criminal adjudication and on social and legal understandings of justice. Toward this end, chapter 1 begins with a review of the various legal responses to drug use during the twentieth century leading up to the years just prior to the drug court movement. Chapter 2 considers in some detail the initiation and expansion of the drug court movement by exam- ining the structural and cultural causes of the movement, an analysis which reveals limitations in the conventional political categories typically used to make sense of phenomenon like the drug court. Chapter 3 investi- gates the unique features of the drug court theater, that is, the radically redefined roles of the various actors in the courtroom drama and the sub- sequent tensions sometimes created by these new roles.

The next three chapters consider some of the intended and unintended consequences of the drug court model. Chapter 4 evaluates the extent to which the drug court, particularly as it concerns the new role of the judge, departs from the American common law tradition. Chapter 5 analyzes the centrality of storytelling to the drug court drama and considers the extent to which the poignancy of a "good story" becomes an increasingly plausible criteria for evaluating the success of judicial programs. Chapter 6 assesses the manner in which a growing number of criminal behaviors (not just drug offenses) have, in the context of the drug court, been redefined in pathological terms, thus making increasingly obsolete—both philosophically and practically—the legal salience of "guilt."

Finally, the last two chapters specifically focus on the meaning of justice. Chapter 7 situates the drug court within a broader discussion of philosophical and cultural understandings of the goals of punishment, moving from the retributivist theories of Kant and Hegel in the early modern period to the "rehabilitative" ideal of the first part of the twentieth century. Chapter 8 investigates the manner in which the drug court's quintessential embodiment of therapeutic jurisprudence theory represents a significant break from previous understandings of the purposes of punishment and criminal adjudication. Taken together, the unique qualities and consequences of the drug court movement portend to redefine the very meaning of justice.

The new form of legal social control represented in the drug court movement is not perceived today as "cruel and unusual" as Uriah Levy's disciplinary practices were in his time. The absence of protest, however, says as much about American culture and its understandings of punishment and justice as did the hostile reaction to Levy's actions. At an earlier moment in American history, one could imagine a very different reaction to the drug court movement. Today, however, the widespread popularity of the drug court movement suggests that its defining philosophy and forms are consistent with the dominant sensibilities of American culture, a theme to which we will return in the pages ahead.

One _____

Drugs and Law

AN HISTORICAL PERSPECTIVE

> America has a long history of drug use—
> sometimes rich and colorful, other times ugly
> and tragic. . . . Americans grappled with drug
> use using moral suasion, medical treatment,
> legislation, and education. These efforts have
> sometimes succeeded, sometimes failed, and
> sometimes been at odds with each other.
> —Patricia Tice

THE HISTORY of the social control of drug use in America is a long and somewhat complicated story. Different systems of moral understanding have informed social responses to drug use in varying ways over time. Recognizable in public debates during the nineteenth and twentieth centuries and in the scholarly literature on the topic are three distinct "root metaphors" or "legitimizing values" that have informed efforts to socially control drug use in the United States.[1] The cultural dominance of one metaphor over another has played a critical role in shaping the direction of drug policy.

The first legitimizing value that has influenced public views on drug use is the moral or the religious perspective. According to this value system, the use of drugs is immoral. That drug use is morally wrong is a judgment that, according to William Eldridge, "lies in the ethical and philosophical foundation of our moral and religious culture."[2] From this point of view, the individual is responsible for his or her actions, and drug use represents decidedly irresponsible behavior. As conceived within this paradigm, the use of drugs is an evil, a bad habit, a weakness in virtuous character, a vice which leads to further debauchery and immorality. In the United States, "ultimate philosophical and religious tenets" have played "a large part in the social judgment concerning narcotics."[3]

The second value that has informed the social control of drug use in American society is the therapeutic paradigm. From this perspective individuals who use drugs are not immoral. Instead they are understood to have a disease or disorder that needs some form of treatment. The disease interpretation of drug use can be divided into two categories—the physiological and the psychological. During the nineteenth century and first part of the twentieth century, medical treatment of drug users was pursued primarily through the application of some type of physical remedy. Only later did the psychological or, more specifically, the psychoanalytic model become the dominant medical approach to treating drug users.

The third legitimizing value that has shaped popular and legal views on drug use is the utilitarian perspective. Most commonly, the utilitarian orientation has provided a basis for opposing the use of drugs; from a utilitarian perspective, drug use is believed to inhibit the efficient and productive capacities of a modern capitalist society. As Wayne Morgan observes, to Americans the use of drugs solely for the sake of pleasure "seemed especially unsuitable to a modernizing industrial society whose success depended on hard work, rationality, and the mastery of complex facts."[4] The use of drugs for the purposes of pleasure, therefore, were seen as incompatible with "a system that rested on efficiency, rationality, and predictability."[5] Likewise, Howard Becker points to our "strong cultural emphasis on pragmatism and utilitarianism" to explain why "Americans usually feel ambivalent about ecstatic experiences of any kind" including drug use.[6]

Utilitarianism, however, has also been drawn upon to resist legal regulation of drug use on the grounds, for example, that heavy taxes on pharmaceutical products hurts the pecuniary interests of drug manufacturers and retailers. Pharmaceutical companies in the latter part of the nineteenth century derived substantial profits from importing, processing, and selling opiates. As one late-nineteenth-century pharmacist explained of his economic dependence on the sale of opiates: "If it were not for this stuff and my soda-water I might as well shut up shop."[7] As we will see, the utilitarian argument has remained an enduring theme in discussions about drug policy, including most recently in public advocacy of the drug court movement.

Social responses to the use of drugs has relied on each of these legitimizing values in varying ways throughout American history. Different institutional spheres draw more heavily, though certainly not exclusively, on one legitimizing value over the others. For example, most central to the legal system, historically, has been the moral or religious orientation. For the majority of the twentieth century the makers and the enforcers of law ignored the medical community's disease view of drug addiction. In fact, the law's involvement in this area of American social life is a relatively new one. Prior to the turn of the century the legal system played virtually no role in controlling the use of drugs. Up to that time the medical and pharmaceutical communities regulated drug use, and the legitimizing value most central to the medical community was the therapeutic perspective. Finally, the pharmaceutical community has been informed in large measure by the utilitarian perspective, in that pharmacists were (and remain) concerned with making a profit.

Since particular metaphors are more dominant in certain institutional spheres than others, the question of which institution has authority for controlling drugs plays a significant role in determining how drug use will be interpreted and controlled. As Bakalar and Grinspoon put it, "Disputes about when drug use is illness and when it is crime are often in effect jurisdictional disputes between the medical and police professions."[8] In other words, a profession's basic history, structure, and institutional focus will dispose it to one perspective over another, and, correspondingly, the dominant societal interpretation of drug use will depend in part upon which institution regulates drugs.

Legal responsibility for drugs did not really begin until the first part of the twentieth century. The story of the drug courts is the final stage of a process whereby meaning systems whose public expression historically rested in two distinct institutional spheres—the moral/religious in the legal and the therapeutic in the medical—came together. Both institutions served the societal function of socially controlling drug users, but they did so in fundamentally divergent ways and with little philosophical common ground or structural overlap. To tell the full story of the social control of drugs in the United States, therefore, one must necessarily begin with an examination of medical efforts in the nineteenth century, which not only provided the primary means by which drug use was socially controlled in the nineteenth and early twentieth centuries but which also embodied the evolving therapeutic perspectives that would eventually find a more central place in the adjudication of drug offenders in the American criminal justice system—an evolution that would ultimately find its fullest expression in the burgeoning drug court movement.

Medical Social Control

As mentioned above, during the second half of the nineteenth and the first two decades of the twentieth centuries the principal means by which Americans addressed the use of narcotics was through the authority and practices of the medical community. Many argue that physicians played a major role in creating the problem of drug addiction, particularly morphine addiction.[9] Unaware of the harmful and addictive qualities of morphine, physicians prescribed the drug for a number of ailments, most popularly in the forms of laudanum or paregoric.[10] For example, just prior to the Civil War, Oliver Wendall Holmes, Sr., then Dean of Harvard

Medical School, asserted that "the constant prescription of opiates by certain physicians . . . has rendered the habitual use of that drug . . . very prevalent."[11] During the Civil War morphine addiction became so widespread among soldiers, who were given it to relieve the pain of battlefield injuries, that it became known as the "army disease."[12] John Burnham estimates that by the end of the nineteenth century "approximately 200,000 Americans were addicted to opium in one form or another."[13]

In this first period of the social history of narcotics control in the United States, the medical community focused most of its efforts on finding a physiological cure to the problem of addiction. Implicit in this approach, of course, was the belief in the disease view of drug addiction. Consider the stated position of the *American Textbook of Applied Therapeutics* from 1896: "Morphinism is a disease both of the body and the mind, caused by chronic poisoning by morphine. When the disease is developed there exists an irresistible craving for the drug, and it is this artificial appetite that is the chief difficulty to be overcome in the treatment."[14]

Explanations for the disease of drug addiction varied. Some held that opiates and alcohol caused a physiological change in the nervous system that actually created in the user the perception that a state of normality could only be achieved through continued use of the substance. Even if initial use was only experimental, the drugs effected a physical alteration that created a irresistible physical compulsion. This "craving," as C. L. Case argued in 1910, was "a physical condition," just as real as "typhoid fever or pneumonia."[15] Others held that addictive tendencies were hereditary. Not unusual, for example, was the opinion of the physician, J. B. Mattison, who in 1876 wrote of "a well-marked hereditary tendency towards a debilitated state of the nervous system" among addicts,[16] or William G. Thompson's views expressed in the 1902 *Text-Book of Practical Medicine* that victims of morphinism are "those who have a strong neurotic inheritance . . . and often give evidence of feeble will-power by addiction to other habits."[17]

In short, drug addiction was understood to be a physical disease.[18] The few physicians who disagreed with this position, including Dr. Charles W. Earle, recognized that they were in the clear minority. Writing in the *Chicago Medical Review* in 1880, Earle expressed a view reflecting a moral/religious perspective, where he compared drug use to alcohol consumption, gluttony, licentiousness, and other "habits frequently followed with dreadful results." Drug use, according to Earle, was not a disease that excused the individual of responsibility for his or her actions. "That the responsibility of taking the opium or the whiskey, or the gluttonous use of food . . . or the undue and unbridled gratification of the sexual passions, is to be excused and called a disease, I am not willing for one moment to admit, and I propose to fight this pernicious doctrine as long as it is necessary." But Earle fully realized that few of his colleagues shared his perspective. "I am aware," he wrote, "that I am expressing an opinion at variance with that believed by the majority of the profession."[19]

In keeping with the disease view of drug addiction accepted within the medical community, physicians sought to discover a medical curative to the problem. Among the plant derived substances experimented with to conquer opiate, bromide, and morphine addictions were coca (or cocaine), cannabis, and *Viola Sagittata*, also called "husa." Synthetic opiate derivatives were also used as hoped-for remedies, including codeine and then later heroin.[20] As is well known today, many of these ostensible antidotes simply replaced previous addictions with new ones. Use of these and other substances were often combined with the voluntary removal of the patient to a rural retreat site or sanitarium for treatment. An estimated one hundred of these sanitariums existed by 1910.[21]

One of the most famous sanitariums was the Keeley Institute in Dwight, Illinois. The treatment regimen developed by Dr. Leslie E. Keeley in Dwight and, then subsequently, at franchises in most major cities in the United States, combined the prescribing of Keeley's famous and secret "Bichloride of Gold" remedy with a kind of treatment program foreshadowing practices more common today. In addition to receiving regular doses of Keeley's secret formula, visitors to the Dwight Center encountered self-help philosophies, group therapy sessions, and other treatment modalities of the late twentieth-century type. Still, Keeley's approach, like most in the late nineteenth century, was fundamentally geared toward curing what practitioners believed was a physiological, rather than a psychic, disease. Though Keeley, and others like him, employed therapeutic methods implicitly oriented toward psychological processes, fundamentally "Keeley believed that inebriety had a physiological basis."[22]

After years of experimenting with different medical antidotes, however, physicians largely failed to discover a medicinal remedy to the problem of narcotics addiction. "By the beginning of the new century, addicts and experts alike had experimented with almost everything that conceivably could affect the withdrawal process. There was no magic bullet."[23] At this time, around 1920, the psychological explanations for addiction emerged as plausible replacements to the failed physiological explanations and treatments. Beginning in 1920 "psychoanalysis could be invoked as an explanation of dysfunction and as a source of effective therapy."[24] In an important 1920 American Medical Association (AMA) report, the medical community argued that it was the "newer psychology" of "psychoanalysis" that now provided "the greatest hope for salvation" to the habitual drug user.[25] Given the admitted failure of physical remedies, treatment would therefore turn to psychology and psychiatry to guide its curative efforts.

Ironically, the shift from physiological to psychological explanations for drug addiction facilitated the emergence of legal and political involvement in the social control of drugs. The strictly physiological explanation necessitated strictly medicinal remedies, including maintenance prescriptions and clinics. The psychological interpretation, on the other hand, though it explained addiction through reference to psychoanalytic symbols, viewed the behavior as an intolerable menace. Having admitted that ambulatory treatment had "proved a failure . . . and should be forbidden," the most important goal to the medical community in 1920 was "to get the patient off the drug as soon as possible."[26] Therefore, both law enforcers and advocates of the psychoanalytic approach interpreted drug addiction as deviant behavior in need of control. As David Musto notes, the psychological interpretation of drug addiction as deviance "lined up the AMA leadership and federal antinarcotic agencies on the same side."[27]

The alliance was, however, tenuous at best. Though there was common ground in the medical and legal interpretations of drug use as something in need of termination, there were wide differences in how to handle the drug addict. Not only did the legal world not adopt the medical world's shift to psychological explanations for addiction, it largely ignored the disease concept of addiction altogether, choosing instead to draw upon a perspective derived from a moral or religious interpretation of the behavior.

Legal Social Control

Government involvement in narcotics control was initially spurred by international developments, which themselves were born out of religious predilections. Opium use first emerged as an issue of national concern following the U.S. acquisition of the Philippines in 1898, when it was discovered that the territory had a serious problem with opium addiction. Individuals such as the Episcopal Bishop to the Philippines, Charles H. Brent, believed the United States had a "moral duty to abolish the opium trade."[28] Moreover, with the sour memory of its nineteenth-century Opium Wars with Great Britain, the Chinese government, in the first decade of the twentieth century, remained concerned with its own opium problem and sought to restrict the importation of the drug from India— its not always welcomed supply source for many years. Pressured by "missionaries and other reformers" to "foster a liberalism in China that accorded with Christian values" and recognizing an opportunity to garner useful ties with China, President Theodore Roosevelt supported efforts to regulate narcotics use on an international scale.[29]

Toward this end Roosevelt requested of Congress $20,000 to support three commissioners who would investigate the opium problem in the United States, China, and surrounding East Asian countries and prepare for an international conference on the subject. The commissioners included Bishop Charles Brent; Dr. Hamilton Wright, a politically ambitious medical doctor; and Dr. Charles Tenney, a former missionary to China. Bishop Brent was asked to chair the commission.[30] By July 1908, all three delegates had accepted their appointments and began preparing for the international conference to be held in Shanghai, China, in the beginning of the following year.[31]

Thirteen nations attended the Shanghai conference, which commenced on 1 February 1909 and continued for approximately four weeks.[32] Because of its status as a "commission," conferees were only given the authority to make recommendations rather than a binding international treatise. Nevertheless, several recommendations were agreed to by the represented nations, including resolutions for each government to regulate and suppress opium use in its own country, to "reexamine" its laws, and to disallow the exportation of opium to countries that prohibited its importation. During the meetings delegates from the United States pressed for the scheduling of another international meeting, one with the status to impose more binding international restrictions.

The Shanghai meetings provided the impetus for the introduction of new federal legislation. Leading the effort on the domestic front was Hamilton Wright, who argued for federal restrictions that would further prohibit the nonmedicinal use of narcotics in the United States. A little over a year after the Shanghai conference, legislation was introduced that, if approved, would control the manufacturing and interstate trafficking of "habit-forming" drugs in the United States both by requiring the Bureau of Internal Revenue to register and collect annual taxes from drug retailers and wholesalers and by prohibiting nonregistered procurers from the interstate trafficking of such drugs as opium, chloral, and coca.

The legislation, introduced on April 30, 1910 by Congressman David Foster of Vermont, never made it out of the House Ways and Means Committee. However, the Foster bill was the direct antecedent to the most transformative piece of narcotics legislation in the history of U.S. drug laws, namely the 1914 Harrison Act. The Harrison Act represented what was in essence the narcotics equivalent to the 1919 Volstead Act. Significant for the purposes of this study, however, were the Congressional discussions about the Foster bill, which provide a glimpse into the manner in which political/legal efforts were informed by moral and religious ideals.

Status Politics and Anti-Drug Law

Before analyzing the substance of Congressional discussion of the Foster bill and other narcotics legislation, it is worth reviewing what others have identified as an important motivating force behind narcotics legislation. One could argue that another legitimizing value that justified the expansion of state efforts in the control of narcotics use was the Protestant establishment's concern with the unfamiliar behavior of immigrants and other non-"WASP" classes. That is, inasmuch as the use of drug behavior was endemic to a particular marginalized but growing class, legal efforts to restrict drug use was actually an implicit effort to "normalize" these classes and to restore the dominant values of the establishment. This "status politics" argument was made famous in Joseph Gusfield's 1963 analysis of the Prohibition effort. Gusfield argues that prohibitionism was really a consequence of nativist, rural, Protestant Americans threatened by a growing urban class of mostly Catholic immigrants and their alleged cultural propensity to consume alcohol. Others have noted the applicability of this explanatory scheme to the antinarcotics efforts of the early twentieth century.[33] Just as prohibitionists were ostensibly threatened by the alcohol-consuming practices of Catholic immigrants, antinarcotics reformers, it is argued, were anxious about large-scale opium use among Chinese immigrants and cocaine use among Southern blacks.

Though class issues, as such, may have played some role in the antinarcotics efforts, the relevance of the status politics model is problematized by empirical evidence that suggests that consumption of drugs in the second half of the nineteenth century and beginning of the twentieth century was not really class specific. Consider one of the earliest discussions of the so-called opium problem put forth in 1867 by Fritz Ludlow: "The habit is gaining fearful ground among our professional men, the operatives in our mills, our weary serving women, our fagged clerks, our former liquor drunkards, our every day laborers, who a generation ago took gin. All our classes from the highest to the lowest are yearly increasing their consumption of the drug."[34] If anything opium use was highest among the upper and middle classes. As John Burnham notes, late nineteenth-century addicts were "the middle and upper classes, respectable people."[35] Troy Duster likewise asserts, "The evidence clearly indicates that the upper and middle classes predominated among narcotic addicts in the period up to 1914."[36] That drug use was most popular among the upper classes calls into question the extent to which "status anxiety" was a motivating factor in antinarcotics efforts. Nevertheless, Troy Duster, among others, still attempts to explain early twentieth century anti-drug efforts as a class issue.

In Gusfield's analysis of the prohibition movement, status politics was a driving force behind the successful efforts to make alcohol illegal. Because the middle class continued to consume alcohol after 1919, the legitimacy of the Eighteenth Amendment was undermined, thus leading to its eventual repeal in 1933. Following Gusfield, but reversing the order of events, Duster argues that the passage of the Harrison Act in 1914 contributed toward a transformation in the consumptive habits of Americans. That is, after 1914 drug use became more pervasive among the lower classes. Only after this shift, according to Duster, was drug consumption perceived as a moral problem and as an activity common to the criminal class. Prior to 1914, when drug consumption was mostly a middle-class phenomenon, it was not seen as a moral issue. As Duster puts it, "The federal law of 1914 was therefore enacted prior to strong moral judgment about heroin use *per se*." Only after passage of the Harrison Act was the drug addict "placed in a class of law-breakers, and . . . associated with the underworld and its 'immoral' non middle-class elements."[37] Linking social responses to drug consumption in this way, Duster, like Gusfield, depicts the moral indignation toward consumptive habits as essentially a matter of middle-class values.

Such a class-based perspective is problematic for several reasons. First, Duster's analysis doesn't really explain why there was enough popular support for passage of the Harrison Act in the first place. It is as though the law just came into existence independent of the dominant values of American citizens. Yet passage of the Harrison Act was preceded by more than a decade of national discussion and several decades of international attention to the problem of opium use. Second, it understates the significance of important cultural factors that may more properly be understood as forces independent of class differences.[38] Finally, and related to the second reason, the empirical evidence simply does not support Duster's assertion that prior to 1914 "there was no moral stigma attached to such narcotics use."[39] To the contrary, as revealed through Congressional deliberations leading up to passage of the Harrison Act, among other sources, moral concerns were a dominant force behind anti-narcotic efforts and served as an important justificatory theme supporting passage of the legislation.

The Foster Bill

Moral concern was certainly evident in discussions about the Foster bill in 1910 and 1911. In the House hearings on the Foster bill, drug users were variously referred to as "dopes," "fiends," "dope fiends," and "habitués." The "secret and vile habit" of drug use was described as "nefarious and soul destroying," as an "evil," a "curse," a "vice," and as that which led to "debauchery" and "crime." An initial review of discussions during the hearings about drug use among Chinese and Southern blacks appears to offer some support to the status politics thesis. That is, use of both cocaine and opium were practices associated with certain marginalized racial groups.

For example, Dr. Christopher Koch, President of the Philadelphia Association of Retail Druggists, testified before the House Ways and Means Committee that cocaine was widespread among Southern blacks. "The colored race in the South," Koch argued, "is very much perverted by cocaine." He stated further that "colored people seem to have a weakness for it," that use of cocaine results in a disregard "for right and wrong," and that "a great many of the southern rape cases have been traced to cocaine."[40] Hamilton Wright testified to similar developments. "This class of negro . . . is known to have become debauched by cocaine."[41] Wright asserted further, "The cocaine habit is greatly increasing in the South. . . . I have most reliable evidence that the crime of rape has largely been caused by the use of cocaine among the Negroes in the South in the last 10 or 15 years."[42]

Reformers worried that drug practicing habits among these groups would ultimately corrupt the white middle-class population. According to Wright, cocaine use was spreading to "our large cities" and was being used in the "white-slave traffic to corrupt young girls" who once habitually hooked on cocaine would in a "short time . . . fall to the ranks of prostitution."[43] The same kind of anxieties were expressed about opium use. Wright, for example, noted that though opium was largely "confined to the criminal classes and the lower orders of society," it was beginning to creep "into the higher circles of society."[44] Koch specifically delineated the process whereby white women were drawn into the world of opium use by Chinese men.

> There is one particular [opium] house where I would say there are 20 white women living with Chinamen as their common-law wives. The Chinamen require these women to do no work, and they do nothing at all but smoke opium day and night. A great many of the girls are girls of family, and the history of some of them is very pathetic. You will find those girls in their younger days went out with sporty boys, and they got to drinking. The next step was cigarettes. Then they go to the Chinese restaurants, and after they go there a couple of times and get a drink in them they want to "hit the pipe." They do it either out of curiosity or pure devilishness.[45]

Implied in these comments, of course, is a fear that habits perceived as common to particular marginalized classes threatened to corrupt the values and practices of the more mainstream white establishment. That advocates of narcotics legislation sometimes played off of these fears is difficult to ignore. Apparently, class concern played some role in legislative efforts. However, drug use itself—rather than the practices of a particular class—seems to have been the perceived evil of greatest concern. In several instances reformers actually pointed to the white middle class, and its corrupting influence, as the real culprit.

For example, Wright argued that it was the contractors in the South who distributed cocaine "among the lower order of their workers" to "stimulate them" and "get more work out of them."[46] Wright even speculated that cocaine was being "forced by contractors on the humble negro worker" to get "more and better work" out of him.[47] Similarly, Koch asserted that it was the "manufacturers and wholesalers, the people higher up" who were selling "these drugs promiscuously." As such, "the poor unfortunate 'dope fiend'" according to Koch, "is more sinned against than sinning." Furthermore, it was because of a lack of "conscience" and "moral" restraint that these "higher ups" were willing to sell and distribute drugs, thus leading to habitual drug use among the lower classes in the first place. Because of the manufacturer's failure on "moral grounds" to institute "sufficient safeguards" against the indiscriminate distribution of narcotics, it was therefore "the duty of the Government to compel him to do it by law."[48]

The Foster bill, therefore, was defended according to moral categories, and lack of moral fortitude, according to testimony, was not a problem exclusive to the marginalized classes. No classes were spared judgment. "Large numbers of all social ranks," Wright claimed, "had become debauched by the misuse" of habit forming drugs.[49] And it was the ranks of the upper classes, in particular, who were seen as the primary perpetrators of this evil. Moreover, drug use was understood to contribute to further criminal behavior among all classes. "Quite apart from the criminal classes it converts the useful, orderly citizen who has become a habitué into a dangerous character. It wrecks him individually and jeopardizes the position of all who depend on him, and in the end drives him to crime."[50] Therefore, though the status politics argument may be helpful in explaining what may have been very real concerns among some in the white Protestant establishment, we cannot understand advocacy of restrictive narcotics legislation exclusively, even primarily, as a product of "status anxiety."[51] Rather, traditional religious morality was offered as a dominant justificatory language to support the Foster bill, and, from the words expressed by reformers, this was a moral problem that largely cut across class lines.

It was, however, the legitimating value of utilitarianism that would win the day in the debate over the Foster bill. Testifying before the House Ways and Means Committee in December 1910 and January 1911 were scores of representatives from pharmaceutical and drug manufacturing companies. They repeatedly argued that though they favored restrictive narcotics legislation generally, the Foster bill contained requirements that were too cumbersome and expensive. Drug retailers and manufacturers "opposed the record keeping, taxation, and potential loss of business" the bill would effect.[52] Typical, for example, was the complaint offered by Albert Plaut, a representative of Lehn and Fink of New York. "The reputable element in the drug trade—and that means the vast majority—has always been in favor, of a proper law, a practicable law, which will regulate and diminish the use of habit-forming drugs. But we want it stripped of all these useless, expensive, and annoying requirements which our theoretical friends consider necessary."[53]

Much to the disappointment of Hamilton Wright and other reformers, further restrictive legislation would not pass through the U.S. Congress before the gathering of the next international anti-narcotics conference, scheduled to meet at The Hague of the Netherlands in December 1911. Nevertheless, the conference would proceed in spite of the absence of national laws, a situation which would slow the ability of the United States to secure internationally binding restrictions, so it was believed.

On December 1, 1911, representatives from twelve countries convened for what would be the first of three international conferences held at The Hague. Chairing the first conference was again Bishop Brent of the United States. Hamilton Wright along with Henry J. Finger, a California pharmacist, made up the rest of the American delegation. At this first Hague convention, delegates from the various countries agreed to rigid stipulations restricting the production and international trafficking of opium, cocaine, and morphine, and signed an agreement toward this end on January 23, 1912. With the goal of garnering wider international support, a second convention was scheduled for the following year. The July 1913 convention was followed by a third in 1914. Over time international support for opium restrictions increased. Ultimately the Hague Convention was made part of the 1919 Treaty of Versailles. From the first Hague meeting in 1911 to the Treaty of Versailles and beyond, these international agreements remained a source of pressure on the United States to intensify its own domestic drug policy.

One example of this pressure is found in the regret expressed by William Jennings Bryan, then Secretary of State to President Woodrow Wilson, in a letter to Congress dated April 21, 1913. Bryan noted that the United States led international effort to suppress the "opium evil" had resulted in "improved domestic legislation in nearly all countries concerned." Disquieting to Bryan, however, was that the United States was not among these, that Congress had failed to take "definitive action for Federal control of the opium and allied traffics in the United States."[54] Only a little over a year after Bryan's letter, however, Congress would finally pass what has come to be recognized as the most important legislative directive in the history of American legal efforts to control narcotics.

The Harrison Act

In response to pressure from international efforts, Congress passed the Harrison Act on December 14, 1914. It was signed into law by President Woodrow Wilson on December 17, and took effect on March 1, 1915. The Harrison Act had three central provisions. First, it mandated that anyone purchasing and distributing narcotics must register with the federal government. Second, those registered to handle the sale and distribution of drugs must pay a special tax. Enforcement of the bill accordingly was established under the aegis of the Bureau of Internal Revenue within the Treasury Department; an institutional location, as we will see, that would have important consequences. Third, the Harrison Act provided that narcotics could only be prescribed by physicians acting "in good faith" and "in the course of his professional practice."[55] The interpretation of these phrases would prove critical in the ultimate direction of drug policy in the United States.

By loosening the more restrictive requirements of the Foster bill, the Harrison Act passed through Congress with little opposition and with very little debate about the "problem" of drug use in the United States. Instead, discussion focused on the rather narrow issue of international treaty obligations. Arguments that were put forth, however, did reflect the same moralistic concerns that characterized discussion of the Foster bill. That is, the bill was defended according to the legitimizing value of morality, and the drug problem was perceived to transcend class differences. Consider, for example, a 1913 defense of the measure by Representative Francis Harrison, the bill's sponsor. "There has been in this country an almost shameless traffic in these drugs. Criminal classes have been created, and the use of the drugs with much accompanying moral and economic degradation is widespread among the upper classes of society. We are an opium-consuming nation today."[56]

The lack of intense debate had more to do with general agreement about the drug issue than it did with some kind of public indifference regarding congressional debate over the measure, as Duster suggests. In other words, a development whereby narcotics became perceived as a "major moral problem in the minds of Americans" did not unwittingly originate with passage of the Harrison Act.[57] Rather, as the record demonstrates, public sentiments regarding the moral status of narcotics use not only *followed* passage of the Harrison Act but *preceded* it, and indeed justified it. As Wayne Morgan concludes, "The law represented a popular consensus against drug addiction and the drug experience that had been building since the 1870s. It was the result of incremental growth in regulation, from local ordinances to a national law. . . . It represented general public fear of disorder and inefficiency, and the belief that society could purify individual conduct in the name of a common good."[58]

Though Duster overemphasizes the class issues related to the Harrison Act, he is certainly correct in his assessment of the critical changes in handling drug offenders that the new law effected. Because the law was technically a tax measure, it would be handled by the Treasury Department. Consequently, the institutional control of drugs was effectively shifted from the medical community to law enforcement, and the legal world would handle drug offenses in the same way that it handled all offenses. As Morgan observes, "Accustomed to dealing with smugglers, tax evaders, moonshiners, and similar lawbreakers, Treasury personnel could not see addicts as medical patients or drug use as a health problem."[59] Thus, what was for years handled as a medical issue became a legal issue, and law enforcement agencies—accustomed as they were to handling offenses according to morally defined legal categories—addressed drug use as they did any other crime, as an indictable offense.

After passage of the Act the government, therefore, began to prosecute physicians, druggists, and addicts who continued to prescribe, sell, purchase, and use drugs now deemed illicit. Prosecutors did not view prescriptions for maintenance as a legitimate medical purpose. The courts, however, at least initially, tended to interpret the law as strictly a revenue measure and were reluctant to view as criminal the act of prescribing drugs to addicts. The Supreme Court took this basic position in its first ruling on the measure in the 1916 *U.S. v. Jin Fuey Moy* decision. In this case a Pittsburgh area physician had prescribed small amounts of morphine to an addict. In a 7–2 decision, the Supreme Court ruled that the Harrison Act did not give the government authority to prosecute addicts in what it viewed as primarily a revenue matter. For Hamilton Wright and other supporters of narcotics legislation, this ruling represented a disappointing setback. However, it would only be short lived.

Even after *Jin Fuey Moy*, prosecutors continued to go after doctors for prescribing what they viewed were illegitimate purposes. As Congressman Henry Rainey put it, "After the decision in the *Jin Fuey Moy* case . . . there was nothing left of the [Harrison] act." Therefore, officials were left to "just bluffing the thing through."[60] For prosecutors this "bluffing," along with the 1919 passage of two Rainey sponsored amendments to the Harrison Act, paid off. Three years after the *Jin Fuey Moy* decision, the Supreme Court handed down two critical rulings, both on January 16, 1919: *U.S. v. Doremus* and *Webb et al. v. U.S.*

The former involved a San Antonio physician, Dr. Charles T. Doremus, who had provided morphine tablets to a known addict. The government argued that though the Harrison Act was technically a revenue measure, "it also had the moral purpose of discouraging the use of the drugs except as a medicine."[61] In a 5-4 decision, the Court upheld in *Doremus* the constitutionality of the Harrison Act and recognized the government's role in regulating this feature of medical practice. In *Webb*, also in a 5-4 decision, the court specifically ruled that it was illegal for a physician to provide drugs to an addict for maintenance purposes. To conclude that a legitimate physician's prescription could be interpreted to include the maintenance of an addict's drug habit would, according to the Court in *Webb*, "be so plain a perversion of meaning that no discussion of the subject is required."[62] These decisions affirmed the prosecutorial bite of the Harrison Act and gave the federal government the authority to indict physicians, pharmacists, and addicts who continued to sell and use drugs. The court essentially ruled that drug addiction was not a medical but a legal issue.

The Jones-Miller Amendment

The strength of moral/legal (along with the persisting influence of utilitarian) views of drug control during this period is evinced further in discussions about an amendment to narcotics laws first considered by Congress in 1920, the year following the *Webb* and *Doremus* decisions. A group of some 450 business leaders from the Seattle area known as the China Club were concerned that narcotics manufactured in the United States were being legally exported to other countries, particularly Japan, and then smuggled back into the United States and into China for consumption, a practice that essentially exploited a loophole in U.S. drug policy. Concerned about the negative effects of drug use in China (primarily because of trade interests) and the United States, the China Club successfully persuaded Representative John Miller and Senator Homer Wesley Jones, both from Washington state, to propose legislation that would prohibit the exportation of narcotics from the United States. A subcommittee of the House Ways and Means Committee heard testimony on the Jones-Miller amendment in December 1920 and January 1921.

As with congressional debate over the Harrison Act, much of the discussion over the Jones-Miller amendment centered on the technicalities of international treaties (e.g., compliance with the Hague Convention and the Treaty of Versailles), rather than the "problem" of drug addiction per se. Nevertheless, some of the testimony before the House subcommittee reveals the extent to which a moral rather than a therapeutic or medical view informed legal understandings of drug trafficking and consumption.

Representative Miller, for example, spoke of drug use as a "wicked habit," and the "nefarious" trafficking of drugs as a "damnable menace."[63] Dr. Howard A. Kelly, a Professor Emeritus in gynecological surgery from Johns Hopkins University, also spoke in moralistic terms. Kelly argued that escaping from morphine addiction "involves not only medical treatment in order to bring about a separation from the drug but it involves a sort of moral status in the persons who desire to cooperate with the doctor."[64] From experiences in his own practice he observed that it was "easy to tell in a few days whether a patient has any moral resistance to cooperate with the doctor; otherwise, it is utterly impossible to do anything with them."[65] That he saw drug addiction as a moral issue was made even more evident when in his testimony he associated it with other "vices," like "race-track gambling," "prostitution," and "prohibition" issues. He admonished Congress to put out the word on these "great evils." "I would appeal to everybody who occupies a high position to send out the message to the Christian people—let it be a message from the United States Government, which professes to be based on Christianity—asking them to cooperate and to get it right in the hearts of the people, and let it go out from such a body as this, from Congress at large, to all of the Christian people and to the churches, which are asleep as to these great evils, these great moral questions which face us."[66]

Also testifying before the House subcommittee, a Frank Chase of Boston, in rather poetic terms, cited Shakespeare and Kipling to illustrate the "measure of degradation that dope produces upon man." In describing his encounters with drug addicts in the Boston area Chase likened himself to the children in Dante's *Inferno* who would say to each other, "There goes a man who has been in hell."[67] Even the Assistant Surgeon General, Dr. J. W. Schereschewsky, testified in support of the amendment on the grounds that drugs were "extremely bad for the individual" and resulted in "physical and moral deterioration." Moreover, according to Schereschewsky drug addiction is a "very destructive habit and one that is bad for the country."[68]

Therefore, discussion of drug addiction, by both those inside and outside the medical community, leaned toward the moralistic rather than the therapeutic perspective, at least as put forth in this legal setting. The general disregard of the medical perspective was made most apparent in the testimony of a proponent of the disease view. Though testifying in support of the proposed measure, Dr. Charles E. Terry, a New York City physician representing the American Public Health Association, expressed deep frustration with public understandings of addiction and the corresponding application of drug laws based on these understandings.

Terry lamented, "Heretofore the narcotic-drug control problem has been considered a purely police problem and . . . it has been delegated to the police department, when as a matter of fact it is strictly a medical and public health problem."[69] Comparing drug addiction to venereal disease, Terry argued further, "There is no other disease we would attempt to regulate for a moment solely by police measures. Even venereal diseases, where the occasion of the disease is *prima facie* evidence of immorality, we do not attempt to regulate simply by police measures."[70] The issue, according to Terry, was that in administering the Harrison Act, the pathological view of drug addiction was being ignored. In sum, the problem, as Terry saw it, was that "one million, possibly more, sick men and women in this country . . . under the administration of the law are not receiving proper treatment because expert medical advice has not been consulted in the administration of regulations over a strictly medical topic."[71]

Though treated with collegiality by the committee, Terry's medical advice was received in a manner commensurate with his own diagnosis of the situation. As David Musto puts it, "[Terry] was heard politely by the Congress but without any sign of agreement,"[72] illustrating once again the extent to which the legal world was at this point largely indifferent to therapeutic interpretations of drug using behavior.

Narcotic Clinics and Hospitals

Once the Supreme Court ruled in *Webb* that doctors could not prescribe narcotics for the purpose of maintaining a drug addict's habit, physicians generally retreated from the practice of providing narcotics to patients for this purpose. State and local government officials feared that as a consequence they would have large numbers of addicts in their localities whose only option would be to secure drugs through illicit means. In response to this fear, some states and cities established drug distribution clinics between 1915 and 1923. In all some forty-four such clinics were established in forty different cities during this period, with New York having more than any other state. The ostensible purpose of the clinics was to maintain addicts until they could get into some form of institutional treatment and/ or to help cure them of their addictions. It was an effort which proved highly controversial. Clinics did little in the way of treatment and were unsuccessful in curing users of their addictions. They were also plagued by allegations of political impropriety, and the inflated salaries of clinic physicians did little to assuage public concerns.

Because drug users were not being cured of their addictions, Treasury Department officials concluded that the clinics were nothing more than maintenance centers for addicts. Supported by the Supreme Court's interpretation of the Harrison Act in *Webb* and *Doremus*, the Treasury Department threatened to bring charges against the clinics if they did not close. By 1925 all the clinics had shut down.

Several years later Congress again attempted to provide some kind of treatment for addicts. Given the direction of drug policy, it is not surprising that the treatment offered would find its place in a legal rather than a medical context. In 1928, Congressman Stephen Porter introduced legislation to establish narcotic farms for drug offenders. Though Public Health Service officers were asked to run the farms, administration of the narcotic farms ultimately fell under the auspices, once again, of the Justice Department and the new Federal Bureau of Narcotics, established within the Treasury Department in 1930. The Porter bill became law in 1929, and within the next decade two narcotics farms were built, one in Lexington, Kentucky, in 1935 and one in Fort Worth, Texas, in 1938.

The narcotics farms had the same fate as the general application of the Harrison Act. That is, the legal community did not recognize, understand, or take into consideration the therapeutic view of drug addiction. Instead, drug addicts sent to these hospitals were essentially treated like offenders in any other prison. Again, it is not that the legal community was openly hostile to the treatment perspective, but rather that the medium of law was at this time neither based on a therapeutic paradigm nor prepared to communicate a distinctly therapeutic message—at least as it concerned the handling of drug offenders. Therefore, even when a legal structure was conceived for the ostensible purpose of providing treatment, as it was in the case of these narcotic farms, the therapeutic message could not be conveyed. In this instance the medium of criminal justice thwarted the message of therapy.

Though Lexington and Fort Worth aimed to be hospitals, they ended up being nothing more than glorified prisons for drug addicts. As Wayne Morgan writes of the two experimental efforts, "For all the efforts at humane and individualized treatment, the farms were modified prisons, complete with walls and bars. The aura of law enforcement and social quarantine remained strong." Thus, in spite of the medical intentions behind the effort, the "national emphasis on law enforcement" prevailed.[73] Physicians hired to run the farms felt disaffected and forced to deliver services oriented more toward law enforcement than medicine. In short, the "hospitals" amounted to little more than "additional prison space for convicted addicts."[74]

The Anslinger Era

At the time the narcotic farms were finally built, legal control of drugs in the United States had already come under the influential leadership of a man who would symbolize the direction of drug policy for the next three decades. In 1930 Harry J. Anslinger, a former Prohibition officer, was appointed the first U.S. Commissioner of Narcotics and remained in the position until 1962. Though he did not so much shape as reflect popular attitudes towards drugs, his reign as "federal narcotics czar" defined an era when the approach toward drug policy became harsher and more oriented toward law enforcement than ever before. While U.S. narcotics laws tightened, discussion continued in the therapeutic communities about the psychological basis of drug addiction, though it had little impact on the legal system. As illustrated even in the most therapeutically oriented programs of the period, law enforcement remained the *modus operandi* for national drug policy. Anslinger continued in this basic direction, believing that the most effective way to handle drug using behavior was "a policy of high fines and severe mandatory prison sentences for first convictions."[75]

Anslinger and his agents worked with state authorities to strengthen state laws, an effort aided by the 1932 National Conference of Commissioners on Uniform State Laws which passed and endeavored to promulgate a Uniform Narcotic Drug Act. By 1937 many states had even made marijuana illegal, a substance not identified in the original Harrison Act. In 1937 Congress passed the Marihuana Tax Act, "designed to stamp out use of the drug."[76] As with other features of drug control, Anslinger followed rather than determined popular sentiments toward marijuana. Politically astute, Anslinger was reticent to initiate legal management of something as widespread and difficult to control as the marijuana plant. Given growing public antipathy to marijuana, however, he eventually became an important spokesman for federal legislation suppressing its use. As Morgan notes, "He seemed to respond more to pressure for legislation that came from local and state authorities than to seek it himself."[77] Nonetheless, once he ascertained that popular sentiments favored restrictive measures toward marijuana use, he became a forceful public advocate. Shortly before passage of the Marihuana Tax Act, for example, Anslinger wrote, "How many murders, suicides, robberies, criminal assaults, hold-ups, burglaries, and deeds of maniacal insanity [marijuana] causes each year, especially among the young, can only be conjectured."[78]

Such a calculated response to public attitudes was typical of the politically savvy Anslinger during his reign as the United States' first drug czar. Even Edwin Schur, a critic of Anslinger and an advocate of a medical approach to U.S. drug control, concedes that Anslinger, "could never have pushed through his policies if they had not conformed with the public disposition."[79] It was a cultural disposition that largely favored a moral—waning though it may have been—rather than a medical understanding of drug abuse; a perspective which, again, was reinforced by the institutional location of drug-controlling efforts in the legal community. Anslinger himself made this very point in 1957 when responding to the issue of whether drug addiction might not best be understood as a psychiatric issue. Equating drug addiction with "hoodlumism," Anslinger stated, "In a sense it may be true that every hoodlum is a psychiatric problem, but in a practical sense one must treat the bank robber, the gambler, and thief as criminals."[80] In other words, inasmuch as the law enforcement world is asked to handle a matter, including drug using behavior, it does so according to the practical demands of standard operating procedures. Such a perspective, not surprisingly, exasperated those in the medical community. Dr. Lawrence Kolb of the U.S. Health Service perhaps put it best when in 1961 he wrote, "People with only a police training have secure commanding positions in the formulation of narcotics policies; sound medical opinion based on careful research is cried down or ignored."[81]

Up until the 1960s this, most assuredly, was the case. During the World War II and postwar period, federal narcotics laws would continue to ignore the medical perspective and would become even more severe than before. One could say that a purely legal perspective on drug use reached its apex during this period. Consider the views of an official from the Boston office of the U.S. Attorney's office in 1943. According to this spokesperson, the drug problem was "primarily—I might say almost wholly—a law-enforcement matter, and resolves itself into one of control of narcotic addiction through control of illicit narcotic traffic. The medical aspects are merely incidental and supplementary."[82] This basic sentiment certainly colored drug policy through the 1950s, when two of the most punitive measures in U.S. drug policy history were approved by Congress. In 1951 Congress passed the Boggs Amendment, which established stiff mandatory minimum sentences for drug offenders. Then in 1956 it passed the Narcotics Drug Control Act which gave juries the option of the death penalty for the sale of drugs to minors and allowed federal narcotics agents to carry firearms. Morgan concludes of the era, "the consensus against drug use and for enforcement seemed stronger than ever."[83]

The Emerging Dalliance

Just when the legal system seemed fully immune to any consideration of the disease view of drug addiction, the Supreme Court rendered a decision in apparent conflict with the basic trajectory of drug policy over the previous fifty years. In 1962, the same year that Henry Anslinger finished his tenure as Commissioner of Narcotics, the Supreme Court handed down a decision that would open the door for greater cooperation between law and therapy, as it concerned the issue of drug regulation. The reasoning offered in the decision foreshadowed the kind of philosophies that would guide the practices of drug courts. In *Robinson vs. California* the court ruled that drug addiction was not in itself a crime—that to convict and sentence someone for a drug addiction was cruel and unusual punishment in violation of the Fourteenth Amendment.

More important, however, was the reasoning offered in a concurring opinion by Justice William Douglas. First, Douglas states that he does "not see how under our system *being an addict* can be punished as a crime." He then compares drug addiction to insanity. "Each has a disease and each must be treated as a sick person."[84] Douglas affirms the disease view of drug addiction. However, the disease view, according to Douglas, does not eliminate the need for social control; rather it provides a new guiding philosophy for it. Just because the drug addict is sick, according to Douglas, does not eliminate the need for confinement. "He may, of course," Douglas opines "be confined for treatment or for the protection of society." What Douglas objects to regarding the California statute in question is that its purpose is "not to cure, but to penalize." As long as curing is the goal, confinement is fully acceptable. Thus, what is "cruel and unusual" about the punishment, according to the court, is not "confinement," but "convicting the addict of a crime." The latter results in "stigma and irreparable damage to the good name of the accused," while the latter can be justified "as a means of protecting society."[85] Thus, the disease view is used to interpret drug use but not to eliminate the possibility of involuntary treatment.

Four years after *Robinson* Congress passed the 1966 Narcotic Addict and Rehabilitation Act which gave the courts statutory authority to commit drug offenders involuntarily to residential and outpatient treatment programs as an alternative to incarceration. With these legal changes in place the stage was set for greater cooperation between the justice and therapeutic communities. During the 1960s, California, New York, Massachusetts, and Illinois established involuntary civil commitment programs for drug offenders, the practices and philosophies of which interestingly foreshadowed some of the same themes and concomitant tensions between justice and treatment that would define the drug court movement of the 1990s.[86]

In the civil commitment programs, for example, residents were viewed in pathological terms. Consequently, program length was sometimes indeterminate (a resident was released when "cured," not according to a fixed sentence), and the criteria for evaluating success was made problematic (i.e., should the relapse of a disease constitute failure).[87] Moreover, all aspects of the program were conceived as part of the therapeutic enterprise, and clients were "forced to maintain the appearance of a strong commitment to the therapeutic principles."[88] Complying with the overall treatment regime and telling the right story, therefore, was often a vital prerequisite for release (as reflected in the "pet phrase" of California program residents: "If you wanta walk, you gotta talk").[89] Civil commitment schemes also, in some instances, had net-widening qualities. For example, a California program included offenders with prostitution charges (albeit, when drug use was suspected), resulting in concerns about civil liberties violations.[90] As we will see, similar issues are evident in the contemporary drug court movement. The civil commitment programs attempted during the 1960s, however, were short-lived, limited in number and size, and "of dubious effectiveness."[91]

Court diversion programs initiated just after the civil commitment projects, on the other hand, were longer lasting and much more widely disseminated. Among the more important of these was TASC (Treatment Alternatives to Street Crime), a court diversion system initiated in 1972 by the Nixon administration in association with the Law Enforcement Assistance Administration (LEAA).[92] In the same year, the first TASC program opened in Wilmington, Delaware. Within six years the LEAA had funded seventy-three projects in more than twenty-four states, and by August of 1991 there were 178 TASC programs in thirty-two states.[93]

TASC serves the purpose of linking the justice system with the medical community. Instead of proceeding through the traditional adjudication process, a drug offender who qualifies for TASC is diverted to treatment for a specified period of time. TASC serves the function of placing the client in an appropriate treatment program. Upon completing the program TASC redirects the client back to court where some kind of disposition is served, usually the dismissal of a charge, the reduction of a sentence, and/or the expungement of an arrest. TASC, as such, establishes a link, conduit, or bridge between the judicial and treatment communities. As Matthew Cassidy, Associate Executive Director of TASC, explains, "TASC provides an objective and effective bridge between two groups with differing philosophies: the justice system and community treatment providers. The justice system's legal sanctions reflect community concerns for public safety and punishment; whereas the treatment community recommends therapeutic intervention to change behavior and reduce the suffering associated with substance abuse and related problems."[94]

TASC is the natural precursor to the drug courts in several important ways. First, the rationales offered for starting TASC were similar to those eventually used to justify the initiation of the first drug court programs. Because of punitive drug laws, especially those passed in the 1950s, the criminal justice system was becoming overwhelmed with drug offenders. TASC was initiated, in part, as an effort to relieve the justice system of low-level drug offenders. As Johnson and Waletzko write, "It was becoming increasingly evident that longer, harsher jail and prison terms were resulting in overcrowded jail cells, burgeoning prisons, unwieldy court calendars, and the related higher cost to state taxpayers."[95] TASC, it was argued, would take pressure off the system.

Also like the drug courts, TASC clients were offered the incentive of having "their charges dropped and their criminal record expunged upon successful program completion."[96] Additionally, TASC foreshadowed developments in the drug court movement, as we will see, in that once underway, the parameters for program qualification expanded over time. As Johnson and Waletzko put it "a 'net-widening' effect occurred with TASC to include . . . others previously not considered appropriate candidates for treatment under the original model."[97] Most importantly, however, TASC laid the foundation for a closer link between the treatment perspective and criminal justice as it concerned the social control of drugs. It provided the first step in drawing together the historically disparate institutions and the distinct root metaphors that defined them.

However, TASC differed from the drug court in one very important way. In the former, treatment was still structurally separated from the adjudicative process. Conducting the treatment were those trained in the therapeutic community. Having served the time in treatment, the client was released or returned to the court where a legal decision was made. Justice and treatment remained separate entities, serving distinct, though more directly linked, functions. In the drug court, justice and therapy are no longer separate enterprises. Instead they are fully merged into the common endeavor of therapeutic justice.

It should be noted, before proceeding to a discussion of the emergence and widespread proliferation of drug courts in the United States, that the convergence of law and therapy as manifested in the drug court movement is distinct from what has come to be known as the "rehabilitative ideal," a defining feature of the American criminal justice system during much of the twentieth century until it first came under criticism during the late 1960s and early 1970s. Curiously, rehabilitative justice took hold at approximately the same time that drug laws were first established and then progressively strengthened in American criminal law. As we will consider in the last two chapters of the book, however, the "rehabilitative ideal" is distinguishable from the "therapeutic ideal"—as realized in the drug courts and related developments—in important ways.

Very briefly, applications of the rehabilitative ideal were most often realized in postadjudicative settings, that is, in probationary practices, prisons, and parole policies, whereas the therapeutic ideal realized in drug courts is played out in the adjudicative process itself. Even where the rehabilitative ideal did influence courtroom practices, as in the juvenile courts of the first part of the century, it did so, as we will see, in ways distinct from the drug courts. Moreover, though related in certain

respects, there are important differences between the ideological substance of the rehabilitative and therapeutic idioms. Where the former can
be characterized by the corrective, reformist tendencies of what John
Steadman Rice refers to as therapies of "adaptation," the latter, with its
focus on the emotivist concerns of the esteemed self is more commensurate with Rice's description of the newer therapies of "liberation."[98]

Francis Allen, in what is perhaps the most careful analysis of the decline of the formerly dominant rehabilitative ideal, observed in 1981 the
curious process whereby the rehabilitative ideal in American criminal law
precipitously fell out of favor at the same time that "therapeutic man"
emerged in a new "psychocivilized" society. So important is this "new
psychologism," according to Allen, that he identifies it as one of the principle characteristics of contemporary American culture and as "sharply
distinguishable" from the rehabilitative ideal.[99] The drug court movement, as will be made clear, is the institutionalization of the "new psychologism," or what I have referred to elsewhere as the "therapeutic
ethos." The drug courts are, in fact, a direct and pure application of a new
theory of "therapeutic jurisprudence" first promulgated in the early
1990s. The differences between these two cultural/legal impulses will be
considered more fully in chapters 7 and 8, where the consequences of
rehabilitative justice are directly compared to the outcomes of therapeutic
jurisprudence, as manifested in the drug court movement.

One final and rather obvious difference between the two judicial forms
is worth noting. Namely, in the case of the drug courts, therapeutic tendencies were introduced into the criminal justice system via the growing
"problem" with drug use in American society. The rehabilitative ideal, in
contrast, was a more general judicial approach not related to a particular
type of criminal activity. It therefore follows that to make sense of the
birth and expansion of the drug court movement, one must necessarily
understand the history of drug control (legal and otherwise) in the United
States—our concern in this chapter—and the particular pressures that
ultimately led to the initiation and widespread adoption of drug courts in
the United States—our focus in the next.

Two

The Drug Court Movement

All human behavior occurs within sociotemporal
contexts, and a full understanding of social
phenomena requires knowledge of the zeitgeist—
the general intellectual, moral, and cultural
climate of the time—in which that behavior
occurs. In the context of this discussion, the
phenomenon is something called drug courts.
  —James A. Inciardi, Duane C. McBride, and
    James E. Rivers

As mentioned in the introduction, the first drug court was established in
Dade County, Florida, in 1989.[1] Janet Reno, Florida's State Attorney at
the time, was among those who spearheaded the effort. In response to the
growing number of felony drug cases in Miami, Associate Chief Judge
Herbert Klein of Florida's Eleventh Circuit was commissioned to study
the problem and offer an alternative approach. Klein's proposal led to the
initiation of America's first drug court—a judicially supervised treatment
program for drug abusing offenders. In the United States, since 1989,
more than eight hundred similar courts have been started or are in the
planning and implementation stages, and more than one hundred and
forty thousand individuals have been enrolled in a drug court program.
Drug courts have been launched in all fifty states as well as in the District
of Columbia, Guam, and Puerto Rico. To support and provide leadership
to this burgeoning judicial development, some two dozen legal practitioners, mostly judges, gathered in 1994 to start a national association for
professionals involved in drug courts. Just two years later, nearly seven
hundred drug court practitioners gathered for the second annual conference of the National Association of Drug Court Professionals (NADCP).
By 1998 more than 2,500 drug court professionals attended the fourth
annual conference of the NADCP, and in 1999 attendance at the annual
conference exceeded three thousand.[2] The rapid expansion of the drug
court model has led participants and observers alike to label the phenomenon a "movement," even a "revolution" in criminal justice.[3]

The drug court offers drug offenders the option of court monitored
treatment as an alternative to the normal adjudication process. The drug

court differs from TASC in that the court rather than a treatment center is the focal point of the treatment process. Defendants participate in various treatment modalities, including acupuncture, individual and group counseling sessions, and Alcoholics Anonymous (AA) and Narcotics Anonymous (NA) 12-step groups. Offenders also submit to periodic urinalysis testing and regularly (every one to four weeks) report back to the judge, who oversees their overall treatment program. The program is usually expected to last one year but often lasts much longer. Most drug courts offer defendants, as an incentive for participation, the dismissal of their criminal charge or the expungement of their drug arrest upon successful completion of the program.

To participants who succeed in the program—for instance, graduating to a higher level (courts may have as many as three or four stages of treatment)—judges offer praise, applause, and prizes. Among the small incentives judges might hand out for good performance are T-shirts, key chains, donuts, pens, mugs, colored star stickers, and candy. Graduation ceremonies are celebrated with cake, speeches, graduation certificates, individual testimonies by graduates, and visits from politicians and other local dignitaries. Failure to comply with treatment, on the other hand, can result in the imposition of sanctions, which may come in the form of increased participation in 12-step groups, community service, one or two days sitting in the jury box during drug court sessions, or short stints (usually lasting several days to two weeks) in the county jail (what Judge Stanley Goldstein in Dade County euphemistically calls "motivational jail" or "my motel").

The drug court fundamentally alters the traditional adjudication process. For example, the relationship between the judge and defendant/client fundamentally differs from that of a normal criminal court. The judge engages the clients directly, asks personal questions, and encourages them in the treatment process. Judges interact with clients in a manner more like proactive therapists than dispassionate judicial officers. The role of attorneys is also substantially different in the drug court than in a traditional court. Not only is the relationship between public defender and prosecutor no longer adversarial, but lawyers generally play a less prominent role. In many drug courts the lawyers do not even show up for the regular drug court sessions, and even when they do, it is often difficult to determine just which persons in the courtroom are the attorneys.

Though all the courts follow the essential style and format established in the Dade County model, each drug court has its own unique features that depend on funding, the level of community support, personnel, and other contingencies. As Philip Bean puts it, "What one finds is that there are as many variations in the locus of Drug Courts within the legal system as there are Drug Courts themselves."[4] Among the important differences are the criteria that each court uses for determining the eligibility of potential participants. According to a 1997 Justice Department survey of ninety-three operational drug courts, 12 percent of the courts allow only defendants with no prior criminal record. Another 26 percent restrict eligibility to defendants with three or fewer prior offenses. The remaining 57 percent accept individuals with any number of prior offenses, as long as they meet all other eligibility criteria. Among the factors that might disqualify an otherwise eligible participant are gang membership, additional pending cases, and out-of-county residence. Approximately 40 percent of the courts have, since initiating their program, expanded their eligibility criteria, a process of extension similar to what occurred in TASC programs. Most, though not all, courts limit participation to nonviolent offenders.[5]

Courts also differ with respect to the point in the criminal justice process when the client is first admitted to the program. Approximately 30 percent of the drug courts are pretrial/preplea; that is, defendants enter the drug court program before trial and before entering a plea. Another 16 percent of the courts are pretrial/postplea. In these courts, defendants enter a plea (usually "guilty") and are then assigned to the drug court. Upon successful completion of the program, their plea may be stricken. In 12 percent of the courts, participation is post conviction. In these courts the program is essentially, if not actually, a condition of probation. The remaining 42 percent use some combination of the above three categories, depending upon the nature of the charge, the defendant's criminal history, and other factors.[6]

Courts also differ with respect to the types of agencies they employ to provide treatment to drug court clients. The majority (over half) contract for treatment services with local community-based or private treatment organizations. Another 14 percent use county health departments. Handling treatment services in other drug courts are probation departments (9 percent), pretrial service agencies (2 percent), or the court itself (8 percent). TASC still handles the treatment function for a few drug courts. Available to the courts through these services are both outpatient and residential treatment services; even some jails used by the drug courts have in-house treatment services. Again, the kind and availability of the treatment services varies from court to court. Not all, for example, have residential, jail, or acupuncture treatment services.[7] In spite of these differences, most drug courts follow the same basic philosophy and "contain certain essential elements."[8]

The drug court has received considerable local, state, and national support. Attorney General Janet Reno, national "drug czar" General Barry McCaffrey, Florida Governor Jeb Bush, and President Bill Clinton have been among the strong supporters of the program.[9] The U.S. Department of Justice opened a Drug Courts Program Office in 1995, through which planning, implementation, and enhancement grants for existing or emerging drug courts have been awarded. Funding for these grants has increased steadily since the Drug Courts Program Office was established. In fiscal year 1995 the office granted $12 million in grants to drug courts. This increased to $15 million in 1996, to $30 million in both 1997 and 1998, and then to $40 million in 1999.

Support for the programs, however, is not limited to the federal level. While about half of the drug courts have received some kind of federal funding, either from the U.S. Department of Justice (Drug Courts Program Office) Grant Program, the Byrne Grant Program, or through Local Law Enforcement Block Grants, 40 percent of the courts have been at least partially funded by state support, either through state substance abuse agencies or other state funding sources. Other jurisdictions have raised money through special tax assessments, asset forfeiture funds, or fees collected from drunk driving or traffic schools. Some courts have even taken the unusual step of raising money through private, usually locally based, foundations. Even bankrupt Orange County, California, started a drug court without any initial state or federal government support.[10]

Thus, interest in and support for the drug court is pronounced both nationally and locally. As Tim Murray, former director of the Drug Courts Program Office, put it, "It's probably the only movement in the judicial system that has bubbled up from the grassroots to the Federal government."[11] Louisville drug court judge Henry Weber observes the same, asserting that apart from receiving some federal dollars, the drug court movement is "a grassroots kind of movement. It's not something where the bureaucrats in Washington tell you what to do. Each community has developed its own program for its own particular needs and they all deal with it on a local level. . . . It's totally a grassroots kind of thing."

That the drug court phenomenon is a movement within the criminal justice system makes it somewhat anomalous according to conventional social scientific conceptions of social movements. Typically, social movements are conceived as collective social behavior seeking to effect change from outside the political processes. In the case of the drug court movement, contrastingly, the major agents of change are the political (or, more specifically, the judicial) actors themselves. "The Drug Court movement is essentially a judge-led movement."[12] Court officials (internal to the judicial process) often seek to gain support from the public (external to the judicial process), rather than the other way around. Those gathering at the annual national conventions, for example, are almost exclusively insiders to the drug court process—judges, district attorneys, public defenders, acupuncturists, and treatment providers. When they come together, they actually strategize about the ways they can get outsiders to accept and support the drug court program. But the drug court movement is very much a social movement—even according to conventional conceptualizations—in that the various actors have joined together with the express purpose of fundamentally transforming the American judicial system.

This transformation is anything but modest. As Judge Jeff Rosnik of the Miami drug court put it, in drug court "the players' roles are altered, modified, inextricably changed. . . . Legal justice becomes therapeutic jurisprudence. And crime and punishment becomes holistic justice." In short, drug court, according to Judge Rosnik, represents a fundamental "change in our judicial system. What was so sacrosanct has changed so drastically." This new form of justice is spreading not only with the expansion of the drug courts but in the application of the drug court model to other criminal behaviors, such as petty theft, prostitution, DUI/DWI, and domestic violence cases.[13]

Separate domestic violence, juvenile, family, and community courts based on the drug court model have already been established.[14] Beyond the initiation of drug courts and other specialized courts based on the drug court model, judges are also beginning to introduce drug court strategies into regular court dockets, as illustrated by the focus of such conference panels as "Using Drug Court Skills Without a Drug Court." In this particular session, judges discussed the innovative ways they have implemented drug court methods in regular criminal court proceedings. Expanding drug court methods to other crimes is justified in part by the well-documented belief that many crimes are "committed by drug offenders in order to buy drugs."[15] Advocates celebrate the "potential for tremendous growth as this model is adapted to other types of criminal cases."[16] Drug courts have even been exported internationally. Courts based on the U.S. drug court model have in the past several years been initiated in Canada, Australia, and England. Plans are underway for the establishment of drug courts in Ireland and Scotland as well. In early December 1999 the United Nations Drug Control Program (UNDCP) convened representatives from eleven different countries for a week-long meeting in Vienna to discuss drug courts.

In short, there is an enormous amount of energy and enthusiasm behind the movement. Speaking at the 1998 drug court conference in Washington, D.C., Judge Jeffrey Tauber, Oakland's first drug court judge and President of the National Association of Drug Court Professionals (NADCP), triumphantly announced to an audience of more than 2,500 drug court professionals that the drug court movement was strong and driving forward. "I think that we have clearly proven through the work that we've done, through our numbers, through the effectiveness of our courts, that this field, this movement, this organization is ready to take center stage, is ready to move its own agenda forward on both the local, state, and national levels." At the same conference, General Barry McCaffrey, Director of the Office of National Drug Control Policy, went so far as to project that, given the rate of growth up to the time, "we could be up to a thousand [drug courts] or so by the turn of the century."

Structural Causes

But how do we make sense of the rapid development and expansion of this radically new form of criminal adjudication? Social movement scholars would likely point to the conventional structural variables of economic pressures, the expansion of political opportunities, resource mobilization, and the like. To be sure, these factors provide partial explanations for the popularity of this innovative form of criminal adjudication. As with supporters of TASC in the 1970s and 1980s, advocates of the drug court often speak of the structural pressures that they believe gave birth to the movement. The growing number of drug offenses, the high recidivism rates among drug offenders, overcrowded jails, the expense of incarceration (as opposed to the cheaper costs of treatment), and heavy criminal court caseloads, are all justifications given by drug court officials for the necessity of drug courts. Also cited are the pressures put on the courts by increasingly strict drug laws. Beyond measures passed during the Anslinger era, even stricter measures were passed during the 1980s. The so-called "war on drugs" popular in the 1980s led to passage of the Comprehensive Crime Control Act in 1984 and the Anti-Drug Abuse Acts in 1986 and 1988. With these legal developments and the growing popularity of cocaine, particularly crack cocaine, the courts became even more burdened with drug cases.[17]

As it is often argued, the criminal justice system was faced with a situation where something new had to be tried. Thus, the common refrain from drug court officials, "What we were doing before simply was not working." The drug court offers itself as a remedy to these structural problems. It promises to relieve overcrowded jails of nonviolent offenders, reduce the heavy case loads of criminal court dockets, and lower the expense of incarcerating offenders with the alternatively cheaper cost of court monitored treatment. From this perspective, the structural realities of the contemporary criminal justice landscape invited the establishment of a new and more effective method of adjudicating drug offenders.

Judge Diane Strickland, Roanoke, Virginia, drug court judge, is among those who observed this pressure on the judicial system. "I think everyone from the judges to the prosecution to the defense to the law enforcement individuals have found that what we have been doing was not working with these people. Basically, we have had a revolving door phenomenon where we take an offender, lock him up for whatever appropriate period of time, and have him back out in the community without addressing the underlying source of his criminal behavior." Given the limited space in America's jails and prisons, low-level drug offenders are not likely to spend much time in jail anyway. As Strickland notes, "The massive over-crowding everywhere from local jails to penitentiaries limits the amount of time that you're going to have any of these offenders realistically being incarcerated." Therefore, "We have to come up with something else that we can do for these folks if we're going to try and deter their criminal behavior."[18]

In other words, the institutional realities (e.g., limited prison space, high rearrest rate among drug offenders, overcrowded court calendars) put pressure on the judges to come up with other plans for handling this group of offenders. Judge Stanley Goldstein claims that prior to starting Dade County's drug court, Miami jails were so overcrowded inmates had to sleep standing up. As NADCP President Jeffrey Tauber puts it, "Certain options are clearly not open to us. We can't put these people in prison and throw away the key, even if we wanted to. We simply don't have the correctional and jail facilities. The new jail facilities are going to go to more serious offenders, as they should." As Tauber and Goldstein see it, then, structural pressures were an important cause fostering the develop-ment of the drug court.

Judge Weber of the Louisville, Kentucky, drug court, also acknowl-edges the structural impetus for change. "I think that anybody who works in the criminal justice system, in the traditional criminal justice system, realizes how little effect we're having on things. The legal system has to change. . . . Overcrowded dockets and high recidivism rates in the criminal justice system are evidence of problems." Therefore, "the system has to change because between demands of volume and demands of bet-ter outcomes, the system is not able to deal with those things." Such pres-sures force a judicial "recognition that the traditional way of doing things may not be the best." Consequently, "the legal system is slowly evolving into something else." Again, the practical forces of correctional and courtroom costs, the volume of offenders, and limited prison and jail space forced judicial actors to consider alternatives to traditional judicial methods.

Moreover, the ability of certain political actors to highlight these pres-sures on the judicial system and make available necessary economic and political resources has played an important role in advancing the drug court movement. For example, federal dollars for drug courts were sus-tained for fiscal year 1995—after an initial scare that they might be cut—because of the lobbying efforts of drug court judges and the establishment

of the NADCP, the headquarters of which is strategically located in the
Washington, D.C. area. Drug court advocates have also rallied support
and resources through annual national conferences, the establishment of
a national resource center (the Drug Court Clearinghouse and Technical
Assistance Project located at American University in Washington, D.C.),
and the institutionalization of mentoring courts for the purpose of helping emerging drug courts establish new programs.

Furthermore, in December 1997 the NADCP announced the formation of the National Drug Court Institute (NDCI) to "promote education,
research and scholarship for drug courts and other court-based intervention programs."[19] Since 1998 the NDCI has been publishing a biannual
journal on the drug courts. Also initiated in 1997 was the Congress of
State Drug Court Associations. The congress is composed of representatives from the various State Drug Court Associations (which exist in over
half of the states), and aims "to help representatives draft legislation and
impact policy and funding at the state level." In response to pressure from
the state associations, eleven states have successfully passed legislation
related to the planning and funding of drug courts. In California alone
"state legislators have earmarked $32 million for drug courts over the
next four years."[20]

While the institutional pressures and corresponding judicial activism
are important variables that certainly explain part of the emergence and
expansion of the drug court, they do not explain all of it. The structural
developments may provide certain opportunities, but, as the drug court
movement demonstrates, cultural factors—ideas, beliefs, worldviews,
symbols of meaning—drive and give direction to social movements. Recent analyses by social movement scholars recognize the dualistic import
of structural and cultural causes in explaining social movements.[21] This
expanding body of literature provides a welcome corrective to the
" 'structuralist' or 'objectivist' bias of previous formulations."[22]

Again, the drug courts are an excellent demonstration of the indispen-
sability of cultural factors in explaining social movements. As Doug
McAdam argues, "Expanding political opportunities do not, in any simple sense, produce a social movement. . . . They only offer insurgents a
certain objective 'structural potential' for collective political action. Me-
diating between opportunity and action are people and the subjective
meanings they attach to their situations."[23] As such, the pressures of increasing case loads, high recidivism rates, mandatory minimum sentences
for felony drug charges, and so on, provide the "structural potential" for
particular innovations in the criminal justice system. But it is certain cultural sensibilities that give meaning and guidance to these innovative efforts. As Johnston and Klandermans put it, "Culture can be seen as a

characteristic of a movement's environment that functions to channel or constrain its development and that defines what behaviors are legitimate and acceptable."[24] Joel Best likewise argues that social movements draw upon "cultural resources," employ rhetorical strategies that have "cultural resonance," and "need powerful, compelling ideas in order to change society."[25] If culture plays such a defining role in social movements, then what cultural tendencies have justified, defined, energized, and channeled the advancement of the drug court movement?

Cultural Causes

Before discussing the role of culture in the drug court movement, it is important to note that the government has typically followed cultural sentiments in determining the scope and direction of drug policy. Even those disdainful of Harry Anslinger's positions in the 1930s, 1940s, and 1950s acknowledge that he was largely following rather than shaping public attitudes. Thus, the influence of culture on drug policy is not a new thing. What has changed is not the ongoing dynamic between culture and law but the meaning systems upon which the culture, and ultimately the law, rest. Recall that until the early 1960s, the legitimizing value that most dominantly informed drug policy was a moralistic one rooted in religiously derived notions of right and wrong. The potency of this perspective, as discussed in chapter 1, was fostered by the institutional location of drug control in the world of law enforcement, an institution accustomed to and defined by moralistic categories. Two related developments would begin to challenge this deeply ingrained posture toward drug using behavior. First were the legal changes that took place in the 1960s (i.e., the Supreme Court's *Robinson v. California* decision and the 1966 Treatment and Rehabilitation Act).

Not coincidentally, it was also during this decade that scholars began to write about the emerging dominance of a peculiarly therapeutic culture in American society. The most important work in this regard is Philip Rieff's *The Triumph of the Therapeutic*, written in 1966. Following Rieff, Peter Berger, Christopher Lasch, Robert Bellah, John Rice, and John Hewitt, among others, have analyzed the increasingly therapeutic tendencies of American culture. Given the advancement of the therapeutic culture—typified as it is by an elevated concern with the self, by a conspicuously emotivist form of discourse and self-understanding, by a proclivity to invoke the language of victimhood and to view behaviors in pathological rather than moral/religious terms, and by the elevated social status of psychologists and other therapeutic practitioners[26]—it is not surprising

that judicial actors would draw upon this system of moral understanding
to give meaning and direction to the drug court movement.

It is not just that drug court judges experience themselves as newly
reclassified "therapeutic judges," though it is telling that some are willing
to be labeled as such. Consider Judge Robert Fogan's response after being
introduced as one. "I have never been introduced at a gathering as a therapeutic judge. . . . And I would admit to being just that. In this group, I
certainly would make no apologies, and would say quite frankly that I am
proud to be exactly that, a therapeutic judge." The impact of therapeutic
ideals on this movement, of course, goes much deeper than in linguistic
reclassifications such as this. Indeed the entire concept of the drug court
is shaped by a therapeutic perspective. Consider a Justice Department
report describing the defining features of the drug court: "In drug court
the treatment experience begins in the courtroom and continues through
the participant's drug court involvement. In other words, drug court is a
comprehensive therapeutic experience. . . . The treatment and criminal
justice professionals are members of the therapeutic team."[27]

The perspective that informs this "comprehensive therapeutic experience" had to come from somewhere. As stated in the report itself, the
drug court movement "did not develop in a vacuum."[28] Indeed not. The
cultural and legal context within which it developed played a significant
role in determining the style, shape, and scope of the drug court. This is
a topic to which David Garland has given considerable attention. According to Garland, "penal culture," by which he means "the loose amalgam
of penological theory, stored-up experience, institutional wisdom, and
professional common sense which frames the actions of penal agents and
which lends meaning to what they do" is always situated in a particular
cultural context.[29] In other words, the actions, habits of mind, and attitudes of legal actors as well as the various legal processes and programs
they lead are influenced by the broader culture within which the law is
situated. "Consequently, the specific culture of punishment in any society
will always have its roots in the broader context of prevailing (or recently
prevailing) social attitudes and traditions."[30]

This most assuredly is the case with the drug courts, though drug court
activists are unlikely themselves to make such a link between culture and
legal changes. Again, articulating the source of the drug court's guiding
philosophy is not necessary because the therapeutic sensibility has become a taken for granted reality. William McColl notes that judges and
other drug court officials are not typically guided by theoretical considerations. This does not mean, however, that they are not influenced by particular systems of moral understanding. As McColl puts it, "There are
certain underlying beliefs that inform the DTC [Drug Treatment Court]

movement."[31] And these, according to McColl, "are primarily medical, rather than legal."[32] Therefore, though they may only do so unwittingly, movement activists draw upon the culturally dominant therapeutic ethos in determining the essential orientation and scope of the drug courts.

The salience of therapeutic sensibilities is certainly evident in the Justice Department's justification for the drug court movement offered in the same report cited above.

> The traditional adversarial system of justice, designed to resolve legal disputes, is ineffective at addressing AOD [alcohol and other drug] abuse. Moreover, many features of the court system actually contribute to AOD abuse instead of curbing it: Traditional defense counsel functions and court procedures often reinforce the offender's *denial* of an AOD problem. . . . Moreover, the criminal justice system is often an unwitting *enabler* of continuing drug use because few immediate consequences for continued AOD use are imposed. [emphasis added][33]

Notice that both therapeutic and utilitarian values are invoked here. The movement is justified on the grounds that the traditional system both does not work and inhibits therapeutic outcomes. With respect to the latter, the traditional system keeps the defendant in denial and it enables the defendant to continue in his drug abusing behavior. As demonstrated in this reasoning, it was not just the pressures of overcrowded jails and the like that drove the development of the drug court movement. It was certain cultural currents that justified, informed, and gave meaning to the advent of this judicial innovation.

In other words, the drug court is not simply a readjustment of existing judicial resources and processes in response to the pressures of escalating expenses and a growing volume of drug offenders. Additionally, it introduces into the adjudication process an entirely new paradigm, one commensurate with therapeutic tendencies in American culture. Drug court judges readily concede that drug courts "view drug offenders through a different lens than the standard court system."[34] Moreover, they acknowledge that adoption of this new paradigm alters the manner in which the court treats the defendant. "In approaching the problem of drug offenders from a therapeutic, medicinal perspective, substance abuse is seen not so much as a moral failure, but as a condition requiring therapeutic remedies."[35] Thus, the medical or therapeutic paradigm is embraced as the guiding judicial philosophy. Culture, as such, has a marked legal effect.

Drug court judges recognize this new judicial form as fully distinguishable from "the traditional criminal justice paradigm, in which drug abuse is understood as a willful choice made by an offender capable of choosing between right and wrong." Instead, drug courts "shift the paradigm in order to treat drug abuse as a 'biopsychosocial disease.'"[36] Such a shift does not just effect the way judges and other justice officials think about the offender turned client, but it demands a wholesale judicial reorientation. "By treating addiction as a biopsychosocial issue, DTCs force those who work with the standard criminal justice system to alter their orientation away from the traditional role of the court. DTCs shift the paradigm of the court system; therefore judges, prosecutors, and defense counsel must change their outlook and conduct to allow DTCs to function effectively."[37]

Having embraced this new therapeutic paradigm, it is not surprising that previous judicial practices would be reconceptualized in accordance with it. Based on this new perspective criminal justice practices that preceded the drug courts are interpreted is having fostered antitherapeutic legal outcomes. As argued by judges Peggy Hora and William Schma, the traditional criminal justice approach to drug crimes inhibited therapeutic outcomes.

> Non-recovering addicts and alcoholics usually do not accept personal responsibility for their behavior, and they continue to blame "others" or "the system" for their plight. Their respect for law and their own self-esteem suffer. The court's and their acquiescence in mere punishment perpetuates denial. Behind bars addicts can mentally suppress the negative impact of their use on family and friends and their responsibility for it. The failure to acknowledge the presence of these anti-therapeutic elements in criminal behavior avoids its substantive nature, cripples our development of an effective, long term response to the drug problem, and contributes to the prolongation of the crisis.[38]

Therefore, as these drug court judges see it, a major part of the problem with the traditional criminal justice system is its antitherapeutic outcomes. Traditional methods keep defendants in denial, lower their self-esteem, and encourage them mentally to suppress issues related to their drug use. Alternatives, therefore, must overcome anti-therapeutic legal effects with therapeutic remedies. Again, all such reasoning relies on the resonance of a therapeutic sensibility in American culture.

The influence of the therapeutic culture on the drug court movement is evident not just in rationales for initiating the program offered by judges and other advocates of the movement. Indeed, as described in the Justice Department report cited above, the drug court in its operating form is a "comprehensive therapeutic experience." The various features of the therapeutic ethic, outlined by Rieff, Lasch, and others, deeply color the substance and style of the drug court program. While we will explore the cultural impact and consequences of the therapeutic idiom on the drug court movement more fully in the chapters ahead, it is worth briefly noting some of the evident therapeutic tendencies present in the drug court model. Judges, for example, whether or not they prefer to refer to themselves as therapeutic judges, often behave much like therapists or social workers. Moreover, psychologists and other treatment providers play a dominant role in the drug court drama, often a role more pronounced than that of the attorneys. Treatment providers and counselors regularly speak on behalf of their clients and counsel the judge on how the clients should be handled.

In addition, self-esteem is viewed as a core problem in explaining drug use and other criminal behaviors, and one of the main purposes of the drug court is to help clients overcome low self-esteem. The ethic of emotivism, likewise, fully permeates the drug court drama. Not only is the free and open expression of feelings emphasized in group and individual treatment sessions, but emotions are conspicuously displayed in the courtroom. Defendants openly share and sometimes give tearful testimonies about their recovery process. Empathetic words of encouragement, even hugs from the judge, are not uncommon.[39] Finally, drug court clients are understood to be victims of a "biopsychosocial disease," a medically inspired reinterpretation of behavior that has spread from the drug court to other populations in the criminal justice community.

A cursory review of the drug court reveals the significant legal impact of the therapeutic ethic. A more comprehensive analysis reveals not only that the therapeutic influence is as pronounced as this *prima facie* overview suggests but that the marriage between treatment and justice as realized in the drug courts portends a rather substantial redefinition of the meaning and practice of justice. Before proceeding to a closer examination of the influence and consequences of therapeutic jurisprudence as realized in this movement, it is important first to dispel a common misperception of the drug court.

False Dichotomies

One cannot emphasize strongly enough that to be therapeutic is not to be soft on crime. It is a common error to interpret such programs as drug courts according to typical political classifications. The conventional political categories of conservative versus liberal, coercive versus liberating, punitive versus rehabilitative, or tough versus therapeutic are of little value in making sense of the drug court movement. Simply put, these are false dichotomies. Nicholas Kittrie made just this point before a large audience of drug court practitioners in 1995. "Punishment and therapy can be collaborative rather than contradictory goals," Kittrie said. "The traditional dichotomy between these two does not and does not need to exist."

Nonetheless, the common misconception of an inherent incompatibility between the two persists, both in popular discussions and in scholarly assessments of legal social control. Consider, for example, the distinction Donald Black makes between "penal" and "therapeutic" styles of social control. The former, according to Black, is an accusatory style of social control where the goal is punishment and where the hostile conflict between parties results in a clear winner and a clear loser. The therapeutic, contrastingly, is a remedial style of social control where the goal is social repair and normality and where the victim gets "help" rather than "punishment" to improve. According to Black each style has its own logic, its own language, its own way of defining and treating deviant behavior.[40]

The drug court cuts across these heuristic distinctions. Social control in the drug court is at the same time both therapeutic and penal, to use Black's terms. Again, to be therapeutic is not to be soft on crime. The treatment perspective endemic to the drug courts clearly has a logic and language that guides interpretations of deviant behavior. But this interpretation does not necessarily result in the more lenient treatment of the drug offender. Rather, it can actually provide the ideological basis whereby the state exercises greater control over the individual than is typical of a normal criminal court.

One could argue further that the inadequacies of conventional demarcations limit and distort understandings of not only the drug court but also the larger debate over the legalization of drugs. Erich Goode, in his thoughtful analysis of the drug legalization debate, rightly acknowledges that "the political landscape is a maze of contradictions" and that this is "perhaps nowhere . . . more apparent than on the issue of drug legalization."[41] As Goode sees it, "the usual political spectrum is not a very useful road map for finding out where someone stands on drug policy."[42] To be sure: On the legalization debate one finds, on the one hand, such moral conservatives as William Bennett in alliance with such liberal prohibitionists as Charles Rangel opposing legalization, and, on the other hand, such liberal legalizers as Ethan Nadelman lining up with such free-market libertarians as Thomas Szasz and Milton Friedman supporting legalization.[43] Even conservative pundit William F. Buckley, though not easily classified as a libertarian, joins ranks with those supporting the legalization of drugs. The drug legalization debate is, therefore a complicated one involving unusual alliances and heavily nuanced positions.

Most drug court advocates, however, do not support the legalization of drugs. They believe drug abuse should be controlled, but it should be controlled in a different sort of way. Senator Joseph Biden, addressing a large audience of drug court professionals in 1998, decried what he perceived to be a growing receptiveness to the legalization option. "They are talking about legalization because they have given up, because they don't believe that there is anything that we can do about this problem." Biden observed that such public frustration with failed drug control efforts cuts across the political divide. "Whether they are liberal or conservative . . . in their hearts they don't think it can be done." As a sign of hope, Biden recalled a recent conversation between himself and William Bennett, former drug czar under the Bush administration. In this conversation Bennett asked Biden if he "would be willing to go on the road with him again to fight the legalization efforts." Biden pointed out the obvious differences between himself, a liberal Democrat, and Bennett, "a very partisan Republican." Yet they both believe that the legalization of drugs is a bad idea.

Though it is equally difficult to categorize drug courts according to conventional political categories, the drug courts essentially circumvent the legalization debate. The drug courts embrace a disease view of addiction, but this does not remove from the state its role in controlling drug use. Recall the reasoning offered by Judge Douglas in the *Robinson* case, where he argued that drug use should be viewed as a disease rather than a crime. But he still favored involuntary treatment, just based on different categories—for the purposes of "curing" rather than "punishing." This unique combination of a therapeutic perspective with the continued exercising of state control contributes to the drug court's broad appeal. Supporters of drug court span the political spectrum. Conservatives like it because of its tough, intrusive nature; and liberals because of its ostensibly more humanitarian and rehabilitative qualities. Most, regardless of political leanings, support it because of its claims to be efficacious, to save the state money, and to relieve the criminal justice system of needed jail and prison space. Judges are cognizant of which aspects of the drug courts play well to which audiences and do their best to emphasize particular features accordingly. Because of the drug court's versatile and wide ranging appeal, Claire McCaskill, a prosecuting attorney with the Kansas City, Missouri, drug court and board member of the NADCP, sees it as a "political winner."

> It is tough. It is tougher than the alternatives. If we will be honest with people, we will tell them that the majority of the people who are going to drug court would normally be on paper. They are not going to be in our penitentiaries. They are not going to be in our jails. In my state they are going to be part of a massive database. Those of you who are probation officers know that there will be no meaningful supervision, and no meaningful requirements for these people. Sorry, if you are offended, but that is the way it is where I come

from. This [the drug court] is tougher. I have a tax-payer factory. We are taking people who have not worked, who have either been on welfare or stealing, to support their habit. Now they are either in school full time or they have a job.

McCaskill also discussed Jackson County's recent passage of an increased sales tax to fund "anti-drug activities." Earmarked in the referendum were funds for law enforcement as well as treatment and diversion. The measure passed by a 71 percent margin. According to McCaskill the most popular part of the package was prevention, with drug courts coming in a close second.

What this example illustrates is that the public can support both "tough on crime" measures and therapeutic treatment approaches at the same time, and even be willing to have their taxes raised to support both. Consider also the results of a 1996 national survey that asked respondents to rank the importance of various approaches to the crime problem. According to the survey results, 85 percent of Americans think "more treatment and education" is important in solving the crime problem. Ranking not far behind, however, are "harsher sentences" (81 percent) and "more police" (75 percent).[44] Once again, Americans can at the same time be enthusiastic about tough approaches to crime while also favoring treatment. These are not mutually exclusive categories.

In the drug court, these seemingly divergent categories are fully merged into one. Drug courts are tough and therapeutic at the same time. Many of the judges with whom I spoke emphasized this point and acknowledged that support for the drug court transcends normal political labels. Judge William Schma, of Kalamazoo, Michigan, for example, observes that "even dead-rock conservatives" recognize that "you can't keep jailing everybody, that it doesn't do a damn bit of good for an addict, and that what addicts need is treatment." It is not, according to Schma, a liberal or conservative type of issue. "It's a widely accepted principle that crosses all kinds of lines, the color lines, political lines." Schma observes further that Kalamazoo is, in fact, a "very conservative community," and it's "the Republicans on the board" who are the "biggest supporters to this drug court you have ever seen." These Republican board members "talk in terms of not only saving money but getting effective results. And sometimes they even talk about the compassionate thing to do."

Schma argues further that emphasizing the toughness of the drug court is not just a political ploy to appease a particular constituency. "That's not an advertising gimmick," he says. "I tell these people at the beginning, and I'm sure it's true in every other court, you are going to work your ass off in this thing. It is going to be a lot harder to get through this and recover than if you simply went through the system, took your licks, and went on." Schma specifies the various features of his drug court emphasizing just how demanding it is. "They've got meetings to go to. They've got case managers to answer to. They've got to come see me every two weeks. They've got to go to AA or NA. They've got to drop [provide urine for testing]." According to Schma his drug court is much more difficult than a normal court. "You take the typical person, throw them on probation or behind bars and hell that's a cake walk. They don't have to do anything." But in the drug court "the chances that they are not going to get caught when they do something wrong is pretty negligible. These folks are just never out of sight. They are locked down really tight. Their behavior is really monitored closely."

Judge Susan Bolton makes the same argument about her Phoenix, Arizona drug court. In Phoenix the majority of drug court clients are put in the program involuntarily, essentially as a condition of probation. According Bolton the drug court program "is a lot more rigorous" than normal probation. "You have to work hard to be successful in drug court. We put a lot of demands on people. We make them spend at least three hours a week in our group [therapy sessions]. We make them spend at least two more hours a week in a 12-step meeting. We make them do their community service hours. We require them to report all the time to their probation officer. We require them to call TASC on a daily basis. And if they don't do what they are required to do, they suffer a consequence." Consequences may involve jail, but they may also involve additional group sessions, more frequent court appearances, community service hours, or other sanctions. Bolton holds that anyone who watches a drug court program will realize that "it is harder, that seven to twelve months in drug court is harder than twenty-four to thirty-six months in any other program."

Judge after judge with whom I spoke made the same point. Judge Strickland of Roanoke, Virginia, for example, acknowledges that from the outside the drug court may "seem to be a soft on crime approach." But the "realities are that it's actually much tougher." From Judge Strickland's perspective, drug court is more demanding than probation, even more demanding than incarceration.

> The demands that are placed on these individuals are far more extensive than anything they would do whether they were incarcerated or put on probation. Incarcerated they basically have no demands on them except to modify their behavior to suit the terms of their confinement, but other than that they are not asked to do anything. They can do absolutely nothing with themselves all day long, whereas in the treatment court model they are required to be either in counseling, in educational courses, on the job or a variety of other classes all the time and there is a very demanding schedule set for them. They also are

required to stay clean in an environment that is very challenging to them. So I see the drug court as a much more demanding program for them than if they went to jail.

But even in the drug court program, as Strickland acknowledges, defendants are likely to spend time in jail, sometimes even more time than if they had proceeded through the normal adjudication process. Strickland notes:

> Every time they make a misstep they are facing the possibility of some time in jail and I have people in my program who have already spent more time in jail than they would have spent had they just pled straight, served their time, and gone on about their business; because we keep working with them and when they are not succeeding we incarcerate them for a certain period of time and then we put them back in the program. If you add up all those short periods of incarceration you would find that in some cases it exceeds the time they would actually serve.

Some judges even instruct potential clients of the difficulty of drug courts and warn them that noncompliance may result in time in jail, even, as Judge Strickland notes, in more time than if the clients had chosen the normal adjudication process. Judge Stanley Goldstein of the Dade County drug court warns defendants of this potential consequence. In one drug court session, for example, he told clients, "If you play games with me you're going to do more time in jail than if you never came in here in the first place. . . . You could have gone to trial and got convicted and still done less time than you're going to do here if you keep fooling around with me. The only way you can beat me is to finish this program and graduate."

Thus, judges conclude that the drug courts are anything but soft on crime. As Judge Strickland puts it, "So I don't see it as being easy on these people or soft on crime. I see it as being very demanding of them, but in a way that is hopefully more inclined to make a difference." This, of course, is the catch. Because they are doing something that will make a difference, because their aim is to cure, to contribute to the recovery process, the extra incarceration and other demands are justified. The drug courts follow the same basic logic advanced by Judge Douglas in the *Robinson* decision. A therapeutic sensibility can actually translate into very tough, harsh, intrusive forms of legal social control.

Consider as a final example the matter of capital punishment, presumably the harshest form of punishment. As David Garland points out, capital punishment has actually been given legitimacy in the United States because of new quasi medical or therapeutic practices. States that had once abandoned capital punishment reinstituted the practice because of, in part, the more culturally palatable practice of a lethal injection. "The offender, who is strapped upon a stretcher trolley like a patient awaiting an operation, is put to death anonymously, under the guise of a medical procedure, by technicians who do not immediately witness the effects of their actions. . . . The use of 'therapeutic' drugs and medicalized procedures is thus an attempt to generate an acceptably 'modern' mode of execution."[45] Therapeutic sensibilities likewise help to legitimize the drug courts, a program that is in many respects more intrusive than previous criminal justice approaches to drug crimes.

Legitimizing the Drug Court Movement

Therefore, both structural and cultural causes help explain the drug court movement; and the substantive impact of the therapeutic culture is not one that fosters a soft on crime approach, as many intuitively suppose. Furthermore, as noted above, a unique feature of the drug court movement, as compared to other social movements, is its location in the criminal justice system. That is, the major actors in the movement are agents of the state, namely judges. Because the leadership for the movement is generated from within the judicial world, it is all the more important that activists seek to justify or legitimate the program vis-à-vis society according to dominant cultural values, because, as S. M. Lipset argues, "Groups will regard a political system as legitimate or illegitimate according to the way in which its values fit in with their primary values."[46] The drug court movement, because of its location in the criminal justice system, provides an excellent empirical case for linking social movement analyses with theories of the modern state. In the case of the drug courts, the two scholarly endeavors find analytical common ground around the concept of legitimation.

From the theoretical vantage point of the state, we recognize that the therapeutic ethos offers the political order a new source of legitimation. As Jürgen Habermas, David Beetham, and John Schar, among others, argue, there is an ongoing need for state programs (including those within the criminal justice system) to justify themselves according to dominant cultural values. State theorists argue further that the processes of modernity have undermined the saliency of traditional codes of moral understanding. Yet the need to draw upon some kind of justificatory meaning system still exists. This is a constant condition of the state. Legitimacy is, as Daniel Bell asserts, the central or axial principle of the state.

The erosion of traditional legitimizing values, such as religious morality, along with the continued expansion of state authority has resulted in what Habermas calls a legitimation deficit or, to use his more apocalyptic term, a legitimation crisis. It appears that, with respect to the judiciary, drug court judges are cognizant of such a deficit. Judges express concern that the judiciary is not only ineffective and overburdened, but that in relation to society and to the other branches of government, its legitimacy is somehow in question. Judith Kaye, Chief Judge of the Court of Appeals in New York, put it this way: "Courts today face a public that, by and large, is cynical and distrustful of all government, including the judicial system. Courts can no longer assume they enjoy the public's trust and respect. We have to achieve it a new-fashioned way: we have to earn it."[47]

Because drug court is "responsive to today's realities and public expectations," according to Judge Kaye, it is one program that promises to help re-engender public trust in the judiciary.[48] Jeffrey Tauber likewise sees drug courts "as a powerful and innovative way to rebuild a community's faith in its courts and criminal justice system."[49] The drug court movement can be understood in part, then, as an effort to remedy a perceived deficit of legitimation by appealing to dominant cultural values. Thomas Merrigan, a Massachusetts judge, made a similar argument before a large audience of drug court professionals in Portland, Oregon in 1995.

> If we don't change what we are doing in the next few years, and if we don't change how we go about serving the community with more relevancy, with more meaning, we are going to find that in twenty-five years, we have become irrelevant in the minds of the public. They will no longer consider us meaningful. . . . So, for me it's not an option. For me, what we are doing is we are reinventing justice, and we are doing it in a way that is relevant to what are the needs in the community.

A court concerned with its own relevance will, therefore, appeal to pervading cultural sentiments to secure or re-establish its legitimacy. This, of course, is not a new situation. The forms of punishment employed by Uriah Levy during the antebellum period violated dominant cultural sensibilities, and he paid a price for that violation. Forms of punishment necessarily rely upon cultural sentiments for their support. As David Garland observes, "Punishment may be a legal institution, administered by state functionaries, but it is necessarily grounded in wider patterns of knowing, feeling, and acting, and it depends upon these social roots and supports for its continuing legitimacy and operation."[50]

Of the "legitimizing values" (to use Becker's term) that have historically played a role in shaping American drug laws, the two with the most cultural salience in the contemporary context are the utilitarian and the therapeutic orientations. Remember that utilitarian concerns were offered by pharmaceutical companies in the first decades of the twentieth century to prevent passage of early drug control laws and were later used to justify further illegalization measures. While I have highlighted the influence of the therapeutic perspective in this chapter, it would be a mistake to ignore the extent to which utilitarian ideals have continued to play a vital role in fostering the drug court movement. Obviously, utilitarian concerns are central to the structural explanations for the emergence of the drug court (i.e., issues of cost effectiveness and the like). Moreover, utilitarian sentiments remain a major source of justification for the continued expansion of the drug court movement.

As illustrated in some of the above examples, drug court judges continually make reference to utilitarian concerns in their efforts to garner public support for the movement. Recall the common justificatory dictum, "What we were doing before was not working." Consider another example of a judge employing utilitarian rhetoric. Jamey Weitzman, the first Baltimore city drug court judge, recounts her efforts to persuade congressional Republicans to support drug courts.

> I went to the Hill to try to convince these really hardcore Republicans that they should buy into drug court to give us money. They were all pounding on the table saying, "do the crime, do the time." At which point I put my head down and decided "I am going to go home. I'm going to get my head beat in." But I'm glad I persisted. . . . I went to each of the Republicans, and I said to them—I didn't tell many warm and fuzzy stories; they didn't want to hear that. I didn't tell them about all the drug free babies that were born and all of the people that we were saving. So, what I went through was dollars and cents. And I told them that to run a drug court defendant through the state of the art drug court program maybe costs $2,000. And the alternative was $20,000 in jail. They liked that number. And then I told them that the cost to have a neonatal intensive care for the child who was born to a drug addicted mother was about $40,000 as opposed to a drug free baby. They liked that number then as well. And then I told them that the majority of the people who graduate from drug court are now tax-payers. They really liked that.

This kind of reasoning is consistently offered by drug court officials. Recall Claire McCaskill's public strategy of telling potential supporters that her drug court is a "tax-payer factory." Again, such utilitarian arguments are very common in public efforts to defend and garner support for the drug court movement.[51]

Therefore, the drug court can be explained, in terms used by social movement scholars, as the result of the concomitant influences of structural and cultural causes. Relatedly, the drug courts can be explained, in the nomenclature of state theorists, as an effort to legitimize this feature of the American political order according to the culturally dominant therapeutic and utilitarian systems of meaning. As illustrated in the comments of judges quoted in this chapter, judges are deliberate and selective about which features of the drug court they discuss with which audiences. There is, in the Goffmanian sense, a clearly defined backstage (what drug court advocates know and believe among themselves) and frontstage (what they selectively put forth for public consumption). At the conferences, planning meetings, mentoring programs, and other gatherings of drug court professionals, movement actors consciously strategize on how best to discuss and portray the drug court. The dramaturgical image is most appropriate for making conceptual sense of the drug court movement and is, in fact, a metaphor that drug court advocates themselves employ.

Three

Therapeutic Theater

> Drug courts, it has been said many times, are
> theater. And the judge is the stage director and
> one of the primary actors.
> —Judge Jamey Weitzman

SOCIOLOGIST Erving Goffman first made famous the dramaturgical model for interpreting social life in his influential 1959 book, *The Presentation of Self in Everyday Life*.[1] Goffman used the Shakespeare-inspired image of the role playing life to make sense of the essential nature of human social interactions. According to Goffman's scheme all humans are actors playing different roles in various social spheres. Through the management of impressions, individuals present favorable images of themselves to an audience and to other actors in life's ongoing drama. Unacceptable aspects of one's life are kept backstage while less blemished images are displayed frontstage. Because acts are most often performed in teams, actors depend upon others to support the images they seek to project—a sometimes tenuous enterprise. More recently, the dramaturgical model has been adapted to explain the dynamics of social movements. Robert Benford and Scott Hunt, for example, demonstrate—fully in keeping with Goffman's interpretive metaphor—that social movements are scripted, staged, and performed and are interpreted by a viewing audience much like a theatrical drama.[2]

The drug court, in important ways, is a fitting example of a social movement that can be made sense of according to the dramaturgical model. In fact, the life-as-theater metaphor is applicable to the drug courts on at least two levels. First, it provides a useful heuristic for interpreting drug court as a national (and more recently, international) movement. Leaders strategize in backstage contexts on how best to present the most favorable information about drug courts on the frontstage, that is, to the media and the general public. Carefully written scripts and well-choreographed performances are used to communicate a particular image of the program to garner public support and encourage others to join the movement.

Relatedly, the drug court itself can be understood as theater. This is, in fact, a common image used by legal and treatment practitioners to describe the program. Drug court is theater, they say, and the actors in it play new and redefined roles. In the backstage, practitioners conspire about how best to make the courtroom theater communicate a particular message to clients and others in the courtroom audience. At times, as we will see, the two staging arenas intersect, that is, movement actors showcase a local drug court theater as a method of advocacy for the larger movement. Though the two levels of therapeutic theater sometimes overlap, for conceptual purposes we will look at each individually, beginning with a discussion of drama at the level of the movement as a whole.

Movement Dramaturgy

The dramaturgical nature of the drug court movement is evident in a number of different forms, perhaps most conspicuously in the content, style, and focus of the national drug court conferences. Drug court conferences of one form or another have been held annually since 1993. The most significant of these have been the NADCP training conferences, which have been held every year since the organization was formed in 1994. Not only are the conferences themselves heavily scripted and staged events (where actual Hollywood actors with histories of alcohol or substance abuse, such as Martin Sheen, Charlie Sheen, and James Caan, have made cameo appearances), but they also serve as a kind of backstage for drug court movement activists. That is, at the national conferences drug court professionals strategize with each other and educate those new to the scene about how best to present the program to sometimes skeptical audiences for the purpose of garnering public support and financial resources to further the movement.

Consider, for example, the titles of such conference workshops as, "Damage Control: Dealing with the Media," "Getting Local Government and the Community to 'Buy In' to a Drug Court Program," "Strategies for Attracting Community Resources to Support a Drug Court Program," "Accessing Community Resources," and "Dealing with the Press/Politics." Moreover, many plenary sessions focus on providing drug court professionals with a script useful to elicit public support. As social movement scholars propose, "social movement scripts" are typically derived from dominant cultural values. That is, the scripts "include ideas, attributions, norms, beliefs and a universe of discourse."[3] Movement leaders use the conferences as an opportunity to pass along these scripts and inform new members about how best to employ them for the purposes of advancing the movement. Advice offered by Claire McCaskill at one conference provides a useful illustration of this kind of backstage counsel.

McCaskill tells conferees that she is going to provide them with a public strategy for selling drug court to the community, in particular to skeptical prosecutors. "I'm going to give you some stuff you can take home to convince your prosecutor or your district attorney to come on in, the water is fine." McCaskill acknowledges that some prosecutors, who fear being labeled "soft and squishy," might be reluctant to embrace the drug court program. Recall in chapter 2 how she and others debunk the soft on crime perception of drug court by emphasizing the tough and intrusive nature of the program. Instead she talks about how drug courts make offenders into tax-payers, into responsible, contributing members of the community. For McCaskill, this is a deliberate strategy. "Whenever I'm interviewed about this, in the media or anywhere else, that is the way I talk about drug court."

As an example, she recounted a recent occasion when she was asked if the drug courts represent the criminal justice system's recognition that drug offenders are victims. Her response to this inquiry: "I said, 'Please, don't say that out loud. Where I come from that is not the way to get community support for drug court, to paint these people as victims.'" It is not that she doesn't believe that the court clients are victims, but rather that, from her perspective, identifying them as such is not a politically smart way to elicit public support for the drug court. "Now, in reality many of them have been victimized in many ways. In reality, the therapeutic approach is good. But, in my opinion that is not the way to get the community to accept the important work that we are doing." In other words, for the purposes of movement advocacy, particularly among prosecutors, one should keep the victimization issue backstage.

McCaskill advises further that new drug courts should start with a narrow eligibility criteria. "I would certainly say that to start conservative in terms of eligibility is a key." Again, this does not mean that she thinks only low-level offenders should be in drug court, but rather that as a publicly palatable strategy, the program should start out with very narrow eligibility criteria and then expand after achieving greater community support. "You can always grow later as the community and everyone becomes a little more accepting of the premise and realizes that you are not going to be creating axe murderers over night. You can in fact expand your criteria . . . as everyone moves forward in a consensus fashion." That approximately 40 percent of the drug courts have expanded their eligibility criteria over time makes clear that many courts have followed such advice.

McCaskill also offers explicit advice for dealing with the media. A relationship with the media, she believes, must be cultivated over time. "Do not assume that you can explain drug court in all of its glory in a thirty-second soundbite and expect that the people out there are going to get it.

You do have to work out what is the message that you want the community to know about the drug court." How this is presented may depend on the messenger. On her part, as a prosecutor, she emphasizes the themes of efficacy and responsibility. "Every time there is a microphone in front of my face, whether it is at a graduation, or whether it is at budget time, it is, 'We have got a taxpayer factory, we are making these people responsible and more accountable. And we are saving space in prison for the people that need to be there because they are hurting people.' That is the mantra over and over again. And that is the message that I want to be out there."

In his instructions to emerging drug courts, Jeffrey Tauber offers similar advice on how to handle the media. Like McCaskill, he believes it is a relationship drug court practitioners must proactively cultivate. "Develop good relations with your local print and electronic media. Make sure that they are aware of program successes." He further advises drug court judges that they should "spread the credit around. The more agencies and staff responsible for program success, the more will be around to fight for the program's survival."[4] In other words, make sure the audience knows that drug court is not a one person show, but a cohesive team with a common, unified vision.

McCaskill also instructs active and prospective drug court practitioners that graduation ceremonies are excellent venues for positive theater and that the most effective performance involves the presence of the media and local political luminaries. "The graduations are a great media opportunity. . . . In our first graduation we had the governor. We always try to have someone who will draw the media speak at our graduation, because we are sure to get the media there. . . . And when the media sees the graduation they get hooked. They are the best natural high in the world, our graduations." Graduation ceremonies, then, are excellent staged events that communicate the essence of drug court and educe positive media coverage.

Finally, McCaskill admonishes emerging drug courts to set up some kind of evaluation, not because she has any question about the efficacy of the drug courts but because evaluations are a useful tool for selling the program to the community. "And finally, evaluation, evaluation, evaluation. If you think you are going to get money in the future without evaluation, you aren't awake. . . . I'm convinced that this will be the norm in twenty years. And I'm convinced that the way it will be the norm is by showing people the efficacies of it and the cost efficiencies of it, and the common sense that is involved here. And if you keep good evaluative statistics, you will keep everybody in the corral, because it does work." Jeffrey Tauber similarly warns prospective drug court judges, "Programs that can't show immediate and direct results lose out at budget time."

In closing McCaskill reviews the overall strategy and outline of the script for presenting drug court to the community, "Okay, so the mantra is, we are making people be responsible. We are getting tough on a population that has not had meaningful supervision and we are saving jail space for those folks who need to be in jail because they have hurt people." Like a fastidious stage director, she makes sure her actors know their lines, offering advice on which points to accent and which to soften with nuance—all for the purposes of selling the program to local communities and advancing the larger movement.

Notice that in McCaskill's presentation she is clearly speaking to a backstage audience. She is cognizant of certain assumptions shared by movement activists but believes these commonly held ideals need to be tailored and massaged for the purposes of public presentation. Given the perceived popularity of the "three strikes and you're out" policy and "tough on crime" political/societal dispositions, practitioners, like Mc-Caskill, believe they must emphasize the tough features of the drug court to get the most public support or at least to appeal to those who think in these terms. Judge Robert Ziemian of the Boston drug court is also explicit on this point. "You have got to start out this program by talking about how tough the program is, that this is the toughest thing these people are going to do." He even advises emerging drug courts to "get yourself a tough judge, if you can. Don't get a judge who is perceived as being very liberal. Because all those things that you want to do, all the therapeutic things you want to do, you can do later."

Like McCaskill, Ziemian assumes everyone in the audience is on board regarding the validity of the various therapeutic features of the drug court. He fears, however, that if this is the only message that reaches the public, it will fail to generate support. It is not that he sees the tough and therapeutic components as mutually exclusive categories, but rather that he is aware of public misconceptions that typically interpret these as contradictory predilections. Obviously, he would not recommend getting a tough judge if he did not think tough and therapeutic features were compatible.

Mentoring court programs serve many of the same backstage purposes as do the national conferences. Like the national conferences, mentoring court programs are geared to help emerging drug courts tap into necessary resources, establish drug court programs, and communicate the efficacy of the drug courts to local communities. The mentoring court program was initiated in 1996. At the time seven courts (San Bernardino, California; Kansas City, Missouri; Stillwater Oklahoma; Louisville, Kentucky; Pensacola, Florida; Rochester, New York; and Las Vegas, Nevada) were named mentoring court sites. By 1998 this number expanded to seventeen. An express purpose of this program is to keep the leadership of the drug court movement at the local level. As a Justice Department publication puts it, the mentoring court program "nurtures local and regional leadership, moving the focus away from the national to the local level, where the practitioners and most of the resources are found."[5] Teams from emerging drug courts visit a mentoring court site to receive training and learn in a practical manner how a drug court functions. Not only do visiting court practitioners watch the mentoring drug court in action, but they meet with officials from the site and are given advice on how to run and publicly present a drug court.

Thus, as do the national conferences, mentoring court training sessions represent the backstage of the drug court movement. Here the defining ideals and forms of the program are passed on, as are strategies for selling the program to local communities. Consider, for example, the advice offered by Judge Bruce Beaudin, a former Washington, D.C., drug court judge, at a June 1997 mentoring court training session in Rochester, New York. Like McCaskill and other conference speakers, Beaudin told visiting court teams to emphasize the tough nature of the drug court. "In this program, defendants get more attention from the criminal justice system than anyone else. It's not coddling criminals. These people will get more monitoring than anyone else. This argument can be used as a basis of public education." Like McCaskill and Ziemian, Beaudin believes it is politically advantageous to highlight the tough nature of the drug court. It is, in other words, a good theme to emphasize on the frontstage.

Judge Henry Weber offered further advice at a mentoring court session in Louisville, Kentucky. Weber warned prospective drug court personnel to be sure various actors in the drama understood their roles, their relationships with each other, and the common vision of the drug court. According to Weber, many problems can be avoided if the court and treatment are on the same page. "The relationship between the court and treatment is so crucial that you have to get that right. If you get that right the other problems you can take care of. If you don't get that right the program is in jeopardy." The various actors in the drama must know their parts and the overall theme of the play. Conflicts or misunderstandings between actors can destroy the larger story. It is critical therefore, that these issues be dealt with in the realm of the backstage.

At both conferences and mentoring court training sessions, movement-level staging sometimes intersects with local-level performances. That is, at the conferences leaders will sometimes roleplay a certain component of the drug court to illustrate how the program actually functions. At the 1995 Las Vegas drug court conference, in a workshop titled "Drug Court Role Playing," three judges performed mock drug courts to display different styles of courtroom drama. At the 1996 Washington, D.C., conference, drug court officials and actual juvenile drug court clients from the Visalia, California, juvenile drug court staged a reenactment of their local drug court drama in a session titled, "Juvenile Drug Courts II 'Role Play.'" At mentoring programs (and some conferences), participants also view a local court session in action, either through a video feed or through a visit to the court, after which they meet with officials who help them make sense of what they just witnessed.

As recent social movement scholars point out, organizers often work hard to maintain a clearly segregated frontstage so that potential movement supporters are prevented from seeing unfavorable backstage aspects of the movement.[6] To movement activists, it is crucial that actors follow expected or predetermined scripts during frontstage performances. Glitches have on occasion occurred in these staged events, providing audiences with unwelcome glimpses of sometimes unresolved backstage issues. For example, at the Rochester training program, Judge Schwartz presided over the drug court during the mentoring court's training workshop, even though he was not the drug court judge at the time; three months earlier Judge Valentino had begun presiding over the Rochester drug court. The style and protocol of Valentino's drug court is somewhat different from that of his predecessor. For example, Judge Schwartz, borrowing a procedure he learned from Judge Bruce Beaudin, would assign noncomplying clients to sit in the jury box for one of more days as one form of sanction. During his one day return to drug court for the mentoring court program he reintroduced this practice. Dozens of personnel from the media and the eleven visiting courts watched him in action. When Judge Valentino returned the next day (before a much smaller audience) to reassume his responsibilities, several clients were sitting in the jury box, as Schwartz had instructed them to do. Judge Valentino asked them what they were doing there. When they explained that Judge Schwartz had told them to sit there, he retorted with evident irritation, "This is Valentino." They quickly moved to where the other clients were sitting. In this case, the scripts of the two judges did not completely match, which had a direct effect on the drug court performance for that day.

Another interesting example of unexpected, and in this case unwelcome, actor noncompliance occurred when movement leaders attempted another double staging—movement dramaturgy and courtroom theater—at the June 1996 NADCP Drug Court Conference in Washington, D.C. In attendance were over seven hundred drug court professionals. At the time there were in the United States some one hundred drug courts underway or in the planning and implementation stages. Organizers of the conference had arranged for a live video feed of Judge Stephanie

Duncan-Peters' Washington, D.C., drug court, just several blocks away. The express purpose of the exercise was to help the attending legal and treatment practitioners, many of whom were in the early stages of starting or planning a drug court program, see what a "State-of-the-Art Drug Court" looked like in action.

It was in essence an opportunity to showcase the model to a national audience and foster the support and involvement of new drug court professionals. In other words, it was a staging exercise aimed to promote the expansion of the movement. When the feed began Judge Duncan-Peters, in typical Oprah-esque style, walked around the courtroom and began explaining to clients the purposes for the cameras in the courtroom. "We're going to be broadcasting live into a hotel where we have about seven hundred people who are watching our ceremony today, and I want to tell them a little bit about what our ceremony is, because they've never seen one."

As is common in Duncan-Peters's drug court, the judge began the court session with a short motivational talk, this time based on a book instead of a movie. She had recently read a book written by John Lucas, basketball coach of the Philadelphia 76ers. In the book Lucas writes of his former drug addiction problem and of his strained relationship with his sister during this period. As Duncan-Peters recounts, Lucas's sister "felt that looking at him was like looking at a diamond that had been painted over, because she saw him as the diamond, something that was clear, and brilliant, and shiny, because she saw all the talents and all the abilities that he had. And by using drugs, he was just painting over that diamond so that you couldn't see the brilliance of it." Duncan-Peters reported further that, according to Lucas, he took drugs to "keep himself from feeling really strong feelings." This reminded the judge of her drug court clients. She observed from her tenure in the drug court that many of her clients had done the same thing, that in response to the loss of a family member or loved one, they would turn to drugs to cover up the pain.

According to the judge, experiencing the pain of losing "somebody that we care about is part of what makes us feel life. And if you are covering over that pain, that is like painting the diamond, because you are not letting yourself feel. You are not letting yourself appreciate how important those people have been to you. You're covering that all over." She then identified several clients by name and pointed out features of their lives where she could see the potential "brilliance and the sparkle" of the diamond. At this point she invited drug court clients to respond to her observations. Following the judge's cue, several took the microphone and, staying with the script, talked about how they had tried to cover feelings with drugs, how it didn't help their self-esteem, and how drugs only made their problems worse. They also encouraged others to "take it a day at a time," to "stay focused," and the like. So far so good.

Then the judge moved to the awards part of the ceremony. Just before doing so she acknowledged the presence of and briefly interviewed an alumnus from the drug court program. This exchange provided the first signs that not everyone would comply with the overall performance plan. The client acknowledged that the program, when he was in it, had been rough. When Duncan-Peters asked why this was so, the client said, "Cause I had to come and sit here and listen to this crap." Duncan-Peters responded, "So, you had a negative attitude when you first started?" She was also certain to point out, for the benefit of the viewing audience, that another judge ran the drug court when this client was in the program. After testimonies (which were mostly very positive) and the presentation of prizes (mugs and pens) and certificates to successful program participants, the judge asked if anyone else wanted to say something. At this point the performance began to unravel.

Taking the microphone a client began complaining about what he believed was the unfair treatment of clients by some drug court counselors. The judge tried to ease his concerns and move on, but the client kept talking. Back at the hotel uncomfortable giggles rippled across the large auditorium. Finally with comments like, "Okay, so you're discussing that with them [the counselors] about how you're going to handle that" and "So we'll talk with them about that," the judge finally pulled away from this client and gave the microphone to another, but matters did not improve. This next client had advice for the court on how the program could do a better job providing educational opportunities, preparing clients for GED exams, offering better vocational training, and helping clients get social security cards. Again, Judge Duncan-Peters nervously conceded, "I'll talk with them and see if we can work around that, too." Laughter in the hotel audience of seven hundred had by now become less constrained.

Back in the courtroom the judge then moved to another client. This third client picked up on the complaints of the first. She agreed that working with some counselors was problematic. "What I want to say is, when you come into this drug treatment program, you know what you are, you're an addict. And by you working on that, that's enough of a problem trying to keep yourself sober. You don't need someone, like a counselor that doesn't like you, doing little sneaky things." The laughter now rose among the viewing hotel audience. Getting more emphatic, the client continued, "We are here recovering, trying to stay clean, focusing on yourself, not going back to the streets. So when you have a counselor who is supposed to be there in the drug treatment program, they're supposed to be helping you, but all other times she or he is behind your back doing little things. . . ."

When it became clear the judge was not regaining control of the performance, conference officials finally just cut the video feed. "We have to stay on schedule," an organizer deadpanned.

Courtroom Theater

This brings us to the second level of theater in the drug courts, namely, local or micro theater—theater at the level of the individual drug court. In the D.C. drug court debacle, the backstage (difficult relationships between clients and therapists) unexpectedly burst onto the frontstage (the public court proceedings before a national audience) thus disrupting the carefully orchestrated performance. As mentioned above, drug court judges very consciously conceive of the drug court as theater; this is a common metaphor used to describe the program. Jeffrey Tauber specifically invokes the "drug court as theater" image in training new drug court judges. Consider Tauber's instructions: "A Drug Court Judge performs on the courtroom stage before an audience full of offenders."[7] In performance, the judge orchestrates the drama to tell a particular story. That is, the drama should flow in such a way that offenders/clients are conveyed a certain narrative that contains a central message. The predetermined or prescripted order of the court calendar, like the different scenes in a play, provides the structural demarcations of this drama. As Tauber instructs, "Shape your calendar as you would a play, with a beginning, a middle, and an end."[8]

Tauber specifies the progression of the courtroom scenes. "In-custody offenders who have failed in the program should always be seen first before a full audience of offenders." This communicates to other clients the consequences of noncompliance. In the next scene "those appearing for progress reports" are called up. Here the judge should "prominently display" successes "with applause, congratulations, and a diploma" and failures with "short-term remands into custody."[9] It is not always clear what will happen to those sent back into custody. Some may serve a short stint in the county jail, while others may be released with a stern warning against future noncompliance. The remand and the ambiguity of the ultimate outcome are all part of the larger drama. As Tauber explains, "Uncertainty of outcome after a remand, and its accompanying anxieties, can be a useful motivator for both offender and audience; consider ordering the offender into custody without stating any disposition until later, at a hearing out of the presence of the audience."[10] Thus, the defendant is treated in an intentionally ambiguous way to convey a message to the individual client and, perhaps more importantly, to the larger courtroom audience.

Arranging the calendar to produce certain effects is a common practice in the drug courts. In her analysis of fifteen drug courts, Sally Satel also found that all but one judge endorsed this practice, while a little over half actually put it into practice. Both the judge and the director of treatment in the Amherst, New York, drug court are among those who follow this basic strategy. Before the judge comes to the bench, the director of treatment, arranges the calendar to produce the greatest effect. As he describes the process, "So early in the calendar, you saw me up on the bench, I was stacking the deck, how the cases would evolve. It's kind of like I set them up and he knocks them down. That's exactly the way it is to work. We set them up. It's orchestrated. It's a show. You are putting on a show."[11]

Orchestrating the drug court show to greatest effect can be problematic when certain actors don't follow script, as occurred in Judge Duncan-Peters' court. In the D.C. case it was the drug court clients who harmfully improvised their lines. In Syracuse, New York, Judge McKinney finds that the defense lawyers, untrained in the unique features of the drug court, can ruin the larger drama. To illustrate this problem McKinney compares a hypothetical lawyer who understands drug court with another defense lawyer who does not. "So Joe Blow may come in here knowing all about drug court and understanding what the ideal lawyer's role is. Suzy Row comes in five minutes later and says, 'I insist on my client's so and so and so and so, I'm not going to go along with this disposition.' It's like wait a minute." The second lawyer is a problem in McKinney's view because she thwarts the essential message of the drug court drama. "In reality, for the benefit of the people in the gallery, drug court is like a theater, it's judicial theater," McKinney explains. "We pat some people on the back, we slap some people on the rump. We hug some people, literally, and some people we chastise. But it's all for the purpose of making sure that everybody who is here has some understanding that the purpose is all the same." Therefore, the various actors must adjust to the new roles demanded by the drug court drama.

Unfortunate for Judge McKinney, there is not just one defense lawyer assigned to his court, as is the case in other drug courts. In the Syracuse drug court, there can be nearly as many defense lawyers as individual clients. Defense attorneys unaccustomed to drug court often try to function according to traditional roles, a situation that Judge McKinney finds exasperating. When during one drug court session a defense attorney objected to the judge's therapeutically styled questioning of a client, the judge leaned back, shook his head, and smiled with knowing irritation, as though accustomed to dealing with defense attorneys untrained in the peculiarities of the drug court format. As McKinney had explained to me prior to this particular session, "there is little or no place for the normal adversarial lawyer in this context."

Michael Judge, a public defender in the Los Angeles drug court, agrees with McKinney. The drug court drama requires a new role for the defense lawyer. As Judge explains to his fellow defense lawyers, "Now, this isn't for everyone. If you just want to be an advocate or an adversary, if you want to get all your bile at work, and then go home with a smile on your face, this is not for you. If you want to get involved personally, and do something highly worthwhile, and see some tremendous successes, this will be the most rewarding thing you can do in your professional career." According to Judge, defense lawyers must "resist efforts to retreat to the comfort of our traditional roles." Like Tauber and McKinney, Judge believes this readjustment of roles is mandated by the larger purposes of drug court theater.

Because the defense lawyer has a reduced role in the drug court drama, as Judge sees it, any objections of the traditional sort should not be raised in the courtroom session. Instead, according to Judge, "the defense lawyers should engage after the courtroom." By working out backstage typical responses to typical actions, courtroom actors preserve the overall story-line of the drug court drama. As Judge puts it, "I think that it is important that these drug court professionals also sort of orchestrate how they respond in typical kinds of things that happen, because I think that that really helps in terms of making the theater part of the court effective." Michael Judge, therefore, would object to the conflicts with defense attorneys that were played out in Judge McKinney's drug court sessions. It makes bad theater.

In sum, the various actors in the drug court drama must know and understand their special roles in the overall production. Lawyers in particular, as Judge explains, must "get rid of the adversarial attitude that we have been taught so well in law school and taught so well as public defenders," in deference to the larger purpose of fostering "an environment in which this therapeutic approach will thrive." Drug court theater then is therapeutic theater. Therapeutic concerns shape the function and style of the drug court. Traditional roles must readjust to the more important orchestration of this larger therapeutic drama. As Judge John Parnham of the Pensacola, Florida, drug court puts it, "Everything that we do in that court setting, everything that we do in treatment has to have a therapeutic value to it." The therapeutic perspective, as such, informs and gives meaning to all the functions in the drug court drama. Louisville's Judge Weber links the concepts of theater and therapy in a similar way. "My personal belief," Weber states, "is that the courtroom, and what you do in the courtroom, is part of their treatment, in addition to being part of the court system, and that you have got a theater there going—the theater of treatment in the courtroom." Even the imposition of sanctions are viewed as part of the therapeutic drama.

Judges also readjust their roles in accordance with the demands of therapeutic theater. As Jamey Weitzman of the Baltimore drug court puts it, "Drug courts, it has been said many times, are theater. And the judge is the stage director and one of the primary actors." As with the theater at the movement level, the "stage director" of the local drug court works to maintain a definite backstage, one that is clearly segregated from frontstage performances. Judges often meet with other members of the drug court team (treatment personnel, lawyers, clerks, etc.) before the court session to prepare for the performance. Judge Ziemian, of Boston, for example regularly meets with his drug court team to go over each client who will be appearing before him that day. Counselors tell Judge Ziemian how a particular client is doing. The team discusses such issues as employment, urinalysis test results, 12-step meeting attendance, and the client's attitude. Counselors give input on what kind of sanctions or rewards the client should receive.

Curiously, when the clients come before Judge Ziemian he responds to the written information before him as though he were seeing it for the first time. When he then demonstrates unusually extensive knowledge of the client, this conveys the message of care, concern, and interest. As Cathy Delaney, the former director of treatment at the Boston court explains, "The review on Friday morning [before drug court] is for his [Judge Ziemian's] benefit. It is what makes him look to those clients like he knows everything about their life, and that he remembers it week for week. They think he remembers all of them personally week to week. He has a really good memory, but none of us is that good." The judge is well rehearsed, in other words, for his role. It is a practice that effectively conveys the message of judicial care and concern, which according to judges, is one of the most important characteristics of a drug court judge.[12]

As illustrated by this example, judges deliberately and consciously orchestrate drug court theater to produce certain outcomes. Consider the judicial theatrics of other judges. Judge Bruce Beaudin, former Washington, D.C., drug court judge, tells of how he used the theater of the drug court to secure banking accounts and social security cards for the children of program participants. "One of the favorite tricks in our court was the rent-a-baby. Here comes this young dude, and he's up for sentence, and he say's, 'Judge my baby and my baby's mother are here'—never 'my girlfriend' or 'my wife', 'my baby and my baby's mother.' I say, 'Bring them up here.' I walk off the bench, I go down and I say, 'Ohh.' Sometimes I hold the baby and say, 'Isn't he cute.' And this is theater; let's not forget that I've got a full courtroom watching what I'm doing. And I'm very much aware of that." Beaudin explains further how he uses this theater to get the father of the child to open up a bank account and acquire a social security card for the kid. "He's going to have done two legal things. He's going to achieve having opened a bank account, walked into a bank with something other than a criminal thought in his mind, and the baby is going to have a social security number. Now how many times do you see that in the community in which we work?"

Judge Anthony Violante of the Niagara Falls, New York, drug court also employs improvisational acts to effect certain outcomes. It is common in drug courts for clients to register positive urinalysis tests and then deny that they had used drugs. They may claim, for example, that they were around people smoking crack or marijuana, that drugs used weeks prior were still in their system, or that they had taken a form of aspirin with codeine in it. During a session in Judge Violante's court a client claimed that "he couldn't figure out how he got a positive [urine test]." Judge Violante used the theater of drug court to challenge this client's denial of drug use. Jeffrey Smith, director of treatment at the Niagara Falls drug court, recounts the incident.

> The judge plays along with it and said, "Are you sure you weren't around it?" And the guy says, "Oh yeah, oh yeah, I'm sure I probably was around it that day." And the judge said, "Maybe people were doing it around you and you were close to them." The judge played him. And finally he gets to the point and he goes, "Were you maybe holding it?" And the guy said, "Yeah, yeah, it was a pretty big rock and I was hanging onto it in my hand," the guy is saying. And now the judge walks into this sideman thing, and you could hear the audience, the rest of the clients, laughing out loud at this guy now, now knowing that this guy is just done. And judge goes, "Were you squeezing it tight?" And the guy goes, "Yeah I was kind of holding it tight judge." And the judge looked at him and goes, "Do you know how full of bullshit you are?" And the guy looks at him and goes, "I knew I wasn't going anywhere but I had the story."

The judge used the drama of the drug court to reveal this client's deceit. He played off the attention and interest of the audience in the all important judge/client dialogue to extend the client's story to its absurd end. The responsive audience, realizing the judge's method, assisted in the process of helping this client to understand and admit the ridiculous nature of his story. Thus, as with Beaudin's theatrics, Judge Violante uses the dramaturgical format of the drug court to effect certain ends. The drug court judge is cognizant of a definite audience and can play off the audience to bring about a desired outcome.

In the Amherst drug court, Judge Mark Farrell uses the urinalysis test for courtroom drama. Every court session clients are chosen "randomly" to take a urinalysis test, though as the judge admitted to me, some are chosen because the treatment providers are suspicious of drug use. Clients chosen for a test leave the court and return, literally, with a small container of urine, which is tested by the director of treatment in front of the bench. When the test is complete, the treatment provider asks the client, who is now standing before the judge, when the client last used cocaine, smoked marijuana, and drank alcohol. The client is unaware that they cannot test for the latter. Still the inquiry is done for effect. In fact, the whole episode is done for effect. As Judge Farrell explains, "Some of them [the urinalysis tests] are random and they come up negative. Some of it's done for effect. Some of them who haven't used get so scared they might be willing to say they use, just to not put them through the anxiety of going through the test." Judges are thus fully aware, as revealed in these examples, of the dramaturgical qualities of the drug court setting and deliberately use therapeutic theater to effect certain outcomes.

Redefined Courtroom Roles

Also evident in these examples is the radically redefined roles of the courtroom actors in the drug court drama. In a normal criminal court the main actors in the courtroom drama are the lawyers who speak on behalf of their clients and who engage each other in an adversarial manner. The client and the judge, on the other hand, rarely speak in a traditional criminal court. The roles are totally reversed in the drug court, where lawyers are virtually silent (if they are even present) and where the extended discussions between the judge and defendants are the main action in the drug court drama. Like the judge and lawyers, then, the defendant's role is also fundamentally altered in the drug court. That they are called "clients" rather than "defendants" or "offenders" is, of course, not just a superficial alteration in judicial nomenclature. The new label speaks volumes about how these clients are understood and treated. Additionally, as illustrated in the Amherst example above, treatment providers play a much more pronounced role in a drug court than they ever did in regular criminal courts, even in the more rehabilitatively oriented juvenile courts of the first part of the twentieth century.

Given the radical departure from traditional criminal court roles, officials offer prospective drug court professionals specific redefinitions of their roles for the drug court setting. Clearly delineated in NADCP literature and Justice Department reports are the important shifts in thinking and practice judicial actors must assume. A common theme guiding the redefinition of roles is the so-called "team approach" of the drug courts. Instead of operating in conflictual relationships, the various actors in the drug court drama are to work together. "Successful treatment-based drug court programs are built on collaboration. To effectively create a courtroom atmosphere that is rehabilitative, the judge, prosecutor, public defender, treatment providers, and others must work as a 'team' to promote rehabilitation by placing a high priority on the defendant's success."[13]

Such a collaborative approach, of course, directly affects the functions of lawyers and, in particular, the relationship between the defense and prosecuting attorneys. To a group of prospective drug court judges, Judge Tauber offered the following instructions on the role of attorneys in the drug court setting. "A successful drug court depends on the willingness of you and your staff to work as a team. Prosecuting and defense attorneys avoid confrontations in court and work together to sell the program to potential offenders. The defense attorney (literally and figuratively) takes a step back, rarely getting between you and the offender. The prosecuting attorney adopts a conciliatory position. All staff see their job as the facilitation of the offender's rehabilitation."[14] In deference, then, to the larger goal of the client's recovery, lawyers must fundamentally depart from normal practices, acting as cooperative partners rather than legal adversaries.

Not all make the transition to the disease model painlessly. Drug court actors still sympathetic to traditional approaches can come into intense conflict with those operating from the treatment perspective. Often the early planning and implementation of a court are characterized by significant tensions between the various actors. More advanced drug courts have made efforts to help nascent courts identify and iron out differences before a new drug court program is launched. Movement leaders are fully cognizant of the dichotomy and potential tension between the traditional adjudication process which focuses on "the defendant's guilt or innocence" and the treatment approach which "generally adopts a health promotion/disease prevention model in which the treatment professional works with the client to overcome what is seen as a biopsychosocial disease or disorder."[15]

Reconciling these traditionally distinct focuses can be a very difficult process, particularly for those trained in the legal system, who are unaccustomed to and thus leery of—at least initially—therapeutic forms of justice. For some it represents a fundamental challenge to their understanding of constitutional law. Both prosecuting and defense attorneys have problems with the drug court, though the issues over which they struggle differ. That prosecutors, who are typically more politically conservative, and defense attorneys, who are typically more politically liberal, have their own misgivings with the drug court underscores the point made in the last chapter that the drug court is not easily classified according to conventional political categories.

The Drug Court Defense Lawyer

The effect of this non-adversarial team-approach on the defense attorney is particularly pronounced.[16] Traditionally, the defense counsel is concerned with protecting, in a highly adversarial setting, the client's constitutional rights and liberties. The defense function is seen as a protective counterforce against the formidable law enforcement and prosecutorial resources of the state. The defense lawyer's job is to assert every ethical and legal barrier in opposition to perceived efforts against the client's welfare. As stated in the American Bar Association's standards for judicial functions, "The basic duty defense counsel owes to the administration of justice and as an officer of the court is to serve as the accused's counselor and advocate with courage and devotion and to render effective, quality representation."[17] In its service to the overall administration of justice, then, the traditional defense function ideally contributes toward the assurance of a "just" outcome for the defendant. Moreover, defense lawyers have typically been skeptical of alternative "problem solving" approaches to criminal defense.

The drug court, of course, fully departs from this traditional defense posture. Defense lawyers are, in essence, asked to consider the "higher" priorities of helping solve the client's drug addiction problem. As Los Angeles defense attorney Michael Judge argues, the drug court defense lawyer is asked to consider "long term general lifestyle outcomes rather than only the immediate consequences viewed from an adversarial perspective." Or as John Goldkamp puts it, "A critical question for defense lawyers has to do with the priority of safeguarding a defendant's (or, at later stages, a convicted person's) legal rights versus doing what is in the best interest of the client."[18] Reflected in this statement are two important assumptions: first, that the protection of a client's rights and what is best for him or her may be somehow incompatible; and, second, that the drug court program *is* in the best interest of the client.

Regardless of the validity of these assumptions, the shift in courtroom roles presents a quandary for the defense lawyer, particularly when, as noted in chapter 2, the drug court can be much more demanding on the client than the traditional adjudicative process. This was a central concern raised by defense lawyers at 1993 conference in Miami, Florida. Defense counsel present at the meeting worried that "involvement in the drug court treatment program could be more onerous," with respect to both the time the defendant is "subject to court control" and the "degree of restriction of liberty." Moreover defense counsel were concerned that the drug court program might be worse "than whatever else the defendant might receive as a disposition, including a short term of incarceration or probation."[19] As we have seen and as many drug court judges admit, such defense-based fears are often realized.

The "attitudinal shift" necessitated by the drug court paradigm, as Michael Judge explains, requires that defense lawyers reinterpret this potential "loss of liberty" within the larger context of "a total treatment strategy," one that, once again, has "the clients best interests" in mind. Unlike traditional criminal courts, the drug court is a "problem-solving" court that addresses "the root causes of addiction and other issues relating to the social and economic viability of the client."[20] Based on these larger concerns the defense lawyer should willingly "participate in the design of the 'theatre' of the courtroom," and "play a more team-oriented, encouraging, and pro-treatment role in the drug court than would normally be the case."[21] Moreover, among the defense lawyer's new roles, as specified by the Justice Department, is explaining to the defendant "all of the rights that the defendant will temporarily or permanently waive," encouraging the defendant "to be truthful with the judge and with treatment staff," discussing "with the defendant the long-term benefits of sobriety and a drug-free life," and informing the defendant "that he or she will be expected to speak directly to the judge, not through an attorney."[22] In the context of the drug court, then, the defense lawyer very decidedly jettisons some traditional responsibilities in deference to the defining assumptions of a therapeutic perspective.[23]

Not all defense lawyers easily accept their new role in the judicial process. Some are nervous about potential violations to their clients' Fourteenth Amendment due process rights and Sixth Amendment rights to a speedy trial and to a trial by jury. Defense lawyers also worry about equal protection rights, the demanding and open-ended nature of the drug court, and violations of confidentiality laws. The latter becomes a problem when clients speak openly—as they are regularly encouraged to do—in court and in treatment sessions about their drug addictions, their family lives, their jobs, and other activities. Indeed, as noted above, one of the defense lawyer's new roles is to encourage the client "to be truthful with the judge and with treatment staff." Honesty, openness, and vulnerability are defining expectations in the treatment process. A cardinal sin, on the other hand, is to remain "in denial."

But what if the client fails the treatment program and returns to a regular court docket? Can the information gathered during his tenure in the drug court program be used against him? This presents a problem when the drug court judge is the same judge who will hear the case in the regular docket—a practice that occurs in some courts. But even when the judge is not the same, as is more often the case, defense lawyers worry that failed drug court clients will be dealt with prejudicially.[24] Some courts, in fact, are arranged in such a way that failed clients are sentenced based upon the "stipulated facts" of the case, that is, according to the evidence in the police report. In the Sacramento, California, drug court, for example, when clients enter the drug court program they agree that "if they fail . . . the trial will be submitted to a judge on the police reports only." As Judge Gerald Bakarich of the Sacramento drug court explains, "They are going to waive their right to confrontation, waive their right to a jury trial, waive their right to a speedy trial. If they fail for one reason or another, the police report is merely given to a judge and that is his trial. The judge will find him guilty or not guilty based on the police reports." Therefore, though failed drug court clients go back to the regular court system, they may not get a jury trial or even legal representation.

Given these kinds of ethical dilemmas, adjustment to the new paradigm by defense lawyers can be very difficult. In a number of courts, resistance by defense lawyer was one of the main obstacles the drug court team members faced in getting the program up and running smoothly. In Roanoke, Virginia, for example, treatment providers reported that, along with the police department, defense attorneys were their biggest problem. As one treatment provider put it, "Defense attorneys don't want drug court. . . . They don't want to have their client waive all their rights, drop urine three to four times a week, and do all that the drug court requires." Instead, they would rather have their clients go on probation, see a probation officer once a month for a year, and then get their charges dismissed—which, in Virginia, is an option for some drug offenses.

Defense lawyers have also, as discussed above, posed problems in Judge McKinney's Syracuse, New York, drug court. Lawyers who understand the treatment approach, according to McKinney, have been cooperative, but with those who do not "understand drug court and its values" he has had greater difficulties. A recalcitrant defense attorney is, in McKinney's words, "a tough nut to crack." He has had trouble getting them "to abandon their traditional adversary roles" and has been frustrated with their objections to some of the sanctions he imposes, particularly sanctions that include jail time. He reminds defense attorneys, when they make such objections, that they agreed to the unique features of the drug court at the outset, that their clients waived their constitutional rights, and that they were told up front that noncompliance would result in "having to go to jail for awhile."

Defense lawyers in Charlottesville, Virginia, were also initially wary about the drug court concept. One defense attorney, who was part of the planning team, summarized the misgivings of his defense bar colleagues. First, defense lawyers wondered "what was in it" for them and what "ulterior motives" the prosecutors might have for starting a drug court. Second, they were troubled about the virtual "veto power" the drug court team was planning to give to prosecutors. Finally, they were concerned about the swiftness with which defendants would move into the program, not allowing defense lawyers enough time to adequately investigate cases. This last issue is a direct consequence of the introduction of the treatment model into the courtroom. Treatment personnel believe that immediate involvement in treatment is necessary for successful recovery. The shock of arrest serves to make a defendant more open to treatment. A Charlottesville prosecuting attorney, though acknowledging the legitimacy of the defense bar's concerns, responded that "to obtain the benefits of the program, we feel there needs to be expedited procedures." Why? Because this is what "the treatment people feel." In other words, it is what a therapeutic perspective requires.[25]

Related worries were identified by defense lawyers responding to the 1997 Justice Department survey of operational drug courts. In survey responses defense lawyers expressed concern about the "misuse of search and seizure waivers," "increased restrictions on defendants," "prosecution control of entry" into the program, and "dealing cooperatively with the D.A.'s office to protect rights of defendants."[26] Others admitted that adjusting to the non-adversarial nature of the drug court was difficult. Rochester, New York, defense counsel, for example, acknowledged that this was one of the most serious problems they encountered in implementing the drug court, noting that the new method was "very different from how we generally do our job."[27] What these sometimes conflictual adjustments represent is the fundamental difference between the therapeutic approach of adjudicating offenders and the traditional adversarial approach as understood from the position of the defense lawyer. Some judges are concerned that defense lawyers will not move beyond their legal training to accept the basic orientation of the therapeutic approach. Judge Ziemian, for example, worries:

> Our traditions are going to make it very difficult to move in the direction of a therapeutic court. The whole defense bar is totally against that because their ethical considerations are to protect their defendants' rights. And the way they protect their rights is to, no matter what, keep them out of jail. That is their sole concern. This kind of drug court is the beginning of perhaps a wider concern for defense counsel, a more long term concern for them. I am hopeful that we will change.

But Ziemian realizes this change may not come easily, that it goes against the very core of the defense bar's traditionally understood legal responsibility. The traditional legal disposition and method, however, is one that Ziemian and other movement activists see as highly problematic. "What happens [in the normal adjudicative process] is the defendants say things which are lies to the defense attorney. The defense attorney then repeats them in open court." The defendants, according to Ziemian, are "already in denial," and the enabling complicity of the defense lawyer simply makes matters worse. "It is such a detriment to even the beginning of a therapeutic situation," Ziemian argues. "It's awful."

In response to these concerns, movement activists encourage drug court planning teams to address early in the process areas of conflict and disagreement. And though the voices of the defense attorneys are certainly taken seriously, advice in literature produced by the Justice Department and others, is for attorneys to put aside their traditional legal training and adapt to the new program. Therefore, though defense attorneys are encouraged to have a voice in the planning and implementation of the drug court, they must ultimately assume a therapeutically redefined role; the defense lawyer must discard his or her traditional legal training. As the Wilmington, Delaware, drug court defense lawyer, Edmund Hillis, put it, "The defense lawyer doesn't fit well in this system in his traditional role." The best solution, according to Hillis, is to get the lawyer out of the way as quickly as possible.

> Design the programs in such a way that the adversarial nature of the proceedings are over early on, and you can get the lawyers out of the process. Defendants tend to use their lawyers to protect them. And in the therapeutic environment, which is kinder and gentler, that is probably not a productive thing. So, if you get the legal issues out of the way early, provide the representation that is needed, address the concerns of the protection of constitutional rights, and move along in your program, you will be better off.

In the end, then, the defense lawyer adapts or steps aside in order to preserve the integrity of the "therapeutic environment."

The Drug Court Prosecutor

The role of the prosecuting attorney is also fundamentally altered by the therapeutic approach of drug court theater. The traditional district attorney is concerned with representing the interests of the state, protecting offended victims, and making a persuasive prosecutorial case against offenders. As guardians of public safety, prosecutors are concerned with protecting the community from the impact of criminal behavior. As with the defense lawyer, the drug court district attorney is asked to put aside some traditional approaches for the greater ideals of therapeutic justice. As Goldkamp observes, "Ultimately, the prosecutor, like the other actors, must decide that providing the opportunity for treatment is an important and appropriate part of the responsibility to provide justice."[28]

Among the difficult issues that prosecutors face in accepting this expanded understanding of justice is handing over more discretion to the judge and treatment providers than is the case in the normal adjudicative setting. That prosecutors yield authority in this manner is glaringly evident in the drug court setting, where prosecutors, if they are even present at all, play a very limited role. Consider, for example, a description of the district attorney's (D.A.) role offered by the prosecuting attorney in the Rochester, New York, drug court. "I stay out of the way of the treatment providers. I just bite my lip. Instead of opening my mouth, I whisper in [the case manager's] ear, then I whisper to the judge. I try to stay in the background. I try to stay in the shadows." It is not surprising, given this description, that an observer of the Rochester drug court likened the D.A. to a "potted plant." The Rochester D.A. did, however, retain one weapon in his reduced prosecutorial arsenal. When everyone else in the room applauded the client, he did not. "I don't clap because I want them to remember that a district attorney is standing there." During a session in the Los Angeles drug court the district attorney did even less. Not uttering a single word during the entire afternoon session, she limited her involvement to little more than taking notes on a legal pad. The judge hardly acknowledged her presence, except at one point to look her way when telling one client, "I want to help you. The D.A. wants to help you. Normally, she wants to put you in jail."

Adjusting to this new role can be difficult for prosecutors. The 1997 Justice Department survey found that district attorneys had a number of problems adapting to drug courts. Some prosecutors struggle with eligibility criteria and worry that ineligible clients (including those who do not have a drug addiction problem) find a way into drug courts. Others express concerns about reduced possibilities for effective prosecution after program failures. When clients drop out of drug court, it has usually been months, even years, since the original arrest, making it more difficult for prosecutors to investigate cases, interview witnesses (who may have moved or whose memory of the incident is less fresh), and put together satisfactory prosecutions.

Given these kinds of reservations district attorneys have sometimes posed very real obstacles to the initiation and operation of a drug court. In the Key West, Florida, drug court, for example, treatment personnel complained about the state attorney's refusal to "automatically divert first time felony drug offenders" to drug court.[29] Getting the "D.A.s office 'on board'" was also an issue in the Las Cruces, New Mexico, drug court.[30] In Tampa, Florida, treatment providers struggled to get support from the state attorney's office concerning some of the treatment or "nonpunishment" aspects of the court program.[31] District attorneys in Charlottesville, Virginia, nearly derailed the initiation of Charlottesville's drug court program. During the planning stages, prosecutors insisted on a system of graduated sanctions, including a policy of client dismissal after four positive urine tests. The judge and treatment providers argued forcefully against this standard, claiming that such a policy ignored the realities of addiction and that if the policy was adopted, the Charlottes-ville drug court would have no graduates. At one point, in the heat of the disagreement, one treatment provider insisted that she could not profes-sionally and ethically support a program "where people are destined to fail and it would ruin their lives." Another member of the planning team agreed that the policy would cause more failures than successes in the drug court program and suggested that prosecutors "take a longer and closer look at the realities of the addictive needs."

District attorneys caused even more serious problems in Fort Lauder-dale, where they intensely opposed the drug court from its very outset. Broward State Attorney Michael Satz, emphasizing his traditional duty to protect citizens from criminal actions, objected to a program that erased the arrest record of a drug offender. He believed it took away from his ability to press for a stiffer penalty should the client commit a crime in the future. He also believed the drug court shifted too much authority away from the district attorney to the judge. Satz was a constant source of frus-tration to Judge Fogan in operating the Broward County drug court. He even kept a file on Fogan's courtroom statements and on the progress and success rates of drug court clients. Criticism eventually led to a Broward County audit of Fogan's drug court, the results of which faulted Judge Fogan for being too lenient with defendants, even in some cases ignoring the recommendations of treatment counselors who advised stricter sanc-tions. Consequently Fogan was removed from drug court and reassigned to a juvenile court docket.[32]

The outcome of this case, however, is rather anomalous. More typi-cally, prosecutors are forced to get over their hang-ups and adapt to the overall purposes of drug court. Though initially skeptical, many ulti-mately accept this position and the reduction in discretion that it requires. As one D.A. put it in a meeting with other prosecutors, "The D.A. gives up a certain amount of authority. That is something you are going to have to come to grips with." A Justice Department report makes the same basic point. "The prosecutor and defense counsel *must shed* their traditional adversarial courtroom relationship and work together as a team. Once a defendant is accepted into the drug court program, the team's focus is on the participant's recovery and law-abiding behavior—not on the merits of the pending case."[33]

Even D.A.s who support drug court programs, however, run into problems. For example, pro drug court prosecutors have sometimes had difficulty convincing law enforcement officers to accept the program. The relationship with police is one prosecutors value. It is, therefore, impor-tant to get police officers on board early, as Kansas City prosecutor Claire

McCaskill explains. "It is really important that you spend some time with the guys who are actually going through the doors of the drug house, with the bullet proof stuff on, the attack team, the guys who are working under cover, because they are the ones who look you right in the eye and say, 'Let me get this straight, I'm out here risking my life, going to the door of this drug house, and you are going to give the guy a baby-sitter and a job?' And that is a tough question to answer." According to McCaskill, law enforcement officers' input and involvement in the early planning of the drug court is imperative.

To summarize, like the defense attorney, then, the prosecuting attorney is asked to adjust his or her role in conformance with the greater interests of therapeutic theater. Because the therapeutic perspective assumes a more central and defining place in the judicial drama, "the prosecuting attorney," as Jeffrey Tauber puts it, "adopts a conciliatory position." As with other actors in the therapeutic theater of drug court, prosecutors must "see their job as the facilitation of the offender's rehabilitation."[34]

The Adjustment of Other Actors to Drug Court Theater

Lawyers are not the only actors who must adjust to the particular requirements of drug court drama; other criminal justice officials must also substantially alter their roles. Probation officers, for example, are often asked to give over the management of offenders to treatment providers or to substantially change the way they function. Many have actually been retrained in drug therapy to assist in the drug court treatment process. As with some lawyers, not all probation officers have been immediately amenable to their new roles.

In Louisville, according to Judge Weber, "more than prosecutors and police officers, the probation people do not like this. They do not like it." Like lawyers, however, probation officers can make the adjustment. Weber tells of one who started with a very skeptical attitude toward drug court. After the first couple of times a client failed a urine screen, the probation officer argued, "Well, I'm going to make a revocation motion." Judge Weber responded in kind, "You go right ahead and do it. I'm going to hear it." According to Weber, it took the probation officer "awhile to understand what I meant by that." Over time, however, the probation officer adjusted to his new role. Something that helped in this process was "having him go to some other places, conferences and listen to other people, so he's not hearing just from this one crazy judge." While this probation officer eventually "really bought into" the drug court program, other probation officers in Louisville have remained skeptical. As Weber explains, "His colleagues over at the Probation Department still are having a very hard time with this notion. . . . The probation officers just do not get it."

In Oakland a similar reluctance and period of adjustment was necessary for probation personnel. "Several probation officers said they resented trading familiar tasks like writing reports for new ones like running group counseling sessions and having their discretion eroded."[35] In this case, however, it was reported that "they quickly found their new roles more satisfying than the old ones and the results inspiring."[36] Today in the Oakland drug court, probation officers play a central role in providing treatment to drug court clients.

In addition to criminal justice officials, the drug court changes the offender's role in the criminal court, something we have already touched on and will discuss in greater detail in following chapters. Suffice it to say here, though, that the defendant's role in the drug court drama is radically altered. In a typical criminal court the offender says very little, if anything. Normally defendants are represented by counsel, the experts in legal matters, who speak on their behalf. In the drug court, the client directly engages the judge, and is asked to be open and honest with the judge about all sorts of issues. In the drug court, a client not only talks openly about his or her drug use but about employment, family, friendships, and financial concerns. Perhaps even more significantly, the drug court client not only discusses behavior but feelings, thoughts, attitudes, and beliefs. It is not surprising, therefore, that Judge Ron Spivey of the Winston-Salem, North Carolina, drug court could say, "In a regular court, we know very little about the offender before us. . . . [In drug court] I know almost everything about the offender before me."[37]

In the theater of the drug court, as already mentioned, the main act is between the judge and the client. In many courts the client stands alone before the judge. To emphasize the central importance of the conversation between judge and client, some courts actually microphone the client so that everyone else in the audience can hear the conversation. One judge has even contemplated moving the client "off to the side" so that the audience can have a better view of the main two players in the drug court drama. The Denver drug court even uses a split screen television set to allow the rest of the gallery audience to see "both judge and participant and hear the proceedings."[38]

The importance of the dialogue between the defendant and the judge is also revealed in participants' perceptions of the drug court. In the 1997 Justice Department survey, responses from 250 participants in the final stages of treatment from fifty different drug courts reveal that participants view the intensity of the client/judge relationship as central to the success of the program. Eighty percent of the respondents report that they would not have stayed in the program had they not appeared before a judge as a part of the program.[39] Seventy-five percent of the clients report that it is "very important" that "a judge monitors my progress."[40]

In facing the judge in the courtroom, the client will occasionally have a lawyer standing at his or her side. More often, however, if the client is accompanied by anyone, it is a treatment counselor or the director of the treatment program. Counselors advise the judge on how the client has been performing in the program and may suggest to the judge some kind of sanction or reward. This exchange between judge and counselor, as we have already seen, is often rehearsed, with the sanctions or rewards pre-determined. The presence of treatment personnel in the courtroom setting is, of course, one of the unique qualities of the drug court drama and symbolizes in a tangible manner the centrality of the therapeutic para-digm in the courtroom drama.

Outside of the court, of course, treatment providers play an even more central role. Counselors handle the day-to-day treatment of the drug court clients. They administer urinalysis tests, run individual and group therapy sessions, provide acupuncture treatment, and help clients with GED testing and job placement. With the possible exception of acupunc-ture treatment, these are the same basic functions treatment providers performed in TASC. The major difference is the regular contact with the court and the added authority vested in the treatment providers by the backing of the court. As often as once a week the client returns to court where treatment providers update the judge on the client's performance. Urinalysis test results, attendance records, job status, receptivity to differ-ent treatment modalities, and attitude are among the pieces of informa-tion treatment personnel pass along to the judge.

Treatment providers, of course, are the personnel representing the other major partner in the drug court's marriage of treatment and crimi-nal law. The impact of the therapeutic worldview, however, is much more profound than the physical presence of therapists in the courtroom, as significant as this is. That is, the role of the treatment provider represents just one component of the larger impact of therapeutic sensibilities on the adjudication process. The unique role of the treatment provider in the drug court drama is given further consideration in chapter 6. Here I will briefly discuss what is perhaps the most critical adjustment issue faced by the treatment community when it plays a role in the new drug court drama.

As with defense counsel, confidentiality is an important issue for treat-ment providers. Because confidentiality is a highly valued, indeed legally protected, feature of the usual treatment relationship, the drug court set-ting poses a dilemma for those in the treatment community. In drug courts, clinicians regularly report to the judge on the client's progress, and clients sometimes sign waivers allowing for the disclosure of confidential information. Figuring out how to handle confidential client information was a particularly difficult issue in the Brooklyn drug court where, according to one treatment provider, the drug court team members devoted considerable study and discussion to the matter. This treatment provider is still concerned that judges and district attorneys do not have enough respect for treatment's concern with confidentiality. "I will say this," she began. "There is a notion sometimes on the part of judges and on the part of defense attorneys, district attorneys, everybody in the team, to want to know everything about participants, about their history, so that they too can be part of the whole process. And while it is a partnership, there really has to be a certain amount of respect for the parameters of the treatment world."

The director of treatment of the Boston drug court, following squabbles with probation officers over access to information, took measures to ensure that these parameters would be respected. She maintains two files to protect confidential information given by clients to treatment providers. Consider her explanation for this practice: "There have been some rifts. Treatment has strict confidentiality laws. Probation has none. Probation can talk to who they want to talk to. They can tell whatever they want to tell. So, we are very careful with what information we give to our probation officer. I have two sets of files. One is a treatment file. One is a probation file. The only file that people can get at through the freedom of information act is the probation file."

Questions may arise, however, when treatment providers discover certain kinds of information. What if a treatment provider discovers in therapy sessions that the client is actually a dealer and doesn't really have a drug addiction problem? (Incidentally, this occurs more often than many movement advocates would care to admit.) One treatment provider with whom I spoke admitted that as many as half of the drug court clients in his program were not addicts but dealers.[41] Another described the following incident that took place in her drug court. "Our probation officer was trying to get a client to open up and made the mistake of saying, 'This is just between you and me, but what is going on?' And it came out that he [the client] is dealing drugs. So in treatment team she [the probation officer] came in and told us this, and as a treatment provider I'm not supposed to have this information. I still haven't been able to deal with this." Occurrences such as these raise difficult questions. Having discovered this information, should the treatment people not pass it along to the judge? If they do, does this not represent a violation of therapeutic confidentiality? Could it be used in another court case should the defendant face other charges, which is also not an uncommon experience?

Given these concerns, treatment providers have had to work through competing allegiances, and not all have entirely resolved them or arrived at the same conclusions. Consider the quandaries of a treatment provider in the San Bernardino drug court. On the wall of the treatment center where he works, which is just down the road from the court house, is the following aphorism: "What you say here let it stay here." The treatment provider says of it, "That is a golden rule." Therefore, when he talks with the judge, he may speak in generalities or deliberately withhold potentially problematic information about a client. "I don't always tell the judge that stuff, because I'm treatment." In the context of drug court, however, if the judge pointedly asks about a particular matter, this treatment provider will be forthcoming. As he explains, "If he asks me, I am going to tell him. But I'm also going to say, 'Judge, please don't bring this up in open court.' And he is understanding of this." The treatment provider offers these warnings to the judge because of past occurrences when previously disclosed information was subsequently discussed by the judge in the courtroom drama. "Now, when we first started doing this, he put some things out there . . . I won't say they were inappropriate. It is hard for me to correct a judge. So, we all have been learning. I've been teaching him about my role, and he has been teaching me about his."

The director of treatment services in Miami likewise summarized the emphasis of the usual treatment approach: "We have always been very client centered. Okay, that is the point of treatment. It is to focus on the client, the client's needs, the client's problems." In drug court, on the other hand, "one of the main things that the treatment providers have to do is to reorient themselves as to who they serve. We don't just serve the client anymore. We now serve the client and the court. And that is hard to do. That is where you get into the issues of confidentiality." The National Drug Court Institute (NDCI) released a document identifying this tension, in which it is argued that the disclosure of information is vital for the proper functioning of a drug court. "Tension between confidentiality laws and drug courts can arise, however, because confidentiality laws restrict the spread of information, while drug courts can only function if information is shared among the members of the drug court team."[42]

The conflicts that emerge as a consequence of this tension can be overcome, according to this report, "by adjusting drug court procedures or by obtaining consent from participants."[43] Regarding the latter, the report provides sample waiver forms for use by courts to permit the disclosure of confidential information in the drug court context. Accepting this practice, and the unique qualities of the drug court more generally, some treatment providers have fewer scruples than others about disclosing confidential information to judges and other members of the treatment team. A treatment provider from the Las Vegas drug court, for example, asserted that because drug court "is such a different sort of animal," he doesn't have a problem sharing information with other members of the drug court team. As he put it, "I honestly believe from the bottom of my heart and gut and soul that the judge and D.A. and public defender are a part of my treatment team."

Thus, in drug court the treatment provider also must adapt his or her role to the new setting. All actors in the courtroom drama must adjust their roles in the context of a program that merges therapeutic and traditional criminal justice perspectives. As one judge put it during a panel discussion at the 1999 Miami drug court conference, "I think judges should be judges. I think therapists should be therapists, and so on. But when we come together a new thing happens, and that is therapeutic justice." To achieve this "new thing," as another judge added, "everybody gives up turf. In a drug treatment court, everybody, every single one of us is giving up turf." A probation officer, in response to this judge, took it one more step. "I think you have to go further than that," he said. "I think you have to actually take on a little bit of everybody else's role as well. We have to sort of learn to meld together."

To summarize, the therapeutic theater of drug court requires fundamental role transformations for the major actors in the courtroom drama. While new actors are added to the scene (treatment providers) and others have substantially reduced roles (attorneys), the main drama takes place between the client and the judge. In this chapter we have considered the transformation of courtroom roles and the concomitant tensions these changes sometimes create. The one actor to whom we have given only scant attention is the main actor in drug court theater, namely the drug court judge. Because the judge is the leading figure both in the courtroom drama and in the drug court movement, we turn now to a fuller discussion of the judge's transformed role in the drug court context and the consequences, intended and unintended, that this transformation effects.

Four

The Un-Common Law

Judges in these courts have a new role. No longer
remote umpires of legal disputes, Drug Treatment
Court judges play an active role in the treatment
process: monitoring compliance, rewarding
progress, and sanctioning infractions.
  —Judge Judith S. Kaye

One dramatic departure from the traditional
model is the role of the drug court judge. These
judges are not neutral factfinders. . . . This novel
judicial role confers great institutional power. . . .
[I]t departs considerably from the traditional
American conception of the judicial role.
  —Harvard Law Review *(May 1998)*

IN THE LAST chapter I considered the extent to which the theater of the
modern drug court represents a fundamentally new type of courtroom
drama, with traditional courtroom actors playing decidedly untraditional
roles. In this chapter I give more focused attention to the drug court
judge, whose role in the drug court drama is perhaps the most altered.
The redefined role of the drug court judge is hard to miss. Even those with
only limited exposure to the U.S. criminal justice system would find the
actions of the drug court judge clearly out of the ordinary. The profundity
of the change, however, is even more significant than it first appears. The
drug court and the actions of the judge in it represent an important departure from the U.S. common law tradition, a change that is, as we will
see, commensurate with broader changes taking place in the American
judiciary.
  But first, what is the common law from which the drug court has allegedly disengaged? The common law refers to several different things. For
one, it is to be distinguished from the Roman-based civil law tradition of
continental Europe, what Weber described as the prototypical embodiment of formal legal rationalism. The common law, contrastingly, is
judge-made or case law, and has its origins in the English system dating
back to the middle ages. In the common law tradition, judicial decisions

are not made through reference to an aggregate and comprehensive legal code—as is the case in the civil law tradition—but to judicial precedent and in accordance with a particular method of decision making. In other words, the common law refers both to an evolving body of law that is developed on a case by case basis and to the particular process of reasoning that goes into deciding these cases. As Roscoe Pound, then Dean of Harvard Law School, put it over a half century ago, the common law is both a "body of authoritative materials" and a "judicial process"—a process that is itself defined by a particular cognitive disposition or "frame of mind."[1] The judicial "frame of mind" endemic to the common law tradition requires a high level of restraint, discipline, craftsmanship, and careful reasoning. It is a legal orientation that has "always," as Pound explains, "imposed upon itself limitations."[2]

Writing in the early 1960s, Karl Llewellyn offered a similar understanding of the common law. For Llewellyn, like Pound, the common law refers to a distinctive "way of thought and work," a particular "manner of doing the job," a kind of "craftsmanship in office."[3] The common law judge, according to Llewellyn, strives toward impartiality, avoids cases in which he may be personally interested, and endeavors to discern the "true essence" of a conflict from "accidents of person, personality, and the like."[4] The impartial, common law judge, moreover, works within a tradition that is deeply connected to the past yet allows for the "ongoing renovation of doctrine." This renovation, however, occurs only gradually. In Llewellyn's words, it does not have the "smell of revolution or . . . of campaigning reform."[5] Adjudicating within the common law tradition, then, is not for the maverick or the revolutionary. Rather, as classically conceived, the role of the common law judge requires a great deal of restraint.

Mary Ann Glendon characterizes the nature of this restraint as threefold: "structural restraint," or those limits placed on the judge by the other branches of government, by the federalist system, and by the court's place in the hierarchy of the judiciary; "interpretive restraint," or those limits required by judicial deference to constitutional precepts, statutory law, and legal precedent; and "personal restraint," or the limits the judge places on herself in her efforts to be fair, impartial, objective, and dispassionate.[6] The common law, as such, requires a certain kind of judge, trained in a particular tradition, who operates within the confines of important structurally and personally imposed limitations. It is a passive rather than an active posture, which, again, distinguishes it from the civil law tradition.

The common law judge, as Lawrence Friedman explains, "sits on the bench as an august, reverend umpire," whereas the civil law judge is one who will actively "investigate" and "develop evidence" for a particular case.[7] The common law judge literally and figuratively stays behind the bench, while the civil law judge, often behaving more like an American lawyer, does not. According to comparative law scholars these contrasting judicial roles represent a major point of difference between the two legal systems.[8] The more passive role of the common law judge was, in fact, a defining feature of the American judiciary that so impressed Tocqueville in his famous early nineteenth-century investigation into American culture and society. American "judicial power is, by its nature," Tocqueville observed, "devoid of action; it must be put in motion in order to produce a result. . . . It does not pursue criminals, hunt out wrongs, or examine evidence of its own accord." To do so would "do violence to the passive nature of his authority."[9] As traditionally understood, then, the common law judge is one who operates within a particular system, is committed to carrying on a certain tradition, and employs a unique frame of mind—approaching the adjudicative process with disinterest, impartiality, passivity, and restraint.

Abraham Lincoln once worried that a thirst for distinction might remain a defining feature of American leadership, and that in such an established democracy as the United States a passion for distinction would prove "highly dangerous." In its place Lincoln argued for "the sober judgment of Courts," for "unimpassioned reason, . . . general intelligence, sound morality, and, in particular, a reverence for the constitution and laws."[10] Could passionate leaders desirous of distinction, Lincoln asked, be content to support and maintain a system handed to them by others. "Think you these places would satisfy an Alexander, a Caesar, or a Napoleon? Never! Towering genius disdains a beaten path."[11] The common law, and the kind of deference to tradition and precedent that defines it, is precisely this—a beaten path—deviations from which are forged only very slowly, cautiously, and with considerable judicial restraint. But are American judges still willing to exercise the restraint necessary to carry on a tradition, a system, a temperament, a manner of reasoning, a form of adjudication, "an edifice," as Lincoln put it, "that has been erected by others?"[12]

Observers of the Supreme Court in the second half of the twentieth century argue that they decidedly are not. Nathan Glazer first observed in 1975 that the American courts have "changed their role in American life." They are "now more powerful than ever before" and "reach into the lives of the people . . . deeper than they ever have in American history."[13] The kind of judicial activism which defined the Warren court between 1954 and 1968 did not retreat with the confirmation of four Nixon appointed justices in the years following. Instead, what Glazer calls the "imperial judiciary" sailed at full tilt through the Burger court years, with justices laying down decisions "even more far-reaching" than in the Warren court years. Glazer predicted then that the assertion of judicial authority realized between 1955 and 1975 was not a passing fad, that it had become the expected posture of the court, transcending the varying philosophical tendencies of the different justices.

Glendon, writing nearly two decades after Glazer, argues that the trend has indeed continued. In fact, Glendon holds that the "'conservative,' 'moderate' justices on today's Supreme Court are often more assertive and arrogant in their exercise of judicial power than the members of the 'liberal,' 'activist' Warren Court."[14] The classical judge characterized by "impartiality, prudence, practical reason, mastery of craft, . . . and above all, self restraint" has given way to the romantic judge who is disposed instead to be "bold, creative, compassionate, result-oriented, and liberated from legal technicalities."[15] The romantic judge is less bound by tradition, by precedent, and by a cautious and careful approach to judicial decision making. The traditional ideals of disinterest, humility, and restraint have given way to the new ideals of "judicial boldness, energy, and compassion."[16] Consider one rather telling anecdote. On June 29, 1992, the day of the *Casey* decision, Justice Anthony Kennedy invited a reporter to follow him around for the day. While a crowd gathered outside of the Supreme Court building, in view from Kennedy's office window, Kennedy said to the reporter, "Sometimes you don't know if you're Caesar about to cross the Rubicon or Captain Queeg cutting your own tow line."[17]

More significant than Kennedy's unusual invitation of a reporter to shadow him on the day of a widely observed ruling or the disturbing hubris of his self-comparison to Caesar is the degree to which the attitude reflected in this statement characterizes the disposition of the Supreme Court in the last several decades and the extent to which this new orientation represents a notable departure from the common law tradition. No longer, it seems, is the judiciary primarily a custodial vocation for those willing quietly to carry on and carefully to advance an inherited tradition. Rather, in direct contrast to Lincoln's musings, the imperial leanings of a Caesar may well find (or at least seek) satisfaction in the role of a judge.

Glendon and Glazer concentrated their observations on developments at the Supreme Court. In this chapter I will show that the same type of transformation is mirrored in the judicial activity of the local drug courts. Here too judges are casting off the shackles of common law constraints in their efforts to make a mark, exercise compassion, and bring about real change. It is important to note, however, that judicial activism, as such, is not quite so unusual at the local or district court level where judges have always had more discretion and flexibility. This was the main reason that Charles Wyzanski declined an offer in 1959 to be considered for a position on the U.S. Court of Appeals for the First Circuit. As he wrote to

Senator Levertt Saltonstall at the time, "The District Court gives more scope to a judge's initiative and discretion." In the letter he discussed the "width of choice" his position allowed him not only in how he sentenced defendants, but in "many other instances."[18] So independent was the local judge that Wyzanski worried about the "perils of individualism" and the dangers of "the nigh universal sin of pride" to which the district judge was particularly vulnerable.

In the final analysis, however, Wyzanski recognized that even the district judge must exercise restraint. Here, too, rules, legal precedent, and judicial attentiveness determine the "proper function" of the judge. As he put it, "It is within the proper function of a District Court not merely by rules and decisions, but by an informed, intelligent, and energetic handling of his calendar to effectuate prompt as well as unbiased justice."[19] Thus, though there is a greater place for judicial innovation at the local level, "unbiased justice" is still the desired telos. All U.S. judges, after all, take an oath to "administer justice without respect to persons" and to "faithfully and impartially discharge and perform all the duties incumbent" upon them under the Constitution.[20] This is the common law disposition traditionally salient to all levels of the judiciary. An investigation into the philosophy and behavior of drug court judges, however, reveals a deliberate departure from the classical orientation. Like the romantic Supreme Court judges, the drug court judges have jettisoned traditional adjudicative restraints, finding them "too confining, boring, unrewarding, [and] insufficiently responsive to social problems."[21] Instead, they have championed a reinvention of the adjudicative process, one which allows them to be more proactive, personally interested, and responsive to the needs of the clients who come before them.

Judicial Activism

To begin with, the drug court judge deliberately departs from the kind of passive role Tocqueville saw as a defining quality of the American judiciary. Instead, the drug court judge is, on a number of fronts, an activist judge. As we saw in the last chapter, the drug court judge is the main actor in the courtroom drama. But the judicial robe of passivity is also shed when the judge is off the bench. That is, judges actually involve themselves in the lives of clients outside the courtroom. Consider an example from the Boston drug court program. Cathy Delaney, the director of treatment at Boston's drug court, tells the story of Judge Ziemian visiting a client who for months had been unable to secure employment. Judge Ziemian finally "got tough" on this client telling him, "You are going to get a job or you are going to do community service, whichever you want.

You can work for free or you can work for money. Take your pick." Brad, after weeks of no success, finally got a job. Judge Ziemian was so pleased with the news that he personally visited Brad at his new place of employment. And according to Cathy Delaney, "Brad has never forgotten it, ever."

Another who may never forget the actions of a drug court judge was Jeff, a client in the Amherst, New York, drug court, the first suburban drug court in the United States, located just outside of Buffalo. The extraadjudicative activity in this case was communication between the judge and Jeff's mother. In a letter to the judge the mother claimed that her son was still heavily into drugs, was abusive in the home, and was bragging to friends, "I've got this judge eating out of my hands." In response to the mother's letter, the judge severely dealt with Jeff at his next court appearance. "This is one judge you don't have in the palm of your hand," Judge Farrell asserted. To the incredulity of Jeff and his father, who, along with Jeff's mother, was also present in court, Judge Farrell put the young man in custody, set a bail for $5,000, and established a new court date for three weeks later. "I don't understand," Jeff protested. "You do, you know very well," Farrell retorted. "Get out of here." As Judge Farrell explained to me later, "You need to catch their attention, break the control there, the domination they have in their families. And I think, in a feeble way, you try to get them to recognize what's going on. . . . But the bottom line is, I had to do what I needed to do." What he did would likely have consequences for Jeff's parents, not to mention Jeff. Because the father didn't know about the letter and was, according to Judge Farrell, still "an enabler" in this situation, when he "finds out Mom has had something to do with it there may be a matrimonial spat." Given the level of tension evident in the courtroom Judge Farrell may well have been speaking euphemistically.

In another case a drug court judge's activism led to the establishment of contact with a client's employer. A participant in Judge McKinney's Syracuse, New York, drug court lost his job. McKinney called the employer and learned that the client was regarded as a "damn good employee" and that the boss would "hire him back in a heartbeat" if the judge could guarantee that he was drug free and that he wouldn't miss any work. So the judge made a deal with the employer. He said to him, "Okay, I'll make a deal with you, you take him back and I'll add another weapon to your arsenal. If he doesn't come to work when he is supposed to, doesn't come to work on time, if he comes to work under the influence of any kind of drugs, I'll put him in jail, on your say so."

McKinney filled the client in on the new arrangement, telling him, "I'll get your job back for you, but you've got to promise you'll be at work when you are supposed to and not take any drugs. Your employer is now on the team of people who are reporting to me. When he calls up and tells me that you are late, or that you're not there, I'm going to send the cops out to arrest you." The client agreed to this arrangement which, according to McKinney, "worked for awhile." McKinney acknowledged that these actions probably violated "the canon of judicial ethics" and that he "would never have done it before as a judge." He justified the actions, however, on the grounds that in the drug court such prohibitions have to be "softened a little bit" because of the "overall purpose and methodology" of the program.[22]

The drug court judge's involvement in the community, however, is not just in relating individually to drug court clients, their relatives, or their employers. The drug court judge also plays a significant leadership role in bringing the whole program together. As described in a State Justice Institute (SJI) document on drug courts, "the judiciary as a whole and the drug court judge in particular must take the lead in promoting the drug court concept in both the justice system and larger community; in developing awareness of the goals it seeks to achieve; and in marshaling the support required to sustain a viable program that meets community needs."[23] The very existence of a drug court is often the direct result of the administrative leadership of a judge. "The fact that a drug court has been established . . . implies that the judicial administration has made the necessary arrangements and adjustments to support the drug court," for it is the judiciary that "provides the leadership, authority, and management capacity to enable the drug court to operate."[24]

Judges are aware that this extra-adjudicative activism represents a departure from traditional understandings of the judge's role. Jeffrey Tauber, for example, acknowledges that "traditionally, judges have played the passive role of objective, impartial referee, only reluctantly stepping beyond the boundaries of their own courtroom." In the drug court, contrastingly, the judge "should be a strong leader with enthusiasm for the court's mission." This new judicial orientation "requires a willingness to work outside the confines of the traditional judicial role," which involves, among other things, exerting leadership "in the promotion of coordinated drug control and treatment efforts, both within the criminal justice system and [in] local communities."[25]

The drug court judge is expected actively to engage the community, campaigning on behalf of the program, pulling different resources and services together, cultivating relationships with the media, garnering support from the police, and so on. Judge Jamey Weitzman, Baltimore's first drug court judge and founding member of the NADCP, clearly understands the role of the judge in this way. Because of a judge's "moral authority and community connections," Weitzman explains, she is in the position, "to cajole, connive, convince, and if necessary, hold in contempt parties who don't want to participate in the program." Though "just kidding" regarding the latter, the comment reflects a self-awareness of the judge's authority and of how it might be unleashed for the purposes of promoting the drug court. The drug court judge, Weitzman explains further, is uniquely positioned to disabuse skeptics of misgivings about the program. "Because of her authority and position in the community the drug court judge is a very effective spokesperson in speaking to the community, educating the media and legislative persons, to convince them that we are not soft on crime, coddling criminals, long-haired hippie, yuppie, bra burning liberals."

In addition to lobbying federal and state legislators to support drug courts, judges have also taken the lead in procuring funding from nontraditional sources. Judge Jack Lehman of the Las Vegas drug court, for example, started a tax-exempt nonprofit foundation (501c3) to support his court. Judge John Schwartz, the first judge of the Rochester, New York, drug court, likewise led efforts to round up support for his emerging drug court. Judge Schwartz tells of being inspired to start a Rochester drug court following a visit to Miami. Though state and local government officials thought his drug court idea a good one, they were not at the time in a position to finance it because of budgetary constraints. Undeterred, Schwartz turned to "non-traditional sources."

> I went to the local United Way and asked them if they would be the fiduciary for all funds I received for drug courts. They agreed. Therefore all the money I raised from city government, county government, charitable foundations, private foundations, is donated to the United Way Service Corporation and that money is dispensed as our drug court team directs it shall be. Whether you like it or not you as a judge are considered a leader of your drug court team. Your team looks to you for inspiration and guidance. So as the leader of that team you must take a very active part in the raising of funds. For the Rochester drug court, I went out and raised all the money from local foundations.

Other drug courts (approximately one in five), following the example of Judge Schwartz and Judge Lehman, have obtained some form of private funding.[26] The 1997 Justice Department survey of drug courts found that nine drug courts had solicited a total of nearly half a million dollars in support from private foundations.[27]

Judge Steven Marcus of the Los Angeles drug court has some concerns about these practices. He thinks drug court judges should "be especially careful about fundraising." "Most judges in most jurisdictions," Marcus notes, "have some strict prohibitions about being directly involved in fundraising. It's an easy ticket to have yourself investigated." To those who question the ethics of judicial fund raising from non-legislative sources, Judge Schwartz answers that prohibitions against such activities are but a "myth," that "the judicial cannons of ethics do not prevent a judge from raising money." Ethical or not, it is an uncommon practice, and one in which American judges historically have not engaged.

Other judges talk about the proactive roles they have taken in securing funds for their program, the many different types of organizations and groups they have approached for support, and the various political strategies they have employed to garner and maintain community support. One judge argued that unelected judges can provide "cover" for elected D.A.s and legislators who sometimes take political risks in supporting drug courts.

> It is up to us, I think, to provide some cover. Because, ultimately . . . it is politics. And if we don't provide them cover . . . In Massachusetts it is easy for judges to provide cover, because we are appointed for life. So, if anything goes wrong, they can just say, you know, the damn judge did it again. So, we can provide the cover that way. I think that it is incumbent upon us to provide that cover, if we expect them to support us.

Beyond fundraising and providing cover for vulnerable legislators, judges also seek the support of other community resources, including groups and agencies that provide health care, education, and job training. Judge Weitzman, for example, sees the judge as uniquely positioned to solicit support from "job training and placement, life skills training, and medical, health services." Syracuse, New York's Judge McKinney tells of how he introduced GED training into his drug court program. He arranged with a particular GED training program to bypass certain eligibility requirements to facilitate and expedite the enrollment of drug court clients. Reflecting on this arrangement McKinney noted the novelty of his role outside the courtroom. "This is something as a judge I would never have done before, because . . . my role was just whatever happened right here in the courtroom. If it didn't happen here, it didn't happen at all." With the drug court, such restrictions are less binding. "But now what we're trying to do is take the courts outside of the courtroom and into the community." Judge McKinney recognizes that the extension of his role in this way broadens the scope and redefines the meaning of justice. "The whole notion of justice is not something that is confined in the courthouse. It is a community responsibility, and the drug courts are a vehicle for pulling in some of these other community entities together. . . . To me the challenge of drug court is to get . . . as many connections and bridges with the community, to have them provide supportive service."

Whether recruiting external resources, providing cover, lobbying, campaigning, coordinating, fund-raising, or talking to the media, the drug court judge is an activist judge. The role represents a clear and intentional departure from the more passive orientation of the classical judge of the common law tradition. As Judge Tauber explains, "It is a system and it is a philosophy that says it is not enough to be a good referee. It is not enough to be up on the law and to know the law." Rather, the drug court judge exercises active "leadership . . . outside of the courtroom." There is nothing to be ashamed of, drug court judges argue, regarding this new role. As Judge Schwartz asserts, "I think the judiciary is an independent branch of the government. We should be leaders. And we shouldn't be afraid to speak up as leaders." That this is a significant departure from previous practices is made clear by Judge Peggy Hora of Hayward, California. "The drug court judge is no longer either the neutral umpire calling the balls and strikes, or the case manager. Instead the drug court judge has taken on a totally different role; a role that judges have never had before in the world, in the history of jurisprudence."

Judicial Compassion

If the classical trait of judicial passivity is absent in the drug court, even less evident are the common law notions of disinterest and impartiality. Drug court judges are actually instructed to be interested and invested in the clients who come before them. As Judge Tauber instructs, "Be less the dignified, detached judicial officer. Show your concern, as well as your toughness. Treat the offender as a person and an individual. . . . Don't lecture the offender, but engage him or her in conversation . . . Make a connection."[28] In the drug court, then, the "assertive and compassionate" is preferred over the "restrained and impartial."[29] As previously noted, this empathetic connection between the judge and the client is a central focus of the courtroom drama. As opposed to disinterest, the judge is encouraged to cultivate interest in and concern for the defendant. When a dozen drug court judges were asked to list the "six most important characteristics of an effective drug court judge," the most often reported response was "the ability to be empathetic or to show genuine concern."[30] Other responses included "acceptance of an unconventional role," having a "sense of humor," and "having experienced personal crises."[31]

A practice started at the Washington, D.C., drug court and emulated at other locations around the country provides a useful example of this unique judicial disposition. For a client who has failed some component of the treatment program—whether missing a counseling meeting, not passing a urinalysis test, or failing to show up in court—the judge may require the client to sit in the jury box for any number of days as a form of sanction. The practice, as Jay Carver, Washington D.C.'s Director of Pretrial Services, recounts, "created much more of a bond with the judge and the defendant and it really seemed to have almost a therapeutic impact." Subsequently, they made it a "standard operating procedure."

> At the end of the day, the judge in that court has a nice little discussion. It could almost be characterized as a group session with defendants who have spent the entire day watching the parade of drug court cases, this parade of misery through the drug court, and it has really strengthened this relationship between judge and the defendant, and we think that it has had a big impact in terms of the very significant benefit we're seeing when it comes to outcome.

Judge Bruce Beaudin, who started the practice, acknowledges that he learned the idea from Michael Smith, an acupuncture guru from New York City. According to Beaudin, jettisoning the role of the disinterested umpire comes with a personal cost. "I'll tell you, if you make a commitment to do it [the jury box practice], you have jumped from being a dispassionate dispenser of justice into a member of a treatment team. And it carries with it a lot of stuff that you take home at night." In a later interview with Beaudin, he elaborated on this point. Like a social worker, he explained, "you start to care" and this caring is so important because so "few of those people [the clients] have ever had anybody care about them for two years, let alone somebody in a position of authority."

Other judges justify the importance of their compassionate acts with the same type of reasoning. The defendants have never been shown care by an authority figure. If the drug court judge demonstrates compassion towards them, it will therefore lead to "empowerment." This is how Baltimore drug court judge Jamey Weitzman sees it. Defendants respond positively to a caring judge "because the judge is one of the few, if the only, authority figure who has ever in their lives taken an interest in them, and shown positive reinforcement." And the reason they are so responsive, Weitzman explains, citing M. C. Hammer, is "because I've got the power." Weitzman talks further about the kind of interaction that emerges out of this "incredible relationship" between the judge and the defendant.

> During periodic progress conferences, as the judge comes to know better the defendants' background, problems, what makes them tick, an incredible rapport develops almost spontaneously between the judge and the defendant. They start doing things because of you. I remember one defendant who said, "Judge, I'm now doing well because I know you were so disappointed in me."

Weitzman does many creative things to encourage her defendants. "We smile and laugh at them. We have them turn around in the courtroom and give speeches. I read the poems they write for me. I play the songs that they record for me. I show pictures." Weitzman may not be overstating things when she concludes that this kind of courtroom activity gives "a whole new meaning to the term 'judicial action.'"[32]

Judge McKinney, Syracuse New York's drug court judge, agrees that this kind of courtroom compassion has "never been done before." In the drug court, "people in an authority position" are telling these clients "I care about you, and I care about some of the things that are troubling you." McKinney believes that this kind of approach should be expanded within the judiciary more broadly. "Let's make these courts more user friendly. Let's just make judges and everyone who is associated with this courtroom business and this justice system a little bit more under-standing"—an understanding that, according to McKinney "leads to compassion."

Judge Weber of the Louisville, Kentucky, drug court demonstrates his compassion and understanding during drug court sessions by literally shedding his judicial robe and the traditional notions of authority that it symbolizes. He intentionally does not wear the judge's customary black robe to communicate a message to his clients. "It's a conscious statement that I'm not the regular kind of judge that you would expect in a criminal court," Weber explains. "This is different. My being there without a robe makes it different." What is the precise message that he wants to get across through this difference? "I'm a real person. I listen to them. I care about them."

At a mentoring training seminar in Louisville, visiting drug court teams discussed this feature of the Louisville drug court. Some believed the robe was a necessary symbol in the courtroom that should be maintained. Oth-ers were more agnostic on the issue: "If the judge wants to wear a robe, fine, if not, that's okay." The majority who spoke up, however, ap-plauded Judge Weber's innovation and "authenticity." One team mem-ber, for example, really appreciated this "symbolic act." In it, he saw the judge putting himself on the same level of vulnerability as the defendants. "You get these people involved in treatment. They are exposing every part of the themselves. . . . The judge may feel that the least he can do as a judge is this symbolic action of disrobing. 'I'm asking you all to lay your dress on the table and involve yourself in treatment. And in response to that I'm taking my robe off and showing you that I am a real person. I'm here to help you.'"

Another agreed arguing that the "traditional thinking" of "respect for the robe and for the law and whatever" has us "where we are now." Therefore, she "liked the fact that there is this alternative." So did an attorney from another emerging drug court in the South. He also "personally liked the act with the robe." He related to the practice in that in his own plea bargaining sessions with defendants he sometimes intentionally dresses down, rather than wearing a suit, to be "better received" by defendants. His rationale was that "you have to consider the people we're dealing with—most of them don't have suits. They are not used to being around people who wear suits. And while we want to show them, I suppose, that we have authority, we also want to show them— particularly in this type of program—that we are going to be their friend in this thing and help them through it."

Judge Fogan of the Fort Lauderdale, Florida, drug court, while he still wears the traditional judicial robe, wants to convey the same message of friendliness to defendants. For example, he regularly asks clients if he can call them by their first name "as a sign of friendship." He also on occasion hugs clients during graduation ceremonies, as demonstrated in a promotional video for the Fort Lauderdale drug court: "At graduation participants receive a certificate of achievement, a T-shirt, and a hug from the judge." Some judges, though certainly not all, forcefully defend this practice. When Judge Ellen DeShazer of the Compton, California drug court, for example, was asked by another judge whether judges should hug clients, she replied with an unequivocal, "Absolutely." She then told the story of one drug court client who "just wanted a hug" and had come to her judicial chambers (a practice she permits of her drug court clients) to receive one.

> I let them come into my chambers. When they say, "Can I speak to the judge?" I never say, "No, you cannot." All she wanted was a hug. And I had to set aside the criminal history information that I had on this person, and say, "this young lady just wants me to give her a hug. And can I do that?" I mean, you are thinking just instantly. You don't have time to think about it later on. So, I just gave her a hug. I mean, what would you do if your child came up to you, and said, "May I have a hug?" You wouldn't say, "Well let me think about this now. You have been bad fifteen times." You would just do it. So, that is what I did. And yes you should [give hugs]. You get a whole lot back. You really do.

One wonders, given this more intimate relationship between the judge and defendant, whether a level of judicial impartiality can be sustained, or even if impartiality and consistency in sentencing are still valued judicial standards. An interesting interchange between a group of judges at a Washington, D.C., drug court conference would suggest that, at the very least, partiality is no longer a value that can be taken for granted. At this particular session, a discussion ensued about the different ways judges impose sanctions on drug court clients who have somehow not complied with the treatment program. The drug court judges who were present offered various strategies. Emerging out of the discussion was the common theme that sanctions should vary according to the individual and according to the particularities of the case. As one drug court judge put it,

"Justice [in the drug court] is taking an individual, it is looking at that individual case, and it is fashioning a disposition in that particular case that is going to benefit not only society, but that particular individual." Such flexibility is important because as Los Angeles drug court judge, Steven Marcus, opined, "So many people in front of you have individual situations." Subsequently, though the Los Angeles drug court "started out with set [sanction] goals, it has become more individualized as we have gone along."

Following this interchange, Judge Patrick Michot from Lafayette, Louisiana, hesitantly took the floor. He was at the time in the very early stages of starting a drug court in his jurisdiction and was visibly perplexed by what he was hearing. "I'd like to ask a question," he asserted. "Is it okay then to be inconsistent in your sentencing? Is that basically okay?" Almost before he could finish his question several more seasoned drug court judges sought to enlighten him. The first was Judge Weber from the Louisville, Kentucky, drug court, who was also moderating the discussion. "Can I ask you a question right back? In your regular court setting are you always consistent?" Somewhat taken aback Michot responded, "I try to be consistent. What I am hearing here, though, suggests that maybe I ought to rethink that."

Another judge rose to try to bring clarity to the situation. He explained that because the drug court employs a "reinforcement model," the relationship between judge and client is more like "parenting." Therefore, like a parent, "You just cannot have absolute rules." Instead "You have got to be responding." This judge, in fact, based upon input from a therapist, preferred the use of the word "response" over "sanction." Next, Judge Stanley Goldstein, the country's first drug court judge, stood up to offer his insight.

> I just want to make one comment. Just don't lose sight of what you are doing. We are there to get these people off of drugs, to retrain them, rehabilitate them, put them back on the street, let them become tax paying citizens. We are not there to fast track them into jail. We are not there to trick them. We are not there to play any games. We are there for specific purposes. As long as whatever you do is designed to get them off drugs and put them back out on the street in a position where they can fight using drugs, whatever you do to accomplish that is fine.

A little later Judge Roosevelt Robinson, Portland, Oregon's drug court judge, with a tone of indignation, argued strongly against the notion of uniform sentencing. "If you want machines that can determine" a sentence then "you can put a computer up there. . . . The drug court program is a situation where we get an opportunity to deal with human beings, with human problems . . . and when we are through with them, they are better persons, and we have a better society. I would rather be a jurist doing that, than a computer just giving people time."

A British criminologist sent by his government to study and report back on the American drug courts restated Michot's question in a slightly different manner, echoing his concerns about "disparities in sentencing" and wondering if drug court judges are not in fact behaving like social workers. The responses to the criminologist were almost as severe as those to Judge Michot. Judge Hoover, a robust and imposing drug court judge from Bakersfield, California, was the first to respond.

> Are we really just doing social work? Well sort of. But aren't your judges who do civil settlement conferences doing lawyer work. Why the hell do they do that? They are only supposed to resolve disputes in the grandest common law tradition. But they . . . get right in the middle of a civil case, and you don't settle every civil case in the same way. You don't apply pressure on the plaintiff or the defendant in exactly the same way. So they're doing "lawyers" work. It is just that treatment sounds so warm and fuzzy, we always have to apologize for it. Never apologize for it.

With his original question apparently answered, Judge Michot never spoke again. Flexibility and individually tailored sanctions—indeed, "whatever" you need to do to accomplish the goals of the drug court—are fair game. Recall that each of these judges once vowed that they would "administer justice without respect to persons," that they would "do equal right to the poor and to the rich," and that they would "impartially discharge and perform" their duties in accordance with the "Constitution and the laws of this country."[33] Even in the "grandest common law" tradition, no one expected or asked more of a judge than he or she aspire with Judge Michot to "try to be consistent," even realizing that human nature will never make the dispensing of justice as consistent as a computer. A wholesale disregard for this standard, however, is a new notion altogether. Classical judges, as Glendon observes, realized the elusiveness of total objectivity. Yet, borrowing Clifford Geertz's imagery, "they also knew that a doctor who cannot have a completely sterile operating field does not need to perform surgery in a sewer."[34]

The goal of getting the drug court client well, however, now supersedes the goal of consistency and impartiality, and even in some cases, as we will see, strict adherence to statutory law. A common frustration expressed by drug court judges is the unwelcome constraints they experience from legislatively imposed mandatory minimum sentences. Drug courts are liberating in that they allow more flexibility in a judge's responses to a client. As we have seen, judges have a myriad of sanctions available to them. They can put clients in jail for two weeks, mandate increased attendance of AA and NA meetings, require community service, and so on. These sanctions are typically imposed individually and creatively. Often there are no hard and fast rules.

The enhanced discretion that the drug court allows is one of the features of the program that is attractive to Judge Barbara Beck from Santa Barbara, California's drug court.

> You know, the legislature in the state of California has just about taken away all the discretion we have as judges. They now tell us exactly what sentence to impose, and how to do it, and when to do it, and where to do it. This is one of the few areas that we have where we still have some discretion. And that is really what I became a judge for. I wanted to help people. I wanted to make a difference in people's lives. And the drug court is one of the areas that we are still allowed to do that.

Judge Peggy Hora expresses a similar frustration with the constraints of mandatory minimum sentences and like Judge Robinson believes such statutorily imposed constraints reduces the judge's role to that of a computer.

> The more you take away judicial discretion, the more you might as well just have a computer sitting up their on the bench. You know, just punch in the numbers and tell me how long the sentence is. And it gives you nothing that you went to the trouble of becoming a judge for. You know, you didn't become a judge because you liked to sit there and figure out the length of a sentence. . . . When you just see this complete recycling of people through the system, it is horribly unsatisfactory. And if you don't have the discretion to use your own judgment and try to fashion something that might actually work for the person in front of you, then it is very frustrating.

The drug court remedies this problem. As Judge Swett of Charlottesville sees it, "Under the traditional courts there are very few effective options available to a judge." With the drug court, however, "because of the emphasis on treatment, it enlarges the number of options that a judge has available." In other words, it is the court's adoption of the treatment perspective that makes the expansion of judicial authority possible. The traditional adjudicative approach inhibited the expansion of judicial authority, though some judges found ways of getting around mandatory minimum sentences even before drug court.

A drug court judge from the Midwest, for example, claims that he has always "felt free to use [his] discretion."

> We have some mandatory stuff here . . . but frankly we've been playing games with it for years. For example, if somebody sells less than fifty grams of cocaine they by law are supposed to go to prison for one to twenty years. And with the full cooperation of our prosecutor's office we're doing all kinds of things to get

one year on the book. Put them on tether for six months, put them in rehabilitation for six months, and there's your year right there. Sometimes we'll put them
on tether for six months and give them six months in jail subject to review at
the end of their probation period, or something like that, and they never do it.
That's what we've been playing games with for a long time.

This judge could see, however, that for judges from states "where they're
crazy about mandatory sentencing" the drug court "would be very useful
and appreciated." As illustrated in the comments of judges quoted above,
this is certainly the case. One of the main reasons judges appreciate the
drug court and the kind of judicial discretion it allows is the belief that
this new form of adjudication actually works, that is, that the drug court
is effective. It has a utilitarian value.

Judicial Expediency

As discussed in chapter 2, utilitarianism is a fundamental justificatory
principle legitimating the expansion of the drug court movement. Inasmuch as this same "frame of mind" is employed by judges and directs
their adjudicative practices, it ultimately represents another way in which
the drug court departs from the common law tradition. Glendon identifies expedience as one of the defining features of the late twentieth-century Supreme Court.[35] In keeping with the same romantic disposition, the
drug court also aims at "problem resolution." As Judge Weber puts it, the
drug court "actually let's us go to the heart of the matter and solve the
problem." The classical arrangement did not. As a result, drug offenders
were repeatedly recycled through the criminal justice system, a system, as
the judges see it, that did nothing to rehabilitate offenders from their root
problem (i.e., drug addiction). Therefore, something new had to be tried.
"What we did before simply was not working," is the common refrain.
    Thus, judges justify a departure from the common law tradition on the
grounds that previous methods were ineffective; these methods failed to
rehabilitate offenders. Because of this, many judges have no scruples
about trying something new even if it fundamentally departs from an
age-old system. This is clearly the case with Judge Schwartz of Rochester,
New York. He acknowledged that departing from the common law may
be hard for some judges. But, as he put it, "It was never a concern of mine.
As a common law judge presiding over trials, I knew we weren't making
an inch of headway in the drug problem." Schwartz is, in fact, very proud
of the innovative effort represented in the un-common law format of the
drug court. "Oh, it's much different. I'm proud that it is different. It
means that we're willing to advance with the times. I truly believe in sepa-

ration of powers and the independence of the judiciary, but that doesn't mean that the judiciary has to do the same thing for over three hundred years." Again, the willingness to be different is justified on the grounds of efficacy. Consider Schwartz's further explanation.

> We weren't making any headway and we are not stupid. So why don't we try different approaches. Our job is to make sure justice is done. Our job is also to punish, but what's the point of punishing if it doesn't work. I mean, 70 percent of our clientele in the criminal justice system had drug problems. It's about time we learned how to deal with them. When they developed the common law, they didn't have the problem. They didn't have this problem twenty years ago when I started, twenty-five years ago, thirty years ago, actually, when I started practicing law. But we do now, so let's deal with it. Take the business world; they come along with new ideas all the time. Government unfortunately doesn't, and the court system is even slower than government. We have to deal with the problem. It is our problem.

Explanations such as this are repeatedly offered by judges. The utilitarian argument is presented with the perception (an apparently justifiable one) that it is the ultimate trump. If it works, then how could anyone conceivably question it? As Judge Stanley Goldstein argues, "You see the thing here that is different than anything else that has ever been done before is that it works. It really works! People come in who are hooked on drugs, look so bad that they can't stay off it for ten minutes. And a year later they are out working. What the hell is wrong with that?"

So concerned are judges with the inefficiency of traditional methods that they fear the judiciary will become irrelevant without some radical changes. "If you don't make some changes," Judge Hodos argues, "you're going to become irrelevant. I think we really need to change the way we are doing things. We need to listen to the community because they are losing faith in what is happening in the justice system." Hodos's Franklin County, Massachusetts, colleague, Judge Thomas Merrigan, is even more emphatic. Recall his fear that if the judiciary doesn't change and become more relevant, "they will no longer consider us meaningful." As Merrigan sees it, it is therefore incumbent upon the judiciary to change, to become more responsive to the needs of the community.

Merrigan argues further that change is not an option. No other institution has the power to bring about social change as does the judiciary. "The school system, the medical providers, the churches, employers, families, nobody else has the power and the leverage that we do. And to me, it isn't an option, it's an obligation." Therefore, the debate over whether this is an appropriate judicial role is irrelevant. "We in the courtroom have an opportunity to put people on an elevator and take them to their bottom, if they're not already there. But we also have an opportunity to

have an impact on their recovery." Merrigan believes American citizens
fully support this new form of justice. If offered the judicial options of
either the traditional or the drug court approach the public would un-
doubtedly, Merrigan argues, see the latter as an "appropriate judicial
role. . . . There would be no question and there is no question, and we all
know that." Judge Hodos agrees that "the community seems to be behind
the project," and they support it, according to Hodos, for utilitarian reasons. As Hodos puts it, "They knew that whatever we were doing wasn't
working."

Whether or not the "people in the street" agree to such developments
as the drug court for the reasons these judges aver, the utilitarian argument is offered by judges to justify judicial change. Consider Judge
Weber's position on the matter: "The system has to change." Why? Because "anybody who works in the criminal justice system realizes how
little effect we're having on things. . . . There is a recognition that the
traditional way of doing things may not be the best." Like Schwartz,
Weber is glad that through such developments as the drug court movement, "the legal system is slowly evolving into something else." The only
thing slowing it down is "those folks that have an investment in the status
quo . . . who don't want to change." A break with the common law tradition, then, is only seen as something that the change-resistant need to get
over. Any misgivings about such a break with the past are overshadowed
by greater concerns with establishing a system that effectively deals
with the enormous problem of drug dependency and associated criminal
activity.

With the expansion of judicial authority and the perceived efficacy of
the drug court program, judges are more excited than ever about their
new judicial role. They have finally been given the tools and the philosophy that allow them to help clients in ways they were previously unable.
Like activist Supreme Court justices, the drug court judges have "decided
that the other two branches won't act." Therefore they have determined
"to act on their own, and increasingly are intrigued by the opportunity to
go to the root of the problem."[36] For the drug court judge, going to the
root of the problem is a more gratifying model of adjudication.

Judicial Enthusiasm

That the drug court presents the opportunity to play a more satisfying
role is repeated by drug court judges. Judge Tauber sums up the judges'
view best: "Drug Court represents one of the most challenging and exciting innovations in the Criminal Justice System in a long time." Moreover,
he asserts, "I have never talked to anyone who has done drug court for

any length of time who hasn't said that this is the most satisfying thing they have done in their career." Almost without exception this is the sentiment expressed by drug court judges.

With the zeal of a missionary Louisville's Judge Weber, for example, says, "Drug court is something I want to do and it's something that I strongly believe in. When I'm in my regular court it's more like work. It's my assignment. Drug court, I don't have to do it. I'm there because I want to do it." Weber reports that people who have observed him in both situations say "I look like a different person when I'm doing drug court." Like Judge Weber, Judge Diane Strickland, of the nascent Roanoke, Virginia, drug court, works both in drug court and with a regular court docket. The contrast for her is striking. "I get more personal satisfaction out of what I'm doing with the drug court population than with anything I do for the remainder of the week, because I do feel that there is a contact with the offenders that allows me to get at a more personal level and to see true success stories."

Judges are enthusiastic because they believe they are for the first time really making a difference in people's lives. Portland, Oregon's Judge Robinson embellishes this point. As he sees it, criminal court judges are typically involved in sentencing people and sending them to jail, which he believes is a very unsatisfying task. "When that judge goes home, it's hard for that judge to look at himself or herself in the mirror and say, 'Today I made a difference in society.'" In the drug court, contrastingly, "a judge can go home and say, 'Today I know I have made a difference in society.' And the judges are enthusiastic about it." Judge Hodos of the Orange and Greenfield drug courts in Massachusetts is among these. Of his work in the drug courts he says, "I find it very satisfying. It really has renewed my energy in what I'm doing, because I can really observe that we're making a difference." Judge Peggy Hora is another who finds the "successes" of the drug court more exciting than the "failures" of the regular court.

> All you ever see in a regular courtroom setting are your failures. You never see your successes. That is depressing. You know, it is really depressing. So, in that sense, it is much more exciting to be a drug court judge, who sees people actually come back well, sees families be whole, sees people have a job for the first time in their life, sees parents and spouses and everybody in court cheering on the person.

So much more exciting is the drug court than the "horribly unsatisfactory" experience of a regular court, according to Hora, that once "you have done it this way you can never go back again."

Rochester's Judge Schwartz is equally gratified by the drug court experience. "In the other role all we saw was failure," Schwartz explained. In drug court "we see success and it's very heart warming";[37] it's "my most rewarding judicial experience."[38] Judge Carl Goldstein of Wilmington, Delaware, likewise finds the drug court experience an emotionally satisfying one. "There are very few emotional rewards in this job. They come along occasionally but very seldom and I think in this case I think that's what you're dealing with. You're dealing with being able to see in a very direct way, at a very personal level, people benefiting from what you have provided them." In the same way, Judge Schma finds the experience "very rewarding, very satisfying, terribly commonsensical and useful." Judges even go so far as to argue that the drug court has positive therapeutic outcomes for the judge. As two judges write, "Judging in this non-traditional form becomes an invigorating, self-actualizing and rewarding exercise."[39]

I was joined at lunch by the previously mentioned British criminologist following a meeting with a group of drug court judges. One thing this academic could not understand was why judges would choose to participate in such a program as the drug court. I related my discovery that the judges almost uniformly report their involvement in the drug court to be a very exciting personal and vocational endeavor, indeed the highlight of their careers. He noted that he too had picked up on this sentiment. After a pause he then stated, "I find the notion that judges need excitement to be a very frightening one." After a moment of further silence, he then added, "If the need for excitement is what drives changes such as these, what will they do next?"

In sum, then, drug court judges find this new form of adjudication personally fulfilling, liberating in comparison to their traditional role, and invigorating in its allowance of extra-adjudicative activism. To top it off, they believe the drug court works and that they are making a difference in the lives of individual clients. These perceived positive outcomes overshadow any concerns about departing from the common law tradition. Judges even acknowledge compromising (or "playing games with") specific statutory injunctions and standards of judicial ethics in their roles as drug court judges. Any scruples with these means, however, are justified by the more important end of helping the clients on their road to recovery. In short, as Judge Peggy Hora puts it, "It works. It makes sense. It's cost effective. And it makes you feel good."

Five

Drug Court Storytelling

> You are the storyteller. Through the people who
> appear before you and their interaction with you,
> your staff, and the audience, the story (and
> promise) of your program is told.
> —Judge Jeffrey Tauber (*to drug court judges*)

AT BOTH THE local and national levels, drug court theater is led by uncommon law judges. Central to both levels of drug court drama is the
telling of stories. Narrative, in other words, is a defining feature of the
drug court and is visible in several different arenas of drug court activity.
In the counseling sessions, in the regular trips to the courtroom, and in the
graduation ceremonies, clients regularly give testimony about the effect of
drugs on their lives and of the drug court's role in helping them to overcome their addictions. Likewise, the counselors, many of whom are recovering addicts themselves, share personal testimonies about their own
recoveries as they help their clients. Even some of the judges have been
aided by treatment in their own efforts to overcome addiction to alcohol
or cigarettes, and talk publicly and personally about the positive effects of
treatment. At the level of the local drug court drama, narrative is a core
feature of the adjudicative process.

Moreover, as we have seen, a defining quality of drug court narrative
is a concern with judicial empathy and the open expression of emotions,
or the mode of communication Aristotle labeled *pathos* in his classical
treatise on rhetoric. Though pathos, from the classical perspective, was
always present in different types of oratory, it was seen as less central to
political and legal discourse than was either *ethos*, the credibility of the
speaker, and *logos*, the logical viability of the argument. Contemporary
legal and political oratory inverts the classical emphasis and gives much
greater import to pathos.[1] The substance of legal discourse in the drug
court is fully in keeping with this contemporary development.

Moreover, drug court narrative represents a welcome example of what
a growing group of legal scholars endorse as it concerns the place of emotivist storytelling in legal settings. Some see a focus on the place of narrative in law as a welcome adjustment to rational proceduralism. From this
perspective narrative represents a benign, if not more beneficial, supplement to logical reasoning.[2] Advocates of legal storytelling "valorize

narrative as more authentic, concrete, and embodied than traditional legal syllogism" and view it as a more persuasive form of legal argument.[3] "Both critical legal scholars and storytellers find the emotive or nonrational aspects of language much more persuasive than rational argument."[4] Recognized, therefore, is an incongruence between traditional legal processes and the therapeutically based orientation of empathetic storytelling. Cognizant of these differences, Toni Massaro argues that, to conflate these divergent paradigms, "empathy advocates must favor a radical restructuring of court procedures to make them more congenial" to the storytelling method.[5] As we have seen, the law-as-narrative style of the drug court does just this, and emotivism is a defining quality of this new style.

Indeed, the identification, assessment, and communication of emotions are central to the change process that distinguishes the drug court program. Inasmuch as the drug court is committed to treating drug offenders, engagement with the defendant's inner life is a central preoccupation. The judge is not simply concerned with whether or not a "defendant" committed some illegal behavior but is actively involved in the process of helping the "client" or "patient" recover, heal, and overcome an addictive lifestyle. Given this orientation, the judges and treatment providers necessarily explore the inner emotive regions of the defendant to effect this change. The application of emotivist storytelling in the drug court setting, then, does indeed result in a restructuring of court procedures.

This local-level narrative is not unrelated to the larger drug court movement. Often the stories told at the local level are retold to justify the larger movement and to convince others of its merit. As such, these local level stories have national, even international, import. The second level of storytelling, then, is what could be called national- or movement-level narrative; that is, storytelling aimed at garnering public support for drug courts and advancing the larger national movement. As we will see, in practice the distinction between local and national narrative is not always clearly distinguishable. The stories in the former often become the justificatory narratives retold in the latter.

Just as legal scholars have demonstrated a growing interest in the place of narrative in law, so too have social movement scholars given greater attention to the place of stories in advancing social movements.[6] Work in the latter provides fitting categories for organizing and making sense of storytelling in the drug court movement—an empirical case relevant to both fields of scholarly inquiry. As Gary Fine proposes, social movement stories are of three general types: (1) affronts to the movement actor, or "horror stories," which are often recounted to justify one's participation in the movement; (2) collective experiences within the movement, or "war stories," which are often told for the purpose of encouraging the troops to persevere in the battle; and (3) stories that reaffirm the value of the movement, or "happy endings."[7] Each type of storytelling relies on emotional connections to the audience. Thus, emotivist storytelling is central to the drug court phenomenon—both locally and nationally—and Fine's typology provides a useful heuristic for depicting the nature of this form of discourse in the drug court movement.

"Horror Stories"

"Horror stories," according to Fine, are told by movement actors through reference to a time when things were bad, to a time or situation that prompted a change in the teller's own perspective or at least signified to them—and implicitly to others—the need for change. Drug court activists regularly employ this genre of movement narrative to illustrate the deplorable condition of the criminal justice system and the desperate need for reform. Drug court judges speak often of their disgust with the "old way" of doing things, the frustration they experienced with seeing the same people arrested and rearrested, and the legal inhibitions they felt in helping defendants address their "core problem" (i.e., drug addiction). The drug courts, in contrast, as the stories are told, provide opportunities whereby judges can be more directly involved in the lives of their clients, helping them to conquer drug dependency; pass a high school GED test; get a job; and become contributing, taxpaying citizens. The horror stories are told to underscore the viability of this new approach by contrasting it with the old.

Consider two examples. The first story was told by Guy Wheeler, the director of the treatment facility at the Fort Lauderdale drug court. In an interview, he spoke of the benefits of the drug court, in particular, the drug court's policy of expunging the defendant's arrest after completion of the program. "Here is the biggest issue of the movement, why I like the drug court movement: It drops charges. That is the biggest reason why I like it." Wheeler believes a criminal record makes it difficult for offenders to get employment. He told a story about his uncle to illustrate this point.

> [With a criminal record] you can't get a job. It is very difficult to get one. I'm not saying you can't. But, it is extremely difficult. So, guess what? You are going to have crime back in the neighborhoods. I can attest to this. I had an uncle, who joined the army, served, did everything he was supposed to do. He sold some drugs. Boom. Got popped. He could never get a job. I was saying, "You're lazy. You're no good. You don't want to get a job." He says, "Okay, you take me out there to find a job." I took him everywhere to get a job. Everywhere he would go—very bright man, very articulate man—they turned

him down. He couldn't get a job. Guess what, they killed him in the street.
Black on black crime. . . . Somebody killed him. Blew his brains out.

This horror story is told to provide a compelling example of the necessity
of the drug court. Without the possibility of a clean record, individuals
who commit drug-related crimes will be forced to continue in criminal
activity. The drug court helps offenders deal with their drug problem and
avoid future criminal activity.

Wheeler linked the potency of his personal story with the significance
of the drug court movement.

> So, these kids come in here, and they say, "I want a job. Where can I get a job?"
> Their families don't own businesses. . . . So, the biggest reason why I like the
> movement is that it gets charges dropped. We say, "They don't want to work,
> they just don't want to work." And you need to ask the question, who is going
> to hire them? They can't get hired until somebody becomes an advocate for
> them.

The drug court, of course, serves this advocacy role. Through education,
treatment, and the dropping of a criminal charge, drug court offers to
remove the stigma of a criminal record. Wheeler's program even helps
drug court clients find employment. With drug court on the side of the
client, then, regrettable outcomes such as the unfortunate fate of
Wheeler's uncle could be avoided.

Nearly a year after the interview, Wheeler told the story again, this
time to an audience of over six hundred at a drug court conference in
Portland, Oregon. The story came at the end of his lecture and was told
even more dramatically than before.

> It is extremely difficult for these clients to get jobs. You see, I know about this
> personally. I had an uncle. His name was Uncle David, and I loved my Uncle
> David. My Uncle David fought in the Vietnam War and he had a drug charge.
> And Uncle David couldn't get a job. And I kept saying, "Uncle David, you're
> lazy. Get off your butt. Go get a job. Go get a job." He kept saying, "I can't get
> a job. I've got a drug charge." I said, "No, Uncle David, I'll go out and help you
> find a job." Everybody turned my uncle down. Five years later my uncle was
> trying to hustle. . . . Someone blew his brains out on 6th Street and 9th Avenue
> in Fort Lauderdale, Florida. You see, I lost my uncle. If we had had a drug court
> treatment program a long time ago, things may have turned out differently for
> my uncle. Maybe he could be here. He was brighter, he was smarter than me.
> And he could stand here right now. So, I say to you in all honesty, America we
> need programs of this nature. Because if we don't, guess what? We will reap
> what we sow.

At the Portland conference, Wheeler more directly connected the story
about his uncle with the need for the drug courts and used the example to

encourage people to continue with or start a drug court in their own region.

Judge Schma provided another horror story to illustrate the harmfulness of an adjudicative process devoid of the therapeutic qualities of the drug court. In addition to his drug court duties, Judge Schma has a regular court docket where he also employs drug court methods. One example of this is his "First Monday Club," where he tells certain defendants (who presumably are on probation) to come to his court every Monday at 4:00 P.M. During these sessions he engages the clients in a therapeutic encounter. As Judge Schma explains, "It's kind of a way of doing some drug court stuff without a drug court"; a pattern, as noted earlier, other judges have adopted. With the First Monday Club he is still able to put some "therapeutic things . . . into the system."

Schma told the story of a former participant in the First Monday Club named Tim. According to Judge Schma, Tim was a drug addict but entered the criminal justice system for "pushing bad paper" (i.e., writing bad checks). Judge Schma put him on probation, and for six months Tim attended First Monday Club, during which time he allegedly stayed off of drugs. Because of Tim's success, Judge Schma eventually released him from court oversight. Once back on the street, according to Schma, Tim stayed clean for awhile but was encouraged back into drug use by the influence of a police informant. This is how Schma tells the story.

> Well, what happened to this guy when he got back on the streets? He stayed clean, he had a job, he didn't commit crimes, he didn't use. The cops get an informant to work on this guy because he had such a long history in the drug world. The cops get an informant to work on this guy to start dealing drugs with the informant. And the next thing you know he's using and dealing drugs, and he's busted again and this time some other judge put him in prison for four years. Now that's fucking dumb. That is unbelievable. . . . He told me this at the sentencing. I had heard that this is what had happened, but I had him tell me the story.

Schma's story is meant to illustrate the problems with current practices and the contrasting value of the drug court method. The story conveys the need for a transformation, suggesting that without change, more people like Tim will be harmed by the system. Judge Schma makes just this point as he continues the story.

> Now if I had kept that guy in the drug court. . . . I could have hung onto him. I would have known he wasn't going to his meetings. You know, you get so you can just tell by the way they behave what's going on. His slipping back into drugs wouldn't have happened. And I could have done that for him for less than two thousand bucks a year. And now we are paying a hundred thousand dollars [to keep him in prison for four years]. That is just stupid, under

anybody's terms, anybody's definition! That's not a happy story, but it's a real story about why we need to be doing what we're doing.

Judge Schma understands the potency of this story and consciously uses it to convince skeptics about the benefits of the drug court. With pungent indignation, Schma promises to use the story of how Tim was "dragged back into the gutter" to promote drug courts. "I'm going to use this example. I'm going to throw it out to every politician I get a chance to talk to, because it is absolutely insane."

"War Stories"

If horror stories such as these are offered to help convert unbelievers to the movement, the second type of social movement narrative aims to embolden those already converted. "War stories" are put forth to encourage the faithful to stay the course; to press forward; and to resist opposition, however formidable it may be. As Gary Fine explains this second class of stories: "Like soldiers after a battle, members may be exhilarated by the accounts of comrades-in-arms."[8] War stories are regularly offered at conferences and training seminars, where more seasoned drug court officials alert the newly initiated of the likely obstacles they will face and impart advice on how to overcome them. War stories, according to Fine, may recount either triumphs or temporary set backs, both of which are told to strengthen the resolve of the troops.

Consider two examples. The first was told at the 1996 drug court conference in Washington, D.C., by Wendy Lindley, a judge from Laguna Niguel, California. In this particular case, the judge was not officially a drug court judge, but like Judge Schma and others, was attempting to implement the therapeutic methods of the drug court in her regular criminal court docket. Judge Lindley's story is an example of a temporary setback.

Judge Lindley, like many of the drug court judges was frustrated with the conventional adjudicative method. She spoke of her frustration with "just recycling these people" through the system and decided something new must be tried. So, she started a therapeutically oriented court program with offenders who had blood alcohol levels over 2.0 at the time of their arrest. She worked on a bench with thirteen other judges and told them about what she was doing. According to Judge Lindley, they were not receptive to her efforts. "They were so negative," Lindley explains, "They called me a social worker. And I said, 'Thank you.'" The other judges on her bench never embraced her therapeutic form of adjudication. Judge Lindley reflected upon the reasons for this resistance.

> Many, many judges have a very strong sense of feeling that you handle a case in a certain way. You process justice efficiently, and you move on, and you

don't care what happens. And they have said that to me, "I don't care what happens when this person leaves this courtroom. It's not my business. I'm a judge, not a social worker." So, to me, that whole issue obviously brings out quite a bit of emotion, and exposing them to it does not seem to make a difference. I invited a number of them to come watch. I had one judge come watch, and he still didn't do it, in spite of the fact that the stories these people told as they stood up and graduated brought me to tears. So, I don't know what the answer is to this resistance other than just continued judicial education, and hoping to change the way people think about what the job of the judge is in our contemporary society.

Notice that Lindley turns her defeat into an opportunity to encourage herself and others to persevere in helping unbelievers find the true judicial light. Judge Lindley not only found the individual narratives of the clients to be emotively persuasive, but she anticipated that these stories would convince her cohorts of the drug court's worth and was surprised and disappointed when they did not.

Consider a second example of a "war story," or rather war stories, these from Claire McCaskill, the Kansas City prosecutor. Her stories are more representative of triumphs than temporary setbacks. Drawing upon her own experiences she sought to encourage movement participants attending the 1995 drug court conference to overcome potential obstacles. She related her own difficulties in securing support for the drug court, particularly from district attorneys. "The prosecutors in this country are not going for this because they are politically chicken. They are afraid that to be for this concept will somehow give them labels as soft and squishy, that they are looking at defendants as victims, or, God forbid, clients. So, how do you overcome that problem?" McCaskill offered several strategies for winning over the resistant and in the end recalled her success in converting recalcitrant D.A.s. "And all of the prosecutors who have served that capacity in my office have enjoyed the experience and have come to me later, even though some of them went kicking and screaming, and came to me after the fact and said, 'I'm glad I did that. It will help me in my work as an assistant prosecutor.'"

One of her favorite strategies for persuading reluctant prosecutors and other skeptics, interestingly, is making public the stories of successful drug court clients. Once again, the telling of stories is seen as essential to the continued advancement of the movement, and, once again, we have an example of local level discourse taking on national movement significance.

The graduations [of clients who have successfully completed the program] are a great media opportunity. Alumni are a wonderful media opportunity. Give your articulate alumni an opportunity to interact with the media, because they are great stuff. They grab the interest of people, because their histories are usually something that is far afield from the experience of most people who are watching. Most people have a hard time, thank goodness, relating to someone who started using hallucinating drugs at the age of eight. But, we know that those folks are in drug court. When they get better and they become contributing members of society, and they are articulate, we need to give them opportunities to talk to the community.

McCaskill proposes that successful drug court alumni be put on stage, that they be given an opportunity to tell their stories, with the anticipated goal of generating community support for drug courts.

Another obstacle McCaskill's drug court faced was resistance from police officers, some of whom were frustrated with the swift release of the drug offenders they had just arrested. She recounted an experience when a former drug court client had been rearrested for a serious crime.

Now, I won't lie to you. We had a rearrest recently, and anonymously across my desk came the sheet on the rearrest. And it was a rearrest for a serious crime of a drug court graduate. And attached to it was a copy of his graduation certificate. It was a little, "nah, nah, nah, nah, nah," from the police department.

To overcome resistance from police and others in the community, according to McCaskill, drug court officials must highlight the "tough" aspects of the drug court and underemphasize the features that could be interpreted as "soft on crime," a strategy, as we have already seen, that McCaskill and other drug court advocates regularly employ.

At the conclusion of her talk McCaskill reached out to the movement activists in attendance: "We do all feel like brothers and sisters. Welcome to the fold." Comrades-in-arm, to be sure.

"Happy Endings"

The third and final type of story in social movements, according to Fine's typology, are "happy endings," the success stories of individuals who have clearly benefited from the actions and ideals of the movement. These stories, according to Fine, "provide a morale boost and directly reinforce movement involvement."[9] Judges and other drug court officials repeatedly tell stories of clients who have turned their lives around because of the drug court. Most press accounts of the drug court—the large majority of which have been positive—feature a particular client who has done well in the program or who graduated and is off drugs, is working, and so on. In essence, this is the application of the strategy recommended by McCaskill. The important message conveyed in these stories is that the drug court is a cause worthy of support.

Consider two examples of these types of stories. The first story was told by Judge Robert Fogan of the Fort Lauderdale drug court. Fogan told the story of Melanie, a graduate of his drug court who had formerly prostituted herself to support her crack cocaine addiction. According to Fogan,

> Melanie was on the street for years, selling herself to get drugs, hopelessly addicted. She is now in treatment. She was in our first graduating class. . . . She is a beautiful woman now. She is a manager at one of the local restaurants in town. She came from walking the streets into treatment. She was so badly addicted when she first got into the drug treatment program. She knew she was dirty, so she would just call it in. "Hey, Phil, I'm dirty. No sense in me coming in and dropping off [a urine sample]. I'll tell you I'm dirty." So, she gets busted again for another possession charge out on the street. We brought her back into the program. . . . I put her into the intensive residential treatment program, kept her in treatment. She came out. She finally got it, and started moving along.

Melanie is also featured on a promotional video tape that this particular drug court shows to new participants and other interested parties. This is her account of her experience in the drug court.

> I was never clean for the first three weeks. Then I got arrested again—the day I was supposed to go into court. I was in jail the day I was supposed to go in front of the judge. And they let me out 45 minutes before, and I had no shoes on, no nothing. I had to come into the courtroom with no shoes on. That is how I went to my arraignment. And that was pretty scary. I was pretty rough. I wish I could get the mug shot so you could see the before and after picture—two different people. Believe it! So when I came into court for the arraignment . . . I had been up for probably two or three days at that time. So, I was in pretty rough shape. I usually went four or five days with no food, no water, nothing, just smoking. So, when I went into the courtroom, I was not very alert or anything. I wanted to just go to sleep and just not worry about it. But Judge Fogan ordered me to detox.

Like a religious conversion story, Melanie recounts her previous condition, and the moment of crisis that marked the beginning of her turn around. She recalls how she resisted the court's insistence that she go into intensive treatment.

> I cried and screamed and hollered. . . . I was not going to go. Period. They said they didn't care. "You're going. That is the way it is. Either go there or go to jail." I did do a couple hits before I went to detox. I had my boyfriend come pick me up. I was pretty pissed off. My last high. He brought me a dime rock, and he took a hit off of that before he even saw me. "This is my last one, you idiot." So, anyhow, I did get that one last little hit before I went into detox.

Because that is the way I was. I would have done it forever. That is the way of the drug addict. So, I went into detox.

Melanie tells of her experience in detox, in intensive treatment, and then in a halfway house, and expresses her gratitude that she is finally free from drug dependency. "I just thank God I am at where I am at today." So compelling is Melanie's story that the drug court uses it to garner public support for the program. As Judge Fogan explains, "She is one of our best spokespersons. She speaks at functions around town." In Melanie's case we see the very direct connection between the individual story and the larger movement. The story told at the local level is rebroadcast to a much wider audience. The purpose for doing this is literally to gain public support for the movement and encourage its further expansion.

Consider another happy ending, this one told by Judge Schma during a discussion about the importance of self-esteem in the recovery process. This judge, like many, claimed it was key to a client's success in the program. "They've been abused consistently. For many, I'm the first one that they've run into that has not been abusing them and it means the world to them. In terms of self-esteem it changes all that around, just upside down." To illustrate this point, Schma read a letter he had received from a woman graduate of his drug court program.

> I cannot possibly ever repay you for what you have done for me. By bringing me into this program you helped me to realize and accept I have a drug problem. That in itself is such a relief. From there you've helped me find a new way of life. I have to let you know what a positive influence you've been in my life. You believed in me and gave me a chance. I cannot think of one other man in my life since childhood who has not abused me in one form or another, not even my own father, except you who are so caring and kind and concerned and compassionate. . . . If you don't mind my saying so, I sure wish I had a father like you.

Judge Schma interpreted the letter in the following manner. "So you know, this is a woman who grew up with absolutely no self-esteem, nobody ever telling her she was a worthwhile person. She wrote me that letter the day that she graduated. And she has now been clean for a couple of years." Once again, this story is offered as a justification for the drug court. Without the drug court and its self-esteem building impact on individual lives, such people as this client would continue in drug use and other destructive behavior.

Happy endings are also told at drug court conferences. In fact, one judge was so taken by a courtroom encounter with a client that he had the transcripts of the court session copied and distributed at one drug court conference. Recall also from chapter 3 the group of juvenile offenders who were brought to a conference to restage a drug court drama; each client participating in this exercise told his or her individual story. Another judge brought a successful client to a conference to tell her success story. This particular story was aided by courtroom video clips of the client at different stages in the drug court program, as well as by the interpretive expertise of a treatment provider. This is how Judge Frank Hoover, of the Bakersfield drug court, introduced the story.

> The reason why I've come here, and I've brought some people with me, is to tell you a story. And I have to apologize in advance, I'm not a professional story-teller, and the story we tell comes out of drug court. And we are going to tell the story of a woman named Valerie, whom I first met in late 1996. But let me tell you the story in a different way . . . quite often depending on who tells the story and in what context the story is told people draw different conclusions from the story. So, I can only hope in telling the story three different ways to give you all the benefit of three different perspectives.

Judge Hoover offered his perspective first. He described Valerie's initial contact with the criminal justice system and the consequence of having to give up her son, Marcos, to foster care. He also described her encounters with a local hospital, the police department, the county jail, the district attorney's office, the public defender's office, and the court, each of which created separate files on Valerie's situation and/or her criminal status. To demonstrate the impersonal nature of the system, Hoover dramatically placed a new file on the podium for every agency Valerie encountered. Pointing to the stack of files, Hoover argued, "This is what Valerie looks like to many people in the criminal justice system. . . . This doesn't make any sense. All we do is make up files. Who is this person? And why in the world are we prepared to spend so much money on her every two or three months when something bizarre happens in her life? Maybe somebody ought to try to deal with her personally. Drug court does that."

Fortunately for Valerie, according to Hoover, she ended up in a place where she would be cared for personally, the Bakersfield drug court program. Hoover then introduced the second storyteller, Angelina, a treatment provider in the Bakersfield program. Angelina interpreted the courtroom video clips showing Valerie's progress throughout the drug court program. Her commentary, not surprisingly, was sprinkled with the symbolic reference points of feelings and self-esteem that define the therapeutic perspective and characterize the discourse of pathos popular in the contemporary context. Interpreting the first clip, for example, Angelina opined, "Look at her [Valerie's] body language, it's screaming low self-esteem, no self-worth." In another clip, showing Valerie at a later stage in the recovery process, Angelina noted, "In this episode she is looking great, feeling confident. I really think that she's taking a turn in her treatment at this point. By this point she is personalizing it. It is now her treatment and she's become more involved."

Finally, Valerie herself was brought to the stage and asked by Judge Hoover to offer her perspective on the drug court program. She began by discussing her recollections of her very first appearance in the drug court and, much like her counselor, invoked the common themes of therapeutic discourse.

> Okay, the day of my intake I remember feeling dispirited, bankrupt. I remember tremendous feelings of guilt and shame for losing Marcos. Feelings of worthlessness, my self-esteem was gone out the door. I remember being scared, very frightened, not knowing what I was getting into at drug court. And I knew that I wanted help. I believed that I needed the guidance to be shown where to go to get it. Because we who are in our disease feel we don't know which way we want to go for help, we just go to the next place to get high.

Judge Hoover then had the video clips shown a second time, and asked Valerie to offer commentary. After watching one clip Valerie recalled, "I remember feeling just so helpless, so desperate. I mean, in case you didn't notice my voice was just cracking because I just wanted to cry out, and I felt like just nobody was listening to me, and my life was just no longer mine. And in all essence, it was no longer mine. It was in the hand of the court and I'm thankful that it was." Valerie also commented on her desire while in drug court to get her son back. She recalled how in the drug court Judge Hoover had asked her, "Do you want to get the baby back? Because if you want the baby back and you complete this program I will personally call the social worker and tell the social worker that I think you should have the baby back." The prospect of getting her son back was a major incentive to Valerie to complete the program. As she put it, "That carried me, it carried me a little bit further to the next step."

Of a later video clip Valerie commented on her own progress in the recovery process. "Yeah, this is when I started doing better and I started trying. I started realizing that a little bit of effort was going a long way for me. I had a feeling of pride in me, growing inside of me, especially after getting praise from Judge Hoover for doing well. Just my self-esteem was growing, confidence was growing inside of me. After going to court and getting a pat on the back for doing well was like no other, no drug I could find out on the street, no high could ever replace that feeling." Finally, Valerie described what she was feeling in one of the last video clips, in which she was visibly more healthy and alert than in the video of her first court appearances.

> Yeah, the next time after I'd started working my [twelve] steps, and I was getting really involved with my recovery and my program. It was a very emo-

tional day for me, I can remember it so well now. I had to process a lot of feelings as far as with the guilt and the shame with Marcos, and losing my self-respect and feeling like I was a terrible mother. But at this point I started looking forward to going to court, to getting the approval that I knew was well deserved and that I was working hard for.

In the final video clip Valerie is shown telling Judge Hoover that the next time she comes to court she will bring her son. Valerie recalled that getting her son back was "the first accomplishment for me in fourteen years. Since I started using drugs, since I had graduated from junior high this is the first accomplishment in my life." At the end of Valerie's presentation Judge Hoover commented, "That's our story." As in the other examples above, telling the story had a purpose: to demonstrate the worth of drug court. As Judge Hoover himself explained,

> Now I'd like to close by saying that there are Valeries all over this country. . . . There are many stories like this . . . in this county. This is why you do drug court. You don't do drug court to process cases, and you don't do drug court to come up with some moral, civil penance for some misdeed that's being done to satisfy the politicians. What you do drug court for is for Valerie, for her baby Marcos, for her sisters and her brothers and her mother and her father and her friends and the judges and her future employers.

Moreover, according to Hoover, Valerie's happy ending is offered as an incentive to prospective drug courts to press forward with their programs. Drug courts provide the tools "that Valerie found to go to the places in her heart that Valerie did." Like Valerie, if others "can find the strength and the hope and pride to go to those places in their heart and find the dignity that's there for everyone, then they can have their lives back, and that's what these drug court are all about. And that's why you should do them. And we'd all like to thank you very much for watching our story."

Each of the stories—fitting as they do within the typology of social movement narratives—clearly relies on Aristotelian pathos. The emotively compelling stories are offered to justify the movement, to encourage others to join the ranks, and to persuade skeptics of the movement's worth.

Telling the Right Story

It is important, in this regard, that clients tell the right story. Clearly, Valerie followed a particular script. She used the same language and appealed to the same therapeutic symbols as did her treatment counselor. The right story was told, just as the right story must be told in the local drug court drama. That is, clients are expected to accept a particular worldview, a particular understanding of themselves, and they are expected to express this understanding according to therapeutically defined categories. Not telling the right story, moreover, is also interpreted in therapeutic terms. The person who fails to accept treatment—with a certain attitude, using the right words—will be interpreted as being in denial, as not complying, as not buying into treatment. Failure to tell the right story can have serious consequences for the client.

Consider an example from the Dade County court. With a large Hispanic population in Miami, a significant percentage of drug court clients are, not surprisingly, from Latin American countries, primarily Cuba. According to two Dade County treatment counselors with whom I spoke, Hispanic clients often have difficulty, at least initially, accepting therapeutic interpretations of their behavior. They do not readily embrace the belief that they are addicts, that they have a disease in need of treatment. It goes against their cultural sensibilities. As one counselor explained, for many Hispanics there "is kind of a stigma attached to having something wrong with you, to having a disease." The counselors, however, interpret this antipathy to treatment in therapeutic terms. As one counselor put it, "Their denial is bigger." As he sees it, the problem lies in a lack of education about the "facts" of drug addiction. "Education about addiction is very poor in Latin America."

Though they initially may be "very resistant" to treatment, over time, with enough education, "peer pressure," and exposure to therapeutic modalities, "they become more and more accepting of the fact that addiction is a problem that they have to deal with." As they are "more cultured to the American system, Hispanics can become more open" to treatment. Therefore, though it may at first be difficult for a client to say, " 'Hi, I'm so and so and I'm an addict,' after months and months of treatment, then that concept becomes a little easier." This is the ideal perspective to which the Dade County drug court counselors hope to bring their clients. "What we would like to do is have people get over their denial and say 'Hi, I'm Joe, I'm an addict. I'm in treatment to help myself.' "

Treatment providers and probation officers in the Maricopa County, Arizona, drug court spoke of similar cultures of initial resistance. The Phoenix drug court has a racially mixed clientele, including whites, Hispanics, and some Native Americans. Drug court staff noted that, like Hispanics, Indian clients sometimes have difficulty communicating according to the common nomenclature of the therapeutic idiom. Of the Native American clients, one counselor said, "They are very stoic and they don't share readily. Invading their space is something that is contrary to a lot of cultural taboos." Because of the "skill of the counselor," however, these clients, like those in Dade County, eventually go along with the program.

As the counselor explained, "You look for a bridge. Sooner or later they start participating, because they see someone doing that. They can relate to it. You just bring them along a little differently."

That complying with treatment and telling the right story can help a client get through the program was made particularly evident in a visit to the Oakland drug court. The setting was a meeting between the judge and a probation officer prior to a drug court session. In this meeting the probation officer—who in Oakland acts as a treatment provider—reviewed with the judge the different clients who would come before the judge that day. The probation officer recommended to the judge the rewards or sanctions she believed each client deserved. The discussion of one male client was particularly noteworthy. This client, though he did not have clean urine tests, was viewed favorably, according to the probation officer, because "he is buying into treatment." In other words, he had assumed the right attitude, the right disposition toward treatment. He was telling the right story. And though there was no evidence that he had stopped using drugs, the probation officer recommended that he be graduated to the next level of treatment. His case illustrates how telling the right story can benefit a client and expedite his release from the court.

Consider another case where evidently no drug use existed. A client in the Portland, Oregon, drug court reported that she was arrested for having a crack pipe in her car. She claimed that the pipe had been left in her car by a friend. She was pulled over by a police officer and the pipe was discovered. Because crack residue remained in the pipe she was arrested for possession of narcotics. This was the defendant's first arrest, and though she claimed to have never used drugs, she enrolled in the drug court for the purpose of maintaining a clean criminal record. In Portland successful completion of the drug court program results in the expungement of an arrest. This client's claim to have never used drugs was supported by the fact that she had not turned up a single dirty urine test since enrolling in drug court.

How, one might ask, could this client tell the right story according to therapeutic terms? Isn't the purpose of treatment to help someone overcome drug addiction? Though a non-drug user, this client still used therapeutic themes to describe her situation. She realized that though she was not an addict per se, she did have a "liking to drinking" and saw herself as living a lifestyle that was leading to drug use and, ultimately, addiction. Moreover, she had come to see herself as an "enabler" of her drug using friends. As she explained, "I was enabling. I was bailing people out of jail with my college money. I was a people pleaser." Through treatment she came to terms with these "negative" tendencies, so much so that now, she "doesn't help anybody anymore." The client told her story to a small group of drug court personnel who were also at the time attending the

Portland drug court conference. Afterward, two treatment providers who were a part of the visiting group discussed the client's story and her claim to have not used drugs. "At first I thought she was in denial," said one to the other. After the client's therapeutically inspired interpretation of her biography and the confirmation that she had indeed had no positive urine tests, they came to believe her story. Their initial response is nonetheless revealing.

One final example of the pressure put on clients to tell a story about themselves according to the treatment paradigm was offered by Jose Suarez. Suarez is the supervisor of the Criminal Justice Unit of the New York State Office of Alcoholism and Substance Abuse. He recounted to me an incident involving a struggle between one of the counselors he supervised and one of that counselor's clients. The difficulty between the two stemmed from the client's unwillingness to identify himself as an addict. The client had become involved in a Pentecostal church and, in keeping with his religious worldview, saw his drug and alcohol problem not as a disease but as a matter of "demon possession." To the counselor this was unacceptable.

According to Suarez, "The counselor was pissed off." Though the client was admittedly not using drugs or alcohol the counselor still saw the client as being "in denial" and as refusing to "accept the fact that he [was] an alcoholic and an addict." From Suarez's perspective, the client had come to terms with his drug use and "he just wasn't accepting the label of addiction that this institution was imposing on him." According to Suarez, the problem was with the counselor who had a "control issue" and could only see the client's behavior according to a particular paradigm. He could only see the client as "not complying, not buying into treatment, as still being in denial." The problem, in short, was that the client "was not saying what he [the counselor] wanted him to say." In other words, he was not telling the right story.

According to Suarez this scenario gets played out often in the drug court. The court is in a position of "interpreting whether the person is sincere or not." As Suarez acknowledges, "that is very subjective. What constitutes sincerity? What constitutes motivation?" In this situation Suarez admonished the counselor for being too rigid and encouraged him to "go with the demon possession thing." Consider his instructions to the counselor: "Why are you making this person say what you want him to say. So the person won't admit he is an addict, but he is admitting that he is possessed. So what. So he is possessed. You go with that." According to Suarez this situation was salvaged because of "good supervision," though he admits that in "a lot of places the supervision is really poor." If so, one is left to wonder how many similar clients are required to interpret their drug use in a certain way to please the counselor who in many instances controls the client's status in the program.

Storytelling and Drug Court Evaluations

Alongside stories about individual successes the drug courts are also expected to produce evidence that demonstrates the program's efficacy. In investigating evaluations of drug court success rates, one finds an interesting development. The traditional methods of evaluation have themselves been influenced by the storytelling perspective. That is, the viability of modern methods of empirical measurement have been joined or colored, if not called into question, by the predominance of narratives. Consider several examples.

The most comprehensive study of the Dade County drug court offers a fairly substantive, though problematically constructed, comparison of the success rates of drug court participants to those of other offenders in the Dade County court. The study also contains case studies that tell the stories of ten clients as they progressed through the program, included because of the expressed concerns of drug court officials who questioned the traditional standards of what constitutes success.[10] As Goldkamp and Weiland note, drug court personnel argued that the strictly quantitative measures would not accurately "convey the 'ups and downs,' 'zigzags,' and other kinds of 'real-life' behavior actually involved in treatment program progress." In other words, as the authors state, "there was concern that a strictly quantitative approach to assessing program impact be supplemented by qualitative information."[11] For this reason, the stories of individual clients are included to supplement the more traditional empirical evidence.

This practice is typical of the evaluations of the drug courts. For example, a May 1997 Justice Department survey of ninety operational drug courts, includes a 101-page "Participants Perspective" section where drug court clients not only respond to survey questions regarding a number of the features of the drug court but also offer their perspective on how frequently urinalysis tests should be required and how the drug courts could be made more effective.[12] The stories of drug court clients are even more central to an evaluation of the Washington, D.C., drug court where thirty-two pages are devoted to the results of focus group interviews of drug court participants.[13] In this case there is also a fairly rigorous (eighteen-page) statistical analysis of three different adjudicative tracks.[14] But the point remains: The stories were told in conjunction with the more traditional empirical measurements.

One final example involves an evaluation, conducted by W. Clinton Terry of the Broward County Drug Court, where narrative appears to triumph over traditional empirical findings as the most convincing determination of the program's worthiness. As Terry notes in his study: "The question of success based upon rearrest information is an approach arising from within the context of criminal justice issues. *An equally viable approach* would be to examine the question of success from the standpoint of substance abuse and treatment, for, after all this is a population of substance abusers."[15] Based on this perspective, Terry concludes, though he found no real difference in rearrest rates between drug court and non-drug court participants, that "[t]here is absolutely no question that the drug court is having a very positive effect upon the lives of many people." He believes this because at "the personal level, one is moved when hearing the individual success stories of persons who have turned their lives around as the result of the Drug Court."[16]

In this case, then, the stories are viewed as more persuasive and credible than traditional empirical measurements. Narrative-based criteria not only have found their way into evaluations of individual drug courts, but these are the typical justifications offered by judges and other drug court officials in defending the movement. So pervasive is this kind of defense that at one drug court conference, David Mactas, the Director of the Center for Substance Abuse Treatment (CSAT), an agency that funds drug courts, expressed his frustration with the lack of discussion among drug court officials about the empirical evidence that supports the efficacy of the treatment approach, evidence he believes is available. Consider the following complaint offered by Mactas regarding what he hears when activists defend the drug court approach: "What you don't hear is scholarship, discovery, revelation, findings, research, data, outcomes. You hear, 'Oh boy, I was at a graduation last week, and you should have been there. I hugged all those people. It feels great.'" Some question remains, however, about what research and data actually reveal regarding the efficacy of drug courts.

Mactas's critique notwithstanding, it is common for drug courts to report, alongside the individual stories, dramatically reduced recidivism rates, the standard criminal justice measurement for success in programs such as this. Press accounts on the drug courts typically pick up the numbers reported by the courts. For example, the Las Vegas drug court reported a recidivism rate of 2 percent;[17] Ventura, California, 12 percent; Austin, Texas, 25 percent; and Seattle, Washington 29 percent.[18] The Portland, Oregon, drug court reported a recidivism rate of 6 percent for drug court participants who had been out of drug court for six months, and 15 percent for those out of the program for a year.[19] Baltimore reported a recidivism rate of 25 percent,[20] and Los Angeles, 10 percent.[21] Summary accounts of the drug courts offer estimates that reflect these same basic numbers. The *New York Times*, for example, notes that "drug courts report recidivism among their participants in the range of 4 to 28 percent."[22] Another article reported that "statistics are hard to find, but estimates nationally claim that between 70 and 90 percent of drug court participants are successful."[23] Again, these numbers are typically based on what is reported by the individual courts themselves. External evaluations, however, often tell a very different story.

Consider, for example, that the Miami drug court initially reported recidivism rates as low as 4 percent in 1990, a year after the program was initiated.[24] A year later, Judge Goldstein reported a recidivism rate of around 10 percent. As reported in a *St. Petersburg Times* article, "Goldstein estimates that of 3,000 defendants who have been through since drug court started in June 1989, about 90 percent have stayed out of trouble."[25] Then in 1994, Dorothy Fletcher, assistant director of the Dade County Office of Substance Abuse, estimated the rearrest rate in the Miami court at just under 20 percent.[26] A year earlier, however, a study conducted by John Goldkamp and Doris Weiland discovered a rearrest rate among Dade County drug court participants of 33 percent, with 10 percent having been rearrested three or more times.[27]

A *Washington Post* article noted this rather significant readjustment resulting from the study. "Initially, county officials claimed that more than 90 percent remained 'arrest free,' an astoundingly high number compared with traditional recidivism rates. More recently, they have acknowledged that the figure has dropped to 60 percent—and that does not count the large numbers who drop out early in the program."[28] A close examination of the 1993 study of the Dade County court, in fact, reveals that drug court clients actually have a higher recidivism rate than the most appropriate comparison group (i.e., a group composed of offenders who were eligible for drug court, but who chose not to participate), though for reasons not entirely clear, this comparison group is not included in the most widely disseminated version of the study.[29]

Similarly, initial reports from the Denver drug court claimed remarkably low recidivism rates. As Judge Morris Hoffman notes, "Two years after the formation of the Denver Drug Court, its coordinator issued a three-page 'study' reporting a colossal drop in recidivism from the control group of probationary drug defendants in traditional courts (58.3% recidivism) to the target group of drug court graduates (10.6% recidivism)." However, when a "formal study of the Denver Drug Courts was done using the proper target group" the findings were much less favorable: "58% recidivism for the drug defendants in traditional courts and 53% for the drug defendants in drug court."[30]

The most careful and comprehensive review of drug court success rates was issued by the General Accounting Office (GAO) in 1997. Based on an analysis of twenty drug court evaluations, the GAO reported that it could not "reach definitive conclusions concerning the overall impact of drug courts," mainly because of problems and limitations in evaluation design and methodology found in the various studies.[31] "Eleven of the 20 studies did not include an assessment of postprogram criminal recidivism among program participants, and none of the studies included an assessment of postprogram drug use relapse. Also most of the available studies (14 of the 20 studies) involved no comparison between participants and nonparticipant arrest rates after program completion."[32]

Even the six studies that did include comparison groups had significant methodological limitations, among these the problematic comparison groups in the Dade County evaluation identified above. An evaluation of the Broward County drug court, in fact, found rearrest rates (for new felony charges) to be higher among drug court participants (39 percent) than among nonparticipants (30 percent).[33] Moreover, a RAND study of the Maricopa County drug court, which, according to the GAO, had the strongest research design, revealed virtually no difference between the rearrest rates of drug court participants (31 percent) and nonparticipants (30 to 37 percent).[34] Findings from the GAO report, therefore, support Judge Hoffman's critical assertion that of the dozens of drug court impact studies conducted, only a handful have used the proper comparison groups, and that "the recidivism results in that handful of studies are substantially less promising than the wild claims regularly made in informal surveys."[35]

Drug court officials point to more optimistic summary findings found in a follow-up to the GAO report written by Steven Belenko and published in the first volume of the *National Drug Court Institute Review*.[36] But even here, particularly as it concerns the issue of recidivism, evidence in support of drug court efficacy is still rather weak.[37] Belenko, for example, identifies only nine drug court evaluation studies that included both drug court participants and graduates in the "drug court" sample. As Belenko notes, "most studies compare only drug court graduates to a comparison sample, which tends to inflate the overall effect of the intervention."[38] When a more appropriate sample is used, "the differences are not as large."[39] In fact, of the nine studies that "tracked *all* drug court participants," one showed virtually no difference in recidivism rates between drug court and non-drug court participants, and only two reported reduced recidivism rates among drug court clients that were statistically significant. Curiously, the study does not identify which two these were.

Also unclear is the constitution of the non-drug court comparison groups used in the various evaluations. For example, included among the nine ostensibly more valid studies is the Goldkamp and Weiland study of the Dade County drug court mentioned above. However, in Belenko's summary of the Dade County evaluation, as in most versions of the 1993 study, the only really appropriate comparison group is excluded from the analysis. Where the GAO report notes the absence of this comparison sample and qualifies that the results "must be viewed with caution as a result of a lack of comparability between groups," Belenko offers no such caveat.[40] But even Belenko is not blind to these problems. In fact, he ultimately agrees with much of the GAO report and emphasizes to those conducting future research that "careful consideration must be given to the selection of a comparison sample to ensure that it is as closely matched as possible to the drug court sample."[41] Conceding "gaps in our knowledge about drug courts" he also recognizes the need for longer follow-up periods of assessment, more studies using experimental designs, and larger sample sizes to ensure scientifically valid comparisons.[42]

Drug court officials similarly concede that "many, if not all, of the initial DTC reports of success were based upon surveys and methods which used quasi-experimentation instead of true scientific experimentation," and that the "results of the studies were suspect."[43] They also grant that the RAND study of the Maricopa County court represents an "effort to correct the methodological and resulting statistical problems associated with these [other] studies," and that the results of the RAND study "were less than resounding in terms of the effectiveness of the DTC."[44] Moreover, drug court judges "accept responsibility for the GAO's failure to reach 'firm conclusions.'"[45] As Judge Tauber puts it, "Many of the evaluations lacked scientifically acceptable designs. More importantly, virtually all of the studies used different data collection and evaluation criteria, making a comprehensive, national evaluation difficult, if not impossible, to conduct."[46]

Other drug court officials are not quite so ready to make such evidentiary concessions, as it were. That is, they submit that given the nature of the drug court, these traditional measurements are less relevant. Moreover, they claim that it may take time for the results to be fully realized. Tim Murray, for example, has argued that "it's ridiculous to suggest that hard-core heroin and cocaine addicts will be cured as soon as you 'stick needles in their ears and ask them to pee into a cup. . . . This is a long-term process. You must be in it for the long haul if there are going to be any successes.'"[47] Advocates, by appealing to the disease view of drug addiction, argue that relapses and, concomitantly, rearrests are simply a part of the process. Based on this understanding, advocates contend that traditional measurements may need to be reconsidered. As Goldkamp and Weiland note, "The attempt to marry criminal justice and drug treatment goals embodied in the [drug court] complicates design of an empirical assessment."[48] That is, the criminal justice and treatment communities may have different expectations for the offender/client. Consequently, "this difference in expectations . . . translates into differences in approaches to measuring 'outcomes' in an assessment."[49]

Following this line of reasoning, David Mactas makes a case for measuring drug court success rates according to therapeutic rather than traditional criminal justice measurements. Comparing drug use to heart, lung, and kidney diseases, Mactas expresses frustration with the lack of patience people typically allow for recovery in the area of drug addiction. From a treatment perspective, as Mactas portrays it, traditional criminal justice measurements appear absurd. "Can you imagine studying the effectiveness of interventions for heart disease by measuring one year after you have cut off heart medication, one year after you stop the kidney medication, one year after you stop the medication for lung disease?" As Mactas's rhetorical questions reveal, he sees this as nonsensical. According to Mactas, one should have the same skepticism regarding one-year measurements of relapse and rearrest for those who have graduated from drug court.

Mactas's argument points to another important development in the drug court phenomenon, which is addressed in the next chapter, namely, the formidable application of the disease model to the adjudicative process. In this chapter we have seen that storytelling is a dominant feature of the drug court at both the local and national movement levels. The role of narrative not only effects the reconfiguration of the criminal court setting but influences how these programs are evaluated. The stories of individual clients represent an increasingly legitimate basis upon which to judge the success of programs like drug court.[50] An important feature of these stories is the understanding of the offender's behavior according to the disease view of drug addiction. As the history of the social control of drugs in the United States makes quite clear, the disease view of drug addiction is nothing new. What is new, however, is the wholesale appropriation of this perspective within the context of the criminal adjudication process.

Six

The Pathological Shift

> As opposed to using the traditional criminal
> justice paradigm, in which drug abuse is
> understood as a willful choice made by an
> offender capable of choosing between right and
> wrong, DTCs shift the paradigm in order to treat
> drug abuse as a "biopsychosocial disease."
> —Judge Peggy Hora, Judge William Schma,
>   and John Rosenthal

DRUG COURT officials adopting the disease view of drug addiction fundamentally depart from the justice system's historical position. As discussed
in chapter 1, treatment was for many years largely irrelevant to the criminal justice approach to drug-related crimes. It is not so much that the legal
world was openly hostile to the treatment perspective, though there was
some of this, but rather that treatment was simply not seen as something
in which the judicial system was involved. Judges were trained in the law,
not in providing treatment. If a legislature determined that certain behavior was illegal, then the justice system was duty-bound to determine guilt,
and, if found, to impose a "just" punishment for the offense. When the
system did mandate some form of treatment or rehabilitation (prior to the
advent of the drug courts), it was administered primarily in the probationary or correctional rather than the adjudicative setting. Of course, the
evolutionary process that began with the 1914 Harrison Act and culmi-
nated in the drug courts of the 1990s changed all this. The treatment
perspective, like previous understandings of criminal behavior, is not
neutral. It profoundly shapes the way judges view and handle defendants.
Some are fully cognizant of the profundity of this change and are openly
dismissive of traditional judicial interpretations of criminal activity.

In her advocacy of the disease view, Judge Peggy Hora, for example,
avers a pronounced distinction between therapeutic justice and traditional understandings of criminal adjudication.

> There was a time when we used religion to try to deal with drug abuse by saying
> "nice people don't do this." The drunkards were put in the stocks. In Puritan

times religion dealt in different ways with addiction. . . . But it is not a moral failing. It used to be treated as that, but that, in fact, is not what it is. The "just say no" to drugs business. You might as well tell a clinically depressed person, you know, "Just cheer up." It has about as much effect. It is a ridiculous way to approach the problem . . . and I don't think a moral failure model was ever the right place to be.

The treatment perspective recasts the traditional view of human behavior as antiquated and irrelevant. It also fundamentally alters the manner in which drug offenders are handled in the criminal justice system. "In approaching the problem of drug offenders from a therapeutic, medicinal perspective, substance abuse is seen not so much as a moral failure, but as a condition requiring therapeutic remedies."[1] Thus, the new orthodoxy demands a new praxis: treatment instead of punishment. Judge Fogan explains this new perspective to the clients who come into his Broward County drug court. Fogan asks one defendant how long he had been in jail. "Since Friday," the client responds. Judge Fogan empathizes, "Long enough to last a lifetime? You don't ever need to see the inside of a jail again, do you?" The defendant shakes his head in agreement. Fogan then explains to this client and to the others present in the courtroom that the drug court is a different kind of court. "One of the reasons we started this program was so that people—young men and women like yourselves—wouldn't have to spend a lot of time in jail or prison simply because you've got a drug problem. We recognize that a drug problem may be part of an addiction, that it is a treatable disease." According to Fogan, then, jail is not the appropriate remedy because drug use is a disease requiring treatment, not punishment. As Fogan explains, "We are not in the business of punishing people because they have a drug problem. We are going to give you help. It's called treatment."

In a subsequent interview Judge Fogan elaborated on this point, comparing drug addiction to cancer, then later to diabetes. "A better example than cancer would be diabetes," Fogan argued. "You can control it by various means, watching your diet and all that type of thing. But you are still a diabetic even though you may not be going into a coma or having problems like that. But you are still a diabetic. And you have to watch what you eat, watch your insulin, and all that stuff. It is the same thing with an alcoholic or a drug addict. It's the exact same thing." Suggested here is the view common to both AA and NA that one never fully recovers from alcoholism or drug addiction, that one always remains in recovery, even if sober for over twenty years. Thus, the common refrain "I'm a recovering addict" rather than "I'm a recovered addict." Like diabetes, drug addiction is a disease that can be controlled. It can be forced into a sort of remission.

Judicial Adjustment to the Treatment Paradigm

Judges, who have not typically worked within a treatment paradigm sometimes go through a cognitive reorientation or period of "consciousness raising" to understand the full implications of the treatment view of behavior and the kind of patience that it requires. In other words, traditional training prepared a judge to see a dirty urine test as something like a probation violation, which most often required the imposition of some form of incarceration. According to the new treatment paradigm, a dirty urine test represents instead something more like the recurrence of a temporarily latent flue. The treatment response requires patience, compassion, and understanding. This reorientation or "consciousness raising thing," McKinney explains, "makes judges like myself and my colleagues come to grips with the notion that substance abuse is a disease." Once realized, judges can then understand that drug abuse "has to be treated and that there are ways in which it can be treated." They also come to recognize that "we traditionally have punished people who we really shouldn't have punished." McKinney sees relapsed offenders as ones who historically were "wrongfully" punished for their failings. From the treatment perspective judges understand that the relapsing drug user, like the cancer patient whose illness has come out of remission, should not be punished but treated. Relapse is to be viewed as an expected part of the recovery process. "Relapse is a part of therapy," McKinney argues; "it's a therapeutic device."

For Judge Violante of the Niagara Falls drug court, having his consciousness raised in this way was "extremely difficult." Violante accurately notes that the criminal justice system historically rejected the treatment perspective. The criminal justice community, according to Violante, told the treatment community to make itself scarce, a position that the judge himself shared. His previous attitude toward the treatment community was, "Don't tell me how I'm going to sentence. Don't tell me how I'm going accept a plea. Don't tell me he's sick. Nobody forced him on the ground and forced this alcohol or these drugs down his throat." After reflecting on the anemic results such a position yielded, Violante converted to the treatment perspective and discovered the necessity of patience with relapses. "What I don't think I ever really realized was that to facilitate the handling of these people I must understand what dependency is all about, and more important than that, from the point of view of treatment, what recovery is all about. I had no idea that recovery involved an aspect of relapse and relapse prevention." Now Violante realizes that relapse is "what it's all about."

For other judges, transitioning to the illness model of drug addiction was less difficult. It was clear to them that what they were doing before was not working and that something new had to be tried. This, of course, is the same kind of judicial utilitarianism used to justify the departure from the common law tradition, which we investigated in chapter 4. Given the basic logic of the utilitarian argument one could conceivably entertain any number of possible alternatives to current practices. One could imagine, for example, caning or other forms of corporal punishment, public shaming, restitution, chain gangs, or community service as other possibilities. These arguably could replace the ineffectual revolving door of incarceration, release, and rearrest that drug court officials complain about in reference to the old ways of doing things. Though some of the cited examples have come into practice in some jurisdictions, these forms of punishment are not obviously commensurate with the therapeutic sensibilities that presently inform our culture, just as Uriah Levy's punitive practices were not in keeping with the cultural dispositions of early nineteenth-century America. Treatment, however, is consistent with today's therapeutic culture, and is therefore more culturally (and subsequently more judicially) plausible. As David Garland argues, cultural sensibilities significantly "influence the forms which penal punishments take."[2]

The cultural dominance of the therapeutic and utilitarian sensibilities helps to explain why the treatment approach is so enthusiastically embraced. Faced with an ineffectual system, judges must draw upon some meaning system to reorient the judicial process. The erosion of traditional meaning systems and the dominance of the therapeutic culture makes the latter the most obvious choice.[3] According to judges, however, the traditional perspective is not rejected because of hostility toward religious traditionalism per se, but because the old method was not working. Pragmatics rather than philosophical reconsiderations drive judicial change. Consider Judge Farrell's explanation for his assent to the treatment perspective. As he puts it, his acceptance of the treatment approach was "more of a practical" decision than "worrying about whether it was moral." Buying "entirely" into the disease orientation, therefore, was not difficult for Farrell because, as he sees it, "there has been no effective response to the problem. We are pouring money and resources down the drain in terms of the drug problem and not getting anywhere with young people." Again, he "never really looked at it as being a tug of war between society's traditional values versus the disease model. . . . Anybody who is exposed to the problem for any period of time would have to see that the traditional approach just ain't working."

For Judge Farrell, then, "it was never a moral issue, it was a practical issue." Buffalo District Attorney, Barry Zavah, makes a similar case. "Our adversarial system isn't working as well as the community thinks it

ought to. . . . If it isn't working . . . then let's do something different."
Again, change is driven by the perceived ineffectiveness of the criminal
justice system. According to Zavah, the change is not driven by philosophical disputes over the Constitution or the meaning systems that inform it but by the need to institute a system that is more effective. "There
isn't anyone in the drug court," Zavah argues, "who doesn't value the
U.S. Constitution and the liberties that we've had in this country for the
last couple hundred years. It is just that we are trying something different,
and some of it tends to make sense."

Farrell, Zavah, and others, then, see the traditional judicial model as
ineffective, and believe that some kind of new method must be attempted.
The availability of the therapeutic sensibility at the cultural level makes
the treatment approach a plausible alternative. "It tends to make sense,"
as Zavah argues. For many, the disease model has already become a taken
for granted interpretation of drug-using behavior, making acceptance of
this model a cognitively painless process. Noting the cultural hegemony
of the disease model, Judge Karlin, for example, observes, "I think that it
is becoming more and more obvious to people that drugs are an illness
and you have to treat it a little differently than a crime. It seems very
simple." So it does in the contemporary context. As we have seen, however, the disease model was not always so commonsensical, at least not
within the codes of moral understanding that at one time more fully informed criminal justice efforts to control the distribution and use of
drugs.

Curiously, the director of treatment at one of the drug courts I visited
took comfort in the apparent ease with which the judge, defense attorneys, and prosecuting attorneys in his drug court adopted the disease
model. He contrasted this judicial position with the views of some physicians who even today question the physiological and psychological basis
of the disease model, a debate, as we have seen, that has gone on in the
medical community for many years.[4] "It's amazing listening to physicians
say, 'It's not a disease.' It's almost done a reverse. We have people who
are normally not trained in the medical field calling it a disease and those
who are trained in the medical field saying, 'It's not a disease,' that it's just
a lack of guts or lack of intestinal fortitude of the individual. It's a scary
thought." What is scary to this treatment director is the perceived lack of
understanding among the skeptical physicians, not the "enlightened"
view of drug court officials. So fully has the treatment perspective pene-
trated the criminal justice system that for many it is a taken for granted
reality. Any questioning of the disease paradigm, even from those in the
medical community, is nonsensical.

Equipped with the disease view of behavior, drug court judges involve
themselves directly in the recovery process, thereby getting at what they

understand to be the root of the addictive behavior or illness. But what is at the root of this behavior? Why do these people need to use drugs? According to many of the judges and drug court officials with whom I spoke, the fundamental problem is low self-esteem. That is, people use drugs because they don't feel good about themselves. It is held that many drug court clients come from backgrounds where they received little affirmation or encouragement. They were not, it is argued, helped to feel good about themselves. Consequently they have low self-esteem and are more inclined to use drugs and participate in other "unhealthy" behaviors. The questionable validity of this view notwithstanding, it is a common perspective among drug court officials.[5] Correspondingly, judges and treatment providers devote much energy to helping clients build their self-esteem. Tim Smith, a counselor at the San Bernardino, California, drug court, speaks for many when he says, "Drugs are just a symptom of our disease. Drugs are not the problem of the recovering addict." Rather, according to Smith, the root problem is a "low self-esteem." Therefore, the focus of treatment is to help clients "start building their self-esteem."

The Centrality of Self-Esteem

To follow the physiological metaphor offered by the judges, then, one could say that drug addiction is a symptom of a low self-esteem in the same way that fatigue is a symptom of diabetes.[6] Consider the diagnosis offered by Judge Fogan: "Many people use drugs to mask their feelings. And one of those feelings that they sometimes want to mask is their lack of self-esteem. Not everyone who uses drugs has a lack of self-esteem, but many of them do." Realizing this common malady, the judge then must work to raise the self-esteem of clients in the same way that the physician works to raise a patient's insulin level. Thus, the raising of self-esteem is a central component of the drug court judge's role. Judge Schma certainly sees this as part of his job. Consider the following discussion regarding the place of self-esteem in his court. "One of the chronic character traits of addicts is that they lack self-esteem. They've had so many negative influences in their lives, had so many negative experiences, that their sense of self-worth is almost zero." Given this fundamental problem it is the judge's role "to build up that self-esteem. And you can imagine what it does for someone's self-esteem to have a judge come down off the bench and shake their hand; talk to them in their first name instead of 'Hey you'; treat them with some respect and obvious affection to the extent that they spend time with them; talk to them; listen to them; talk about their families; treat them like human beings. You know, they just haven't been treated that way." Judge Tauber makes the same point. "When a judge treats a person like a human being rather than as a case . . . people will respond to that. And I think there is self-esteem in that, that he is treating me like a person, and he cares about me or she cares about me, and wants to work with me."

Judge Bolton of the Phoenix drug court also sees the building of self-esteem as a central part of her work in the drug court. When she affirms clients during court sessions she gets the "impression that it may be the first time in their entire lives that anyone has ever told them that they were doing a good job at anything." Even when people are not really doing that well she looks at them and says, "Boy is this person doing well in comparison to what he used to do. He is doing great for him." Counselors in the Phoenix drug court provide Judge Bolton with reports highlighting even little successes so that she can offer some kind of affirmation during court sessions. "The reports try to put a few things in like that so that I can tell them something specific. Or the counselor will make a specific mention of how well they have presented their first step, or what a good job they did on a particular assignment, so that we can try to pick that out, and say something specific about it, so that they know that we are recognizing that they are doing something good."

Judicial concern with the building of self-esteem is believed to be so vital because, as Judge Swett of Charlottesville, Virginia, explains, "an increasing number of people who come into the criminal justice system have an enormous lack of self-esteem, an enormous lack of a sense of purpose, an enormous void of hope in the future." Because low self-esteem is the fundamental problem, Judge Swett believes it is incumbent upon the court to respond to this issue. Following the example of the "therapeutic community" the court must, Swett argues, try to "build self-esteem, little by little by little, and give these people the sense that there are people out there who care." The drug court can "help them to see that it is possible to address who they are without hating themselves for what they've done."

Swett uses a non-drug crime to illustrate his point. "There was a nine-teen-year-old kid who was involved in pizza robberies. And his reasoning and explanation [for this involvement] made little or no sense. He came from a good background, but he retreated from his good background and went into the projects here in the city and created relationships within the criminal drug element in the inner city. That led to him getting involved in pizza robberies with two other kids—who clearly had behavior problems as well." As Swett saw it, this defendant had the problem of a low self-esteem; therefore the judge wondered whether a long penitentiary sentence was the right answer. "The book would have said that when you put a knife to somebody's throat, you take money from them, there is one avenue for you, penitentiary for a long time." This defendant, Swett explains further, did not have a "disease in the sense of being a drug addict but was involved in a terribly warped struggle to where he was going to get his self-esteem." The answer, Swett believed, was not to put "that kid in the penitentiary for twenty-five years." Instead, Swett gave the young man five years, much lower than the court directed guidelines.

For Judge Swett this was not an isolated case. He claims to see the problem of low self-esteem "all the time" and believes that if the court would help offenders to think more highly of themselves, the effects could be dramatic. As Swett explains, the typical person coming into his court has been told for many years, " 'You've failed, you've failed, you've failed, you are a failure, you are no good, you are not good.' But what if someone were all of a sudden to say, 'I care that you make it and I want you to do this because it is going to be best for you,' and all of a sudden were to say, 'You did well, you accomplished something?' Those are the kinds of things that I think in the long run, at least for these people, will have the best chance of changing their behavior, of changing their values systems." In other words, building someone's self-esteem through affirmation is the key to changing bad behavior.

Guiltless Justice

Self-esteem, of course, has for several decades been a taken-for-granted value in American society, especially in the area of education.[7] When applied to the criminal justice system, however, self-esteem essentially offers itself as a replacement to that which previously defined the essence of the adjudicative process, namely, the determination of guilt. Inasmuch as the therapeutically defined ideals of illness and of self-esteem assume a more central place in the adjudicative process, the notion of guilt is made increasingly less relevant. As the judges argue, the drug-using defendant has not done something morally wrong but rather has a sickness. Guilt, therefore, is philosophically non-germane (as legal practitioners might say) to such a process.

This, precisely, is the fate of guilt that Philip Rieff anticipated over twenty-five years ago in his enlightened critique of the therapeutic culture. "No guilt is true," Rieff writes, "except as it subserves the interdicts."[8] In other words, when therapeutic sensibilities replaced the authoritative presence of transcendent interdictions, true guilt became impossible. "To feel guilt takes a certain submission to authority." Since in a therapeutic society "there is no authority—only power and its theatrical effects," it is not possible to experience guilt. Rieff even foresaw the consequences of guiltlessness, as such, on the legal system. "Under the enlightenments of therapy, teaching orders of law, dependent as they must be upon orders of authoritative persons, appear as penal colonies; we re-educated ones cannot comprehend our own received punitive writ; it is a meaningless legacy, handed down by some presence no longer presiding. It is punishment that will become the crime."[9]

Such a philosophical reorientation has, in the drug courts, taken on structural form. For example, many of the courts are pre-adjudicative. That is, the defendants are never faced with the decision of having to enter a plea of "guilty" or "not guilty." The 1997 Justice Department survey of operational drug courts found that 30 percent of the surveyed courts were "pre-plea" only. That is, these courts are made up only of clients who have not entered any kind of plea. An additional 33 percent include at least some clients (usually the majority) who have not entered a plea.[10] Therefore, 63 percent of the drug courts have clients who have not even faced the predicament of having to state a disposition of guilt or innocence. In a very concrete and practical manner, then, the notion of guilt is irrelevant for many drug court clients.[11]

This arrangement is not some kind of procedural coincidence. It is very much in keeping with the larger therapeutically defined philosophy guiding the drug court program. Judge Robinson, of Portland, Oregon, for example, argues that the Portland drug court, which is pre-adjudicative, was set up this way for a reason. In his mind, it would be problematic to make these people who "already have a very low self-esteem" come in and say they are guilty. "They are people who have been told all their lives that they are guilty. . . . To tell them again that they are guilty would potentially lower their self-esteem still more." For this reason, Robinson explains, "our program is a pre-trial diversion program. We don't require them to enter a guilty plea." Doing so spares the defendants from having to experience "another blow to their self-esteem."

Judge McKinney of Syracuse is even more emphatic about the irrelevance of guilt to the drug court setting. He acknowledges the importance of ascertaining guilt in a typical court setting where the judge's purpose is to determine the validity of particular accusations. But, according to McKinney, that is not what the drug court is about. By volunteering to participate in the drug court program the defendant has circumvented this part of the judicial process. Therefore, McKinney asserts, "we literally leave all that [judicial impartiality, presumption of innocence, etc.] at the doorstep." In the drug court context, "the issue of guilt/innocence is not of concern."

Judge Weber agrees that the drug court does circumvent the notion of guilt in certain respects. "To say that you have a medical problem and we're going to help you with treatment in some ways diminishes the notion of guilt." Weber argues that drug court "is a combination of taking responsibility and also recognizing that some things are beyond the control of the individual. Addiction to drugs is a health problem. . . . We're not supposed to be punishing people for their disease." Therefore, he prefers to use the term "responsibility rather than guilt." Judge Strickland of Roanoke, Virginia, agrees that the notion of guilt is less significant in the drug court. Based on the therapeutic perspective, the drug court judge is "addressing the problems and the reasons for the culpable behavior rather than just dealing with guilt and what punishment should be imposed." She sees the expanding drug court movement offering a welcome corrective or balancing of the therapeutic model with notions of guilt, and she sees this balance "spreading to other areas of the criminal justice system." According to Strickland the notion of guilt will be sustained in this new synthesis because a certain "segment of the criminal justice system . . . must be satisfied." When I pressed her on this point, she agreed that her willingness to maintain guilt as part of the judicial equation had more to do with appeasing a sector of the community than with a personal belief in its significance.

Judge Schma also agrees that in the drug court the admittance of guilt is "pretty much immaterial." More important to him is that defendants "admit that they are addicts. That's what I want them to do." Schma thus makes a distinction between admitting guilt and admitting addiction. "It is more useful," he believes, "to get someone to admit addiction, because people will admit guilt, but not addiction, and then you don't cure the addiction." Again, the right story in this setting is to admit one's illness. To see one's behavior in terms of guilt/innocence, right/wrong, moral/immoral, is "immaterial." The drug court demands a therapeutically revised form of confession: "I am sick" instead of "I am guilty." Of greater importance is the therapeutically correct view that one recognize, come to terms with, and confess one's addiction. Simply to admit guilt, but not addiction, is to remain in denial. Guilt, in the context of therapeutic jurisprudence, is meaningless.

The drug court's eradication of guilt has been a subtle and insidious process. Guilt is not so much challenged as it is ignored. It is not so much disputed as it is made irrelevant. But it is the making irrelevant of something that has long been regarded as the very crux of criminal justice. In the world of literature the centrality of guilt to criminal law is perhaps captured nowhere better than in Dostoyevsky's *Crime and Punishment*. The crime in the Russian classic is double murder. The offender, Raskolnikov, is by contemporary measures mad. He is even encouraged by some to employ a defense of temporary insanity, which he refuses. Instead, he confesses to the police and utters words that represent the climatic moment in the story: "It was I." A similar confession today in similar circumstances might well be considered itself an act of insanity, yet it was the major turning point in Raskolnikov's life. The court in the story having "considered his confession and circumstances mitigating his guilt" handed down a sentence of "hard labor to the second degree." For Dostoyevsky and the cultural reference points within which he operated, guilt meant something, and the admittance of guilt, as illustrated in the life of his protagonist, was an event of epiphanic proportions. The jettisoning of guilt may well represent the most important, albeit rarely reflected upon, consequence of the drug court. If, as Philip Rieff argued, culture is not possible without guilt, one wonders what will become of a criminal justice system bereft of what was once its defining quality.

Expansion to Other Crimes

The notion of guiltlessness (and therapeutic justice more generally) is not limited to drug offenses. Indeed, only a few years after the first drug court began, movement activists began talking about and implementing the drug court model to other types of crime. As early as 1994 the Justice Department reported that "in a number of locations the innovative and collaborative methods characterizing the first generation of treatment drug courts were being adapted to other justice system populations."[12] Commending "remarkable local innovation," the Justice Department reported on the initiation of new juvenile, domestic violence, and community courts based upon the drug court treatment model.[13] By June 1998, the Justice Department reported that "50 juvenile and/or family drug courts have been implemented and another 50 are being planned."[14]

Even existing drug court programs have expanded eligibility criteria to include non-drug offenses. The 1997 Justice Department survey found that many drug courts include offenders with non-drug charges. According to the survey, 22 percent of the drug courts include clients with theft/property charges; 4 percent, clients with check and credit card forgery crimes; and another 4 percent, clients with prostitution offenses. Included among these are clients with charges of grand theft, breaking and entering, possession of a firearm, knowingly concealing stolen property, burglary, fraud, assault, forgery, shoplifting, prostitution, and child neglect.[15] In some drug courts, non-drug crimes constitute a significant percentage of the total drug court population. In Markham, Illinois, for example, 13 percent of the drug court clients were arrested for "retail thefts and burglary"; in Cincinnati, 24 percent for "theft related" crimes; in Rochester, New York, 35 percent for petit larceny, prostitution, or harassment charges; in Buffalo, 32 percent for petit larceny and 3 percent for prostitution; and in Newark, New Jersey, 40 percent for non-drug offenses. In the Pensacola, Florida, drug court, the overwhelming *majority* of the clients were in for non-drug charges. A full 68 percent of the Pensacola drug court clients were arrested for property crimes, while only 10 percent were in the program because of a drug possession charge.[16]

Some drug court judges now publicly advocate the expansion of the drug court to include violent crimes. To an applauding audience of some two thousand drug court practitioners at a June 1998 conference in Washington, D.C., Judge Dierdre Hair of the Cincinnati, Ohio, drug court asserted, "I will confess that it seems to me we are fairly idiotic in our policy of not accepting people with violent histories." Judge Hair speculated that most drug courts do take violent offenders and even confessed to "having taken a murderer" into her court. This particular client, according to Hair, was "one of our most successful drug court people."

For some, understanding drug addiction as an illness is one matter, but expanding the disease concept to include other types of criminal behavior is more problematic. That the justice system would move in the direction of interpreting an increasing number of behaviors through the lens of the illness model, however, makes sense for two reasons. First, as discussed earlier, the overwhelming majority of arrests, court cases, and prison spaces in today's criminal justice system are made up of offenders who have had some kind of involvement with illicit drugs. Many of the offenses, though they may not be purchase or possession charges, stem from involvement with drugs. Offenders commit robbery, larceny, forgery, and prostitution to support their drug habit. Moreover, many domestic violence cases, manslaughter, and other violent offenses result from the lack of self-control and sober reasoning that drug use may effect. If drug use is a disease, and this disease is believed to cause other criminal behaviors, then these other behaviors are themselves symptoms of the disease. This is the conclusion to which many in the drug court have come, and it is the reason offered for including in drug court clients with offenses other than charges for purchase and possession of narcotics.

A second and related reason for the plausibility of the shift is the larger cultural context. As noted above, the very meaning of guilt is called into question in a highly therapeutic culture. When anti-social behavior, criminal or otherwise, can be explained by low self-esteem and other psychological categories, labeling a person guilty for any crime becomes less plausible. Many have reached this conclusion in interpreting the behavior of such individuals as Ted Kaczynski (AKA, the Unabomber), even against his protests to the contrary;[17] Lorena Bobbit, who in a "fit of rage" severed her husband's penis with a kitchen knife; Susan Smith, the South Carolina woman who in 1994 drowned her two boys; and Michael Carneal, the Kentucky boy who in December of 1997 shot and killed three classmates and wounded five others while they participated in a high school prayer meeting.

Typical of the commentary surrounding the prosecution of these individuals, including that offered by legal counsel, was the expressed belief that to have committed such criminal acts, they must have been crazy, even if only temporarily. It is almost as though the criminal act itself is proof either of a pathology, a disorder, or low self-esteem. If, as Rieff argues, our ideas about guilt and punishment are "meaningless legacies" then how can we justifiably interpret any behavior as though someone were wrong, immoral, bad, or guilty? That individuals have difficulty interpreting even such heinous acts as those committed by Kaczynski according to traditional categories suggests, at the least, that the cultural saliency of these meaning systems is waning. To be sure, most Americans are not comfortable extending the disease model so comprehensively. However, given the codes of moral understanding that inform the contemporary zeitgeist, this is the logical end to which the current rationales lead.

I asked the various drug court officials about this matter. Should the drug court model be extended to include other types of crime? The answers were nuanced and complex. No one stated unequivocally that the drug court model should be limited only to drug offenses (i.e., purchase and possession charges). Given that approximately 30 percent of existing drug courts already include clients with non-drug charges, such a finding is not very surprising. Some, however, were personally ambivalent about how far the model should be extended, especially with respect to violent behavior—domestic or otherwise. Not all would agree with Judge Hair that murderers should be included in drug court. Others were uncertain not because they questioned the applicability of the model to other behaviors, but because they did not think the public was ready for it *yet*. In other words, they believe the model should be applied to other crimes but do not think that popular and political sentiment supports this view.

Baltimore's Judge Karlin was one who could see the possible merits of extending the model to others crimes but did not believe the public was yet willing to go this far.

> I think people now are becoming more aware that alcoholism is a disease. I think that from what I have seen, more people are becoming willing to accept that drug addiction is a disease. When you get to some of the other crimes that might be related to some problem that could be solved, such as being abused as a child and the other things that we hear about, I don't think people are ready to accept that. I think that there is probably some merit to it. But, I don't think people are willing to accept that yet as a form of a disease.

Judge Carl Goldstein of Wilmington, Delaware, similarly sees the merit of treating certain other offenses with the drug court model. In fact, he is very enthusiastic about the initiation of a new "restorative justice" program in Wilmington where low-level forgery and theft offenders are offered a program that includes treatment, mediation, and restitution as an alternative to the normal adjudication process. When asked if domestic violence should also be treated with the disease model in mind, Goldstein was much less certain.

> I don't know. I really don't know. I think it would depend on a lot of things. It would probably depend on the victim's feelings about it. It would depend on whatever the state of the therapeutic community is in regard to domestic relations work. I would not have problems with treatment for offenders in these areas, but a therapeutic approach like drug court for anything involving an act of violence or assault, I just don't know whether the system as we have it is pliable enough to accommodate that. And that is a different question from asking whether these people need treatment. I think they do.

Like Judge Karlin, then, Judge Goldstein thinks that some behaviors could be understood in this way and that even domestic violence offenders need treatment, but he is not willing to publicly defend this view because of concerns about perceived political and popular opposition. Fort Lauderdale's Judge Robert Fogan offers a similar analysis. Though he basically supports the relevance of the disease model to other crimes, "political realities" would prevent him from pushing for the extension of the drug court model in this direction. "You cannot get the community leaders to go along with that concept. We barely got it through to take simple possession and purchase cases with no prior felonies." Fogan "definitely" agrees that prostitution, theft, and other non-violent crimes should be handled with something similar to the drug court model, but he also believes that the political realities prohibit such an extension and that the resources to support it simply are not available.

Other judges, without acknowledging political currents, were not sure in their own minds whether it was right to extend the model to non-drug crimes. However, even judges with personal reservations were not definite in their opposition. Judge Duncan-Peters of Washington, D.C., for example, did not think she could give "a definite opinion" about expanding the disease model and thought it prudent to "be a little careful about this domestic violence stuff." Still, according to Duncan-Peters, there were some cases where it might be justifiable.

> I think that it probably wouldn't hurt to have domestic violence cases dealt with where you are treating the entire problem that the person has. They may have a drug or alcohol problem and the victim says he gets violent when he drinks, or when he uses drugs. In those cases it probably would make sense to have some sort of a system set up to deal with the drug problems. But in other

cases when drugs are not the cause of the violence, I wouldn't think there would be any need to treat those people's cases in the same way.

Thus, though hesitant about the expansion of the disease model generally, Duncan-Peters could imagine its applicability to domestic violence cases when some type of drug use was believed to be the reason for the violent behavior. For many drug court officials, this is the critical issue. As long as the crime is somehow related to drug use, then the drug court model is fully warranted. These other behaviors are symptoms of a deeper problem—the disease of drug addiction. The additional criminal behaviors, therefore, like drug addiction can be addressed through therapy. For this reason individuals with non-drug offenses are allowed into drug courts. On this issue, many with whom I spoke were much less equivocal, on the matters of both expanding drug court eligibility criteria and starting new courts geared toward particular criminal populations (e.g., domestic violence courts).

Judge Ziemian thinks the latter option makes perfect sense. "In probably 80 percent of domestic violence cases," according to Ziemian, "substance abuse is a contributing factor." Until "you get to the substance abuse problems and clean up that . . . you can't even deal with those other problems." Cathy Delaney agrees. She holds that "89 percent of the batterers are under the influence of something when they batter." If you deal with the drug issue, "a percentage of them will never ever hit another human being in a battering situation again. I think the model can work." For the same reason Judge Robert Russell of the Buffalo drug court justifies taking prostitution and theft offenses in his court (which together make up 35 percent of the total drug court clientele in Buffalo). "If it's drug driven and a person is stealing in order to support that addiction, or a man or woman, if they are out prostituting and the motivating factor is their addiction, then yes we would entertain having them go through the drug court model." Judge Bakarich of Sacramento, California, agrees. "If you are really going to open this up to the real drug addict . . . you've got to expand it to the second degree burglaries, auto thefts, petty thefts, and grand thefts."

Judge Swett, from Charlottesville, Virginia, offered perhaps the most developed argument for why non-drug offenses stemming from drug related behavior should be included in drug court.

> I can't tell you how many forgery cases I've heard where the sole purpose of forging a seventy-five dollar check was to get seventy-five dollars to turn around and ten minutes later buy more crack cocaine. I don't see any difference between that case and the person who is arrested for possession of cocaine after he bought it with a forged check or somebody who goes in and steals for the

same reason. . . . The criminal behavior is motivated by the desire to get drugs. I don't see the difference. . . . I don't know this, but I would venture to say that most drug courts go through an evolution. . . . If it works, which I think it will based on what we've seen in some of the drug courts, then you enlarge the number of clients or defendants, or whatever you want to call them. You open the doors to let more people into the court.

Judge Swett's assessment, as we have seen, is accurate. Often, courts start by allowing only possession cases and then expand their eligibility criteria to include other offenses. In fact, 40 percent of the drug courts surveyed in the 1997 Justice Department study reported altering their eligibility criteria sometime after their drug court's inception.[18]

Judge Strickland agrees with the basic logic articulated by Swett and believes the scope of the drug court model should be expanded to include other offenses. "In our jurisdiction, I would say that probably upwards to 70 percent of all of our offenders have a drug problem to one extent or another, whether they're before the court on a forgery charge or shoplifting charge or breaking and entering or whatever. You're going to see significant numbers of those people who have a drug problem. So for all of those offenders, treatment would be appropriate."

Courtroom Therapy for Non-Drug Crimes

Judge Strickland also believes treatment is appropriate for crime when no drug use is involved. Consider her reflections on its applicability to domestic violence.

You are dealing with someone with an abusive personality. This is something that they don't have control over anymore, just like someone with a drug problem. . . . In both cases you are approaching an illness, if you will, and you need to treat that illness before you can expect behavior to be changed. If you have an offender who has grown up in a household where violence was the mode then you have a whole childhood of learned behavior that needs to be broken down and unlearned and a new way of learning and dealing with stress and anger that needs to be taught to these people in much the same way as dealing with the addicted offender where you are teaching them that this dependence on drugs is not what is appropriate for their lives and they need to find a new way to approach their personal problems which does not involve the reliance on drugs. So I see them as being pretty analogous.

Here Judge Strickland makes an important leap. Not only should domestic violence cases receive treatment when drug use is involved, but domestic violence constitutes a disease in its own right. Some of the drug court officials with whom I spoke, particularly those directly involved with treatment, share this position. That is, they believe that the illness model should be extended to include other criminal activities, even those that are not directly related to drug use. This is Cathy Delaney's position on the matter: "All this model is, is investing time in people and giving them the tools to do their life differently. And if you want to put it in its simplest form, it doesn't matter whether it's drugs or battering or shoplifting. Basically what you are going to look at is investing time to find out why the people do what they do, and give them the tools to show them how there is a different way."

A treatment provider at the Fort Lauderdale drug court argued the same as it relates to the issue of prostitution.

> I don't think that most women wake up in the morning and think, 'Gosh, what a great thing, to go out and prostitute myself.' To have reached that point they have some major life issues to deal with. My own experience with the bulk of our clients who have come in here who are prostitutes is that the incident of incest is extraordinarily high. I mean incredibly high. So, again, I think that these are people who have real problems. I don't think anybody with a healthy sense of self is going to go out and sell themselves on the street. So, if all we do is basically warehouse them and don't help them address this problem, then what is going to change when they come out? I do think that there are a lot of people who probably need help.

Therefore, a treatment process that helps a person deal with their low sense of self is justifiable, even when drug use is not a part of the problem.

Judge Tauber also holds to this position. For him, it is commonsensical. "You know, once again, this stuff ain't rocket science. It is common sense. If you put people in a system and make it real clear that they are not going to escape or fall through cracks—forgive the pun—and you are going to be on top of them, you are going to provide services, you are going to do better. There is no mystery there. It is a good model. You know, it just makes sense to deal with people in a caring way, but in a very direct and intense way as well." Given the "obvious" utility of the model, then, Tauber could see it applied to domestic violence and to prostitution. "Obviously there are already domestic violence courts. Prostitution also makes a lot of sense, in fact probably even more than any of this other stuff. You know, prostitutes generally get right back out on the streets, and if there were directed and immediate intervention I bet you would have significant success with that particular population. . . . It is a model that makes sense."

Judge Robinson of Portland agrees and sees the model as applicable to a number of crimes, including prostitution, petty theft, and battery. "I think the drug court concept can be used for other areas of the criminal justice system." For example, Robinson believes that a "batterer could be looked upon as a person suffering various psychological dysfunctions." It may be "an anger management problem" that leads this person to batter his "spouse or significant other." Putting this person in jail often does not solve the problem. "A lot of them would just go and serve their jail time and return, and they are still batterers when they get out." However, if instead "we were to set up a situation where we provide treatment, the person has an opportunity to look at himself or herself as a person with a problem who needs some type of therapeutic intervention instead of a person who is a criminal." This, according to Robinson, is "a positive way to look at having the drug court concept go into other areas of the criminal justice system."

Judge Schma offered the most strident defense for the expansion of the drug court model, first as it was connected to drug-related crimes. "It's the breaking and enterings, it's the larcenies, it's the malicious destruction of property, there's a whole bunch of addicts running around out there committing a whole bunch of crimes that are not drug crimes, but they are drug related, because they are doing that—passing bad paper, prostitution, stuff like that—all that because they are addicts and they need the money." But he also saw the treatment model as relevant to behaviors not stemming from drugs. "Therapeutically, from a therapeutic jurisprudence standpoint, it's not just the addict who can be dealt with. There is no question about that. It's anybody who is amenable to a rather intensive program of treatment. It could apply conceivably to a sex offender. It could apply to a habitual thief, you know, the chronic thief. It could apply to a lot of other deviant behaviors."

Partners in the Process

Given the shift to the disease model, it makes sense that the authority of those professionally trained in this paradigm would increase. In other words, judges trained in the law are not always immediately prepared to understand relapse, recovery, denial, and the other therapeutic concepts that define the treatment process. We have already noted how some judges go through a cognitive reorientation of sorts to adapt to the new paradigm. Significantly, it is those trained in the therapeutic vocations who aid them in this reorientation. Judge Bruce Beaudin, for one, speaks of the process whereby he consulted psychiatrists and psychologists to educate himself for the drug court model. Others, as noted earlier, have actually received special training in drug treatment. That judges consult those from the therapeutic community in this way is illustrative of the greater authority vested in treatment providers in the drug court program—both in the treatment centers and in the courtroom. As the role of other courtroom actors has receded, the role of therapeutic experts has expanded.[19] Treatment providers are usually a more visible presence in the courtroom than are lawyers. They speak on behalf of the client, report on the client's progress, administer and interpret urinalysis tests, and so on. Treatment providers also play a very important backstage role. In sessions before drug court they advise the judge on how to respond to clients in the upcoming drug court session. In observing these preliminary meetings and subsequent drug court sessions, rarely did I see a judge do anything other than what the treatment providers advised.[20]

Judges are, in fact, noticeably deferential to the expertise and insights of the treatment providers. They acknowledge their own lack of expertise and are thankful for the presence and input of the treatment providers. Judge Duncan-Peters of Washington, D.C., for example, admits that she does not feel fully qualified in administering treatment. "I'm not sure that I still understand treatment. I haven't really gotten formal training in it." Given her deficit of expert knowledge, she turns to the treatment people to help her out. "So what I do is I just leave that up to the counselors. . . . I understand from them that relapse is part of treatment, and all of that, but I'm no expert in any of those areas, so I figure that I'm going to leave it up to the experts."

Judge Hodos, from Franklin County, Massachusetts, is also uneasy about his own expertise in treatment and likewise defers to the counselors in his court for advice and direction. "There are things that make me nervous because I look at myself and, not having the real expertise in terms of treatment of substance abuse, I wonder whether what I'm doing is right." Given this uneasiness, Hodos, like Duncan-Peters, relies on the treatment personnel to help him out. If he is uncertain about his handling of a client he turns to the treatment provider for input. "After court I talk with the treatment provider. When I have a problem I have people that I can go to." As these two examples illustrate, the treatment providers have more authority in the drug court. Judges value and defer to their expertise. Seasoned drug court judges encourage other judges to relinquish some sense of their "divine wisdom," as one judge put it, for the sake of the program as a whole. "Have courage to yield the turf," another judge admonished, "and learn about stuff that you can't believe you'd ever be doing, and have the courage to stick with it." Or as Judge Schwartz from Rochester, New York, puts it, "Case managers [i.e., treatment personnel] have been given a lot of power and authority. What I say is of secondary importance to what the case managers have to say."

Perhaps the most striking illustration of this phenomenon is in

evidence at the Louisville, Kentucky, drug court where treatment providers actually sit on the bench with Judge Weber. They are symbolically, if
not actually, at the same level as the judge, an observation that Judge
Weber would not contest. A NADCP newsletter describes the Louisville
court in this way: "Judge Weber shares the bench with members of the
treatment team, demonstrating that treatment is an equal partner with the
court. He regularly consults with them, before and during drug court, and
discusses offenders' dispositions while at the bench."[21] At a 1997 mentoring court training session in Louisville, Judge Tauber summarized
what participants just witnessed in viewing the Louisville drug court in
action. "The treatment providers were seated close to the judge behind
the bench almost as if they were partners in the process." Tauber then
asked those present to comment on the physical structure of the court.
Some found the arrangement unusual and undesirable, while others appreciated the innovation. Judge Weber himself defended the practice by
discussing the "moral authority" of the two treatment providers who
were with him on the bench that day.

> Darryl who was sitting up there with me was the bigger guy. Ken was the
> smaller guy. Both are recovering addicts. Ken is Darryl's sponsor. . . . Ken is
> kind of quiet, but Darryl is a very, very important presence for us. I think he has
> only been with us here for a year or so now. But he has a very tremendous
> command and authority, moral authority, not any kind of physical authority.
> He's got a moral authority with these folks. And when Darryl says something—
> he doesn't say it very often, he's very soft spoken—but when he says something,
> people listen to him. Ken, on the other hand, has got a wisdom kind of author-
> ity. He's been here much longer in treatment and recovery.

As Judge Weber makes clear, both treatment providers are themselves
recovering addicts. Interestingly, such a background is not uncommon
among treatment providers in the United States today. Joel Best, for example, observes how common it is in America that "therapists are 'professional ex-s,' individuals with little formal training who, having recovered from victimization, have now begun careers helping others into
recovery."[22] This is the case among drug court treatment providers, many
of whom are themselves former drug addicts. For example, in Los Angeles, both the counselor I interviewed and another I observed lead a therapy group were recovering addicts. The director of a treatment center
serving the Miami drug court told me that two-thirds of her counselors
"are themselves recovering addicts." In Boston, the director of treatment
admitted to having been an addict and disclosed that the same was the
case for half the treatment staff. A counselor from the Fort Lauderdale
drug court likewise asserted that nearly half the treatment personnel serv-

ing the Broward County drug court were former addicts. And a counselor in the Wilmington, Delaware, drug court said that "fifty percent of the staff came into the field through their own process of recovery." She explained further that some had received a drug counseling certificate and some were still working toward obtaining one. Not surprisingly, this is not a question that was asked of treatment providers in the 1997 Justice Department survey.

We do learn from the survey, however, that treatment varies a great deal from court to court. Not only is there variation in the types of services offered to clients, as discussed in chapter 2 (e.g., AA/NA groups, acupuncture, residential treatment, outpatient treatment, etc.), but there is considerable variation in the kind and number of treatment personnel serving the various drug courts. "Dedicated treatment staff" working directly with drug court (as opposed to treatment personnel employed on a contract basis) can include case managers, counselors, social workers, medical doctors, probation officers, acupuncturists, student interns, volunteers, or some combination of the above. The San Bernardino drug court, for example, reports having three full-time counselors, two full-time support staff, and anywhere from one to four volunteers. The latter will co-facilitate groups and help in drug testing and filing.[23] The Kalamazoo, Michigan, court, on the other hand, has one part-time support staff and one part-time acupuncturist and contracts for treatment with two different treatment services.[24] The Modesto, California, drug court, alternatively, has two full-time probation officers managing the treatment component of its drug court.[25] The majority of courts employ or contract with just one treatment provider service and some with more than a dozen different providers.[26] Thus, there is much variation in both the level of expertise and the kind of treatment offered in drug court. Again, this is in keeping with the nature of treatment provision in the United States more generally, where as Best notes, "the professional backgrounds and credentials of therapists using medical language and claiming medical authority vary wildly."[27]

Regardless of background and notwithstanding concerns about infringements of confidentiality, treatment providers appreciate the new authority given to them in this unique judicial setting. For many, this is the first time they have ever had the power of the state to enforce their intervening efforts. Beth Peyton, of Wilmington, Delaware welcomes having the authority of the court behind her "because that is really where you get your power and ability to keep these people doing what they are supposed to be doing." A treatment director in Miami likewise sees the power of the court as that which keeps in the program addicts who would otherwise have given up on treatment. "It's like an albatross," she says.

"You are going to have to answer to the court if you don't attend the program. So, at some point people may say, and I've heard them say, 'I'm tired of this, and I want to get it over with,' and in the process of trying to get it over with, they stop using drugs."

Jeff Smith, the director of treatment at two New York drug courts, is also thankful for the "big stick" of the court. As he explains,

> Treatment has always been able to engage someone while it's been nice. . . . We've always been able to bring people in when they needed us or they felt that we were being very nice to them. But once you confront, once you begin to put the ownership of their disease on them, and put the ownership of the results of their recovery on them, they run, and they hide, and they commit crimes, or they commit more crimes. And we never had anyone kind of playing goalie, slapping them back into play. That's why I define the judge as the big stick, that's what he is, that's what she is. The judge sends them back to treatment, always pushing them to take that hard look in a mirror.

Seven

The Meaning of Justice

> One important example of a cultural form which
> has changed over time and has influenced penal
> practice accordingly is the conception of justice.
> —David Garland

As DEMONSTRATED in the last three chapters, the drug court movement has brought about important changes in the criminal justice system. It dramatically transforms the roles of the courtroom actors and, in particular, provides the judge with an unprecedented (at least in adult criminal courts) forum to proactively and personally engage drug offenders. It makes emotivist storytelling a central feature of the courtroom drama, a development that not only markedly effects the nature of courtroom theater but portends to redefine the standards by which judicial programs are evaluated. Like previous experiments in therapeutic justice, drug courts have conspicuously net-widening tendencies. The scope of the model, with the pathological reinterpretation of human behavior endemic to it, not only has been expanded to include more clients but has been applied to other populations in the criminal justice system. One important consequence of the widening of the pathological lens, as noted in the last chapter, is the elevated authority of treatment personnel in the adjudicative process.

Each of these changes is important in its own right. Taken together they represent a profound alteration in the substance and nature of criminal law. In practice, therefore, the drug court represents a clear departure from traditional methods of executing criminal justice, a departure that the judges and other movement activists both recognize and celebrate. But are these changes so monumental as to represent a fundamental redefinition of justice? In these final two chapters of the book I will argue that therapeutic justice, as realized in the innovative practices and ideals of the drug court movement, advances, both in theory and in practice, a transformed understanding of the very meaning of justice.

Any assertion that justice has been or is being reinvented necessarily requires a discussion about how justice has been traditionally conceived in modern Western law. In this chapter, therefore, I consider traditional understandings of justice (both theoretical and practical) before turning

in chapter 8 to a consideration of the manner in which therapeutic jurisprudence, as realized in the drug court, significantly departs from these.
The purpose of this review is not to defend one position over another
regarding the purposes of punishment, but to demonstrate with greater
clarity the substance of the shift in legal understandings of justice that the
drug court effects.

Defining Justice

In the history of modern Western jurisprudence the purposes or aims of
criminal law have traditionally comprised four essential components: retribution, deterrence (specific and general), incapacitation, and rehabilitation. Though definitions of these legal concepts vary, retribution essentially refers to the infliction of some form of punishment commensurate
or proportional to a crime that has been committed. Specific deterrence is
the repellent or inhibitive effect that punishment is expected to have on
the individual offender; having experienced incarceration or some other
form of punishment, the offender is deterred from future criminal behavior. General deterrence is the effect of punishment on society as a whole;
public knowledge of particular forms of punishment for certain offenses
disinclines or deters others from committing these crimes. Incapacitation
is the physical removal of an offender for the purposes of protecting society from future criminal acts. Finally, rehabilitation is the process by
which offenders are treated, educated, and instructed to reform, rehabilitate, or "normalize" them for reentry and productive participation in society.

The question of which feature is most central to the purposes of criminal law has been heatedly debated over the past two centuries. Theorists
defending the retributivist perspective are said to emphasize a backward-
looking perspective; that is, they see punishment as principally concerned
with the reparation of criminal events that occurred in the past. Defenders
of "prevention" (incapacitation, deterrence, and reform can all fit under
this classification) are said to be forward-looking; that is, they are concerned with the effects or the utility of punishment on society and on the
individual offender. They are less concerned with paying back an individual for a past wrong than they are with protecting society and preventing
the offender from future criminal behavior.

At the end of the eighteenth century, Kant provided a singular argument for the preeminence of retribution theory. For Kant, retribution represented the defining purpose of penal justice; indeed, in his view it was a
categorical imperative. The retributivist perspective advanced by Kant

contains two important principles. First, punishment should be an end in itself, not a means either to deter others or to improve the offender. "Judicial punishment can never be used merely as a means to promote some other good for the criminal himself or for civil society, but instead it must in all cases be imposed on him only on the ground that he has committed a crime."[1] To punish someone for the utilitarian concerns of deterrence and reformation, in Kant's view, reduces the criminal to the level of a thing or an object. Secondly, the punishment must be proportional to the crime committed; a qualitative correspondence must exist between the crime and the punishment. With equality and proportionality the criminal should get what he or she deserves; the punishment must fit the crime. In other words, the offender is to receive his or her "just desert." An important role, therefore, of "the court of justice," according to Kant, is to "determine exactly the kind and degree of punishment."[2]

Hegel likewise supported the retributivist position. From a Hegelian perspective, punishment is the annulment of a crime. The commission of a crime negates the moral law. This negation itself requires a negation to restore the right. Thus, in what Oliver Wendell Holmes, Jr. refers to as his "quasi-mathematical form," Hegel views punishment as the negation of a negation, the nullity of a nullity.[3] Like Kant, Hegel considers utilitarian or forward-looking justifications for punishment as dehumanizing and as direct violations of the criminal's rights. For Hegel, punishment itself represents a right of the criminal. "Punishment is regarded as containing the criminal's right and hence by being punished he is honoured as a rational being. He does not receive this due of honour unless the concept and measure of his punishment are derived from his own act. Still less does he receive it if he is treated either as a harmful animal who has to be made harmless, or with a view to deterring and reforming him."[4]

Implicit in this discussion is the central relevance of desert. That the "measure of his punishment" is derived from "his own act" clearly suggests a concern with fittingness or proportionality. Indeed, Hegel, though acknowledging the complexity of assigning specific punishments to specific crimes, argues that "desert" or "deserving" should be the guiding principle behind punishment. The punishment "is just in its content" only in so far as it has been determined by the retributivist principles of equality and desert. Hegel acknowledges that the other goals of punishment (e.g., rehabilitation and deterrence) have a place, but that the notion of deserving makes punishment just. Consider the following.

> The various considerations which are relevant to punishment as a phenomenon and to the bearing it has on the particular consciousness, and which concern its effects (deterrent, reformative, &c.) on the imagination, are an essential topic

for examination in their place, especially in connexion [sic] with modes of punishment, but all these considerations presuppose as their foundation the fact that punishment is inherently and actually just.[5]

In sum, both Kant and Hegel view retribution theory as the guiding aim of criminal law. Other goals of punishment may be relevant, but only after considerations of desert have been determined. Such an emphasis, according to both men, is most respectful of the rights of the individual criminal and most meaningfully related to the notion of justice.

An argument for the primacy of the retributivist perspective of punishment, of course, did not begin or end with Kant and Hegel. The notion of just desert harkens at least as far back as the *Magna Carta*, where the principle of proportionality is also given clear articulation. "[A] free man shall be amerced for a small fault only according to the measure thereof, and for a great crime according to its magnitude."[6] And nearly a century after the publication of Kant's *Metaphysical Elements of Justice*, Dostoyevsky offered a compelling literary defense of the retributivist perspective. Like Kant, Dostoyevsky rejects as a defining purpose of punishment utilitarian preoccupations with reducing future crime and protecting society from the criminal. To Dostoyevsky too much concern with these features of punishment poses a threat to fundamental human rights. The primary purpose of punishment, in his view, is the "meting out to a responsible wrongdoer of his just deserts." As H.L.A. Hart notes, "Dostoevsky passionately believed that society was morally justified in punishing people simply because they had done wrong."[7]

The retributivist perspective has been severely criticized over the years, most notably in the utilitarian philosophies of Bentham, Beccaria, and Mill. Jeremy Bentham, an English jurist and philosopher, offers one of the most important challenges. For Bentham the backward-looking preoccupations of the retributionists are senseless. "If we could consider an offense which has been committed as an isolated fact, the like of which would never recur, punishment would be useless. It would only be adding one evil to another."[8] In other words, if a person has committed a crime and is likely never to do so again, punishment has no purpose or utility. Rather, as the utilitarian would argue, it has no purpose *because* it has no utility. Bentham views punishment as "needless" if future mischief can be prevented by other means. Instead of retribution, then, Bentham advocates a preventive or forward-looking concern with deterring others from committing illegal acts. The rational and calculating actor weighs the prospects of enduring the pain of punishment for a criminal act, and is thus deterred from committing it. In short, for Bentham, "general prevention ought to be the chief end of punishment, as it is its real justification."[9]

Similarly Oliver Wendall Holmes, Jr., in his late nineteenth century classic, *The Common Law*, describes prevention as "the chief and only universal purpose of punishment." Defending the efficacy of deterrence, Holmes writes, "The law threatens certain pains if you do certain things, intending thereby to give you a new motive for not doing them. If you persist in doing them, it has to inflict the pains in order that its threats may continue to be believed."[10] Rejecting the retributivist perspective, he sees the notion of "fitness" or just desert as little more than "vengeance in disguise."[11] Regarding as somewhat irrelevant the question of which perspective (retribution or deterrence) is logically or morally correct, Holmes believes that, in practice, the criminal law follows the deterrence model. Therefore "the theory of our criminal law must be shaped accordingly."[12] Holmes is equally dismissive of the role of rehabilitation in criminal law, arguing that few would hold to the position that reforming a criminal is the only purpose of punishment. "If it were, every prisoner should be released as soon as it appears clear that he will never repeat his offence, and if he is incurable he should not be punished at all."[13] Had Holmes been writing in the twentieth century he could not so plausibly have dismissed rehabilitation theory because, as we will consider in the next section of this chapter, rehabilitation became more central to American criminal law in the twentieth century.

Twentieth-century discussions of the aims of punishment have been more concerned with reconciling the various justifications for punishment than with defending one position over another, resulting in a number of what Lloyd Weinreb calls "composite theories of justice."[14] Among the more important of these is found in the work of A. C. Ewing. For Ewing retribution still has a place in the larger equation, but it is "of much less importance than some of the other goods secured by [punishment]." For this reason he believes retribution should not be regarded as "the chief or sole reason for punishment" but rather should be held in balance with other justifications like deterrence and rehabilitation.[15]

Still Ewing maintains that retribution theory has redeeming qualities and must remain one of the justifications for punishment.[16] Ewing defends, in this regard, what some have referred to as the limiting role as contrasted to the defining, denunciatory, or affirming role of retribution theory.[17] The latter refers to the perceived need or requirement to give criminals what they deserve, to fully repay them for their misdeeds. Decried by some as state-sanctioned revenge, the affirming principle has been the most criticized and discredited feature of retribution theory. The limiting principle, on the other hand, sees justice as protecting the offender from getting more than he or she deserves. Its emphasis is on the prevention of undue or undeserved punishment rather than the retaliatory denunciation of a criminal act.

It is the limiting principle of retribution theory that Ewing defends. He worries, for example, that an exclusive regard for the forward-looking considerations of the utilitarians would undermine this principle and eliminate from consideration the important place of desert. "To justify punishment merely by reference to its future consequences seems, *prima facie* at any rate, to take from the word 'deserve' all of its meaning." Ewing thus rejects extreme Kantian and Hegelian views of retribution theory, acknowledging that "it has fallen on evil days in the last generation or two."[18] He maintains, however, that aspects of retribution theory are necessary "to express the meaning of words like 'deserve,' 'justice,' and 'responsibility.'"[19] This is the important point as it concerns our present analysis. Regardless of which of the competing purposes of punishment is primary or subsidiary, theorists have continued to point to elements of retribution theory as that which most logically links crime and punishment to the notion of justice. A punishment is just or unjust, fair or unfair, too severe or too lenient. The offender is deserving or undeserving. All such claims rely on the retribution theory of justice.

It is not surprising, then, that other twentieth-century efforts to reconcile the various aims of punishment also strive to preserve this central ideal. Consider the highly regarded work of H.L.A. Hart. Like Ewing, Hart offers a synthesis of the sometimes conflicting assertions about the fundamental purposes of punishment. Also like Ewing, he anticipates the possible mitigation of retribution theory but seeks to retrieve its essential qualities by stressing the "more universal ideas of fairness or justice and individual liberty."[20] He believes these can be sustained within a "principle of responsibility . . . quite independent of the retributive or denunciatory theories of punishment."[21]

That Hart successfully advances the principle of responsibility independent of traditional retribution theory is not entirely clear.[22] Consider, for example, the following argument advanced by Hart in 1949. "It is a mistake to consider the objects of punishment as being deterrent or reformative or preventive and nothing else. . . . The truth is that some crimes are so outrageous that society insists on adequate punishment, because the wrong-doer deserves it, irrespective of whether it is a deterrent or not."[23] Elsewhere he concedes that "the idea of proportion interpreted in this way—as respect for a principle of fairness between offenders—has still a place in an account of the values which a theory of punishment should recognize."[24] In both instances he clearly falls back on defining features of retribution theory.

In discussing the matter of proportionality Hart introduces what he calls the principle of the "distribution of justice." Though he is, once again, reluctant to explicate this notion in relation to traditional retributive theory, generally speaking he means that justice has something to do with the fair distribution of punishment—some deserve more than others.[25] Whether Hart advances an interpretation of justice that is truly independent of unfashionable retribution theory is in some respects beside the point. Whatever one calls it, retribution or responsibility, Hart, like Ewing, seeks to defend ideals of justice as they relate to notions of equality, proportionality, fairness, and just desert.[26]

Another illustration of how the limiting properties of retribution theory have been preserved, even amongst scholars with very divergent views on the matter, is found in an interesting debate that ensued in the pages of the Australian law periodical, *Res Judicatae*, in 1953 and 1954. The four contributors to the debate defended contrasting positions on the purpose of punishment. The utilitarian J.J.C. Smart defended the centrality of deterrence; Norval Morris and Donald Buckle, the import of incapacitation and, to a lesser degree, reform; and C. S. Lewis, the primacy of the retributivist perspective.

Lewis begins the debate. Following Kant and Hegel, he argues that without the retributivist theory, the individual would be reduced to something less than a rights-bearing human being, and that bereft of the ideal of desert, punishment would lose its logical connection to justice. The other goals of punishment, though legitimate in their right place, are theoretically incapable of giving meaning to justice in this way. The following represents the heart of Lewis's argument.

> [T]he concept of Desert is the only connecting link between punishment and justice. It is only as deserved or undeserved that a sentence can be just or unjust. I do not here contend that the question "Is it deserved?" is the only one we can reasonably ask about a punishment. We may very properly ask whether it is likely to deter others and to reform the criminal. But neither of these two last questions is a question about justice. There is no sense in talking about a "just deterrent" or a "just cure." We demand of a deterrent not whether it is just but whether it will deter. We demand of a cure not whether it is just but whether it succeeds. Thus when we cease to consider what the criminal deserves and consider only what will cure him or deter others, we have tacitly removed him from the sphere of justice altogether; instead of a person, a subject of rights, we now have a mere object, a patient, a "case."[27]

In his defense of the retributivist perspective, Lewis, therefore, articulates with greater specificity the importance of desert in linking punishment to justice. According to Lewis, the idea of justice only makes sense when just desert is part of the adjudicative equation used to determine a form of punishment.

Responding to Lewis, Smart begins by making a distinction between what he calls "first-order questions" (e.g., "Ought I to drive on this side of the road?") and "second-order questions" (e.g., "Ought we to have a rule of the road and if so what?").[28] First-order questions are asked by the intuitionist (as moral philosophers use the term), second-order questions by the utilitarian. From the utilitarian perspective, a question about criminal law should be asked as follows: "Will this measure or will some alternative one tend most to promote the well-being of society?"[29] This, according to Smart, is a second-order question, any viable answer to which is necessarily informed by the following three purposes: "(1) to deter people; (2) to protect society by eliminating or removing criminals; and (3) to reform the criminal." Like other defenders of the utilitarian aims of punishment, Smart views deterrence as the value of "greatest importance."[30]

Smart, however, makes an important concession. In the area of criminal law, the utilitarian perspective is the concern of the legislator, whereas the intuitionist perspective is the concern of the judge. "The judge or magistrate must not argue as a Utilitarian" because "it is here, in the thinking of the judge or magistrate, that this concept [desert] comes in."[31] Smart defends deterrence as the primary aim of criminal law, but he does not defend utilitarianism on the grounds that it is just. Rather, in his view, the principal aim of punishment is the utilitarian concern of promoting the well-being of society, not justice per se. Furthermore, he allows that the question of desert still has an important place in the jurisprudential process, namely, in the role of the judge. The courtroom, according to Smart, is the place of first-order, not second-order, questions.

In their contribution to the debate, Morris and Buckle argue that instead of deterrence or retribution, incapacitation should be regarded as the most significant aim of punishment. "To us, the vital purpose of the criminal law is the *protection of the community*."[32] Taking a more communitarian position, then, Morris and Buckle contend that regard for the victims and potential victims of the criminal is more critical than the protection of the criminal's individual rights. Moreover, they defend certain qualified forms of therapeutic intervention for particular types of criminals (e.g., child or juvenile offenders). They also concede however, at least in part, to the limiting view of the retributionist theory. That is, though the protection of the community is, from their perspective, the most important aim of punishment, it may be limited by, among other things, a concern "never to deny the fundamental humanity of even the most depraved criminal."[33] Therefore, though they clearly object to the affirming perspective of retribution put forth by Kant and Hegel, they "do not go to the extreme of denying [the] importance to the community's conception of 'deserved' punishment."[34] At one point they even seem to establish desert as the defining or framing purpose of criminal law: "[T]he community's sense of a just punishment will create the polarities of leniency and severity between which the criminal law may work out its other purposes."[35]

Like the earlier understandings of justice put forth by Ewing and Hart, then, that advanced by Morris and Buckle objects to the extremes of retribution theory but allows for the continued legitimacy of its limiting role. Morris and Buckle do not reject the previously articulated understanding of the critical role of desert in linking justice and punishment. Though they view incapacitation as criminal law's "vital purpose" and reformation as a "desirable thing," they do not argue that these aims of criminal law constitute justice. Indeed, they allow that "just punishment" may well provide the parameters for the working out of the other goals of criminal law.

Interestingly, approximately two decades after this debate Norval Morris offered a more critical view of some of the dangers of rehabilitation in criminal law and a more sympathetic, though still qualified, view of desert. Morris identified the latter as one of the three principles of or preconditions to imprisonment. "[T]he concept of desert," he writes, "remains an essential link between crime and punishment. Punishment in excess of what is seen by that society at that time as a deserved punishment is tyranny."[36] Several years later Morris, along with Gordon Hawkins, issued a letter to the president of the United States in which they forcefully argued against incarcerating criminals to improve them. "We cage them for what they have done; it is an injustice to cage them also for what they are in order to change them, to attempt to cure them coercively."[37]

As illustrated in Morris's evolving position, though the retributivist theory has been partially discredited by moral and legal philosophers, it has remained a part of the criminal justice equation and continues to be viewed as the justificatory aim of punishment that most logically unites punishment and justice. At the end of the twentieth century, then, the four purposes of criminal justice delineated at the start of this chapter remain important justifications for punishment. Instead of giving greater credence to one over another, the most common tendency in recent years is to synthesize the various positions. A final example will demonstrate how this is the case today.

Consider discussions on the purposes of punishment found in contemporary criminal law casebooks used in leading U.S. law schools. In them, the limiting feature of retributivist theory is sustained in conjunction with the other justifications for punishment. In one case book, for example, deterrence is synthesized with retribution theory in the following manner: "The stigma of a conviction can work as a deterrent only if it accords with common moral conceptions that commission of a criminal act 'deserves' such moral disapprobation."[38] Though acknowledging a "modern reluctance to embrace the full-blown concept of retribution as a justification for punishment" the authors of the casebook contend that "most persons would agree that general deterrence needs to be tempered by the concept of proportionality."[39]

This is important because proportionality provides the basis for determining whether the imposition of a sentence "is 'just' or 'fair' in relation to the blameworthiness of the offender and the gravity of the offense."[40] Importantly, the authors conclude that "considerations of individual prevention—special deterrence, incapacitation, and rehabilitation—are relevant mainly to decisions about sentencing."[41] They warn that "these goals of punishment should not play a prominent role in determinations of the substantive content of the criminal law or the minimum conditions of criminal liability."[42] And they conclude in full sympathy with the backward-looking focus of the Kantian and Hegelian retributivist legacy that "individual freedom and autonomy are seriously threatened when the criterion for intervention by the criminal law is a prediction of what a person may do rather than a demonstration of what that individual has done."[43]

In sum, retribution theory has been seriously challenged over the past two centuries and, in its purest form, significantly qualified. Philosophical discussions about criminal justice, however, have been on the whole conspicuously reluctant to drop this concept altogether. Indeed, an emphasis on its saliency has even been reasserted in recent years but in conjunction with rather than in opposition to other defining goals and aims of punishment. As in the above discussion, the ideals of proportionality, responsibility, and justice require that elements of retribution theory remain *an* important part of the larger equation. As important thinkers on the subject have maintained over the past two centuries, it is the one goal of criminal law that logically links punishment to justice. In other words, until now, to talk about the meaning of justice necessarily involves a discussion of the place of just desert.

Justice and Social Change

Thus far, this chapter has focused on philosophical discussions about the meaning of justice. From a sociological perspective we realize that these definitions may or may not be reflected in actual jurisprudential practices. The intersection between philosophical statements, cultural sensibilities, and actual judicial practices are complex and multifaceted. As I have discussed more fully elsewhere, the political order generally, and the law in particular, is influenced by culture even as it influences culture.[44] Culture and law exist in a dialectical relationship. Adding to the complexity of this relationship is the availability (or unavailability) of certain philosophical meaning systems at any given historical moment. These meaning systems also influence the social environment even as they are influenced by the social environment. David Garland expresses well the complexity of the interaction between culture, philosophies of justice, and concrete practices in criminal law. "[W]hile it may be an easy matter to show in broad terms the influence of a particular knowledge, value system, or cultural form upon penal practice, the actual route by which one comes to influence the other, and the exact nature of that influence, are often much less easy to specify."[45]

In only very broad terms, therefore, we now turn to a brief overview of changes effected through the ongoing dialectic between culture and penal practices with an eye for the impact of these changes on understandings of justice. Chapter 2 considered how, until recent years, regard for the important influence of culture on social movements had been regrettably neglected. One could say the same thing as it concerns analyses of the influence of culture on judicial practices. The most lucid and compelling articulation of this void in the literature is found in Garland's *Punishment and Modern Society*, in which he provides a trenchant analysis of the strengths and limitations of Durkheimian, Marxist, and Foucauldian theories of punishment. As an ameliorative to these dominant theoretical perspectives he offers what is essentially a Weberian derived analysis of the important influence of culture on changing penal practices. In particular, Garland argues that forms of punishment cannot simply be explained by competing class interests or sinister efforts to exert power under the ruse of particular knowledge systems.

Rather, cultural sensibilities are an important variable *sui generis*, and bear directly on theoretical and practical understandings of justice.[46] J. M. Beattie's analysis of seventeenth- and eighteenth-century English criminal courts offers a useful starting point for the consideration of changing cultural/legal understandings of justice. Beattie's work reveals the extent to which, in very practical terms, the modern understandings of justice as depicted in the writings of Kant, Hegel, Bentham, Beccaria, and the like, are, in fact, modern. Prior to the reform efforts at the end of the eighteenth and beginning of the nineteenth centuries, the classical notions of equality, proportionality, and just desert were much less in evidence. Beattie, for example, demonstrates how between 1660 and 1800 British "grand jurors were more likely to send one type of case than another to trial." Consistent with the remaining cultural salience of chivalrous sensibilities (at least as it concerned women in the upper classes), the courts "were more prepared to indict a man than a woman accused of the same offense."[47]

Beyond considerations of gender, jurors—who, incidentally, were often very knowledgeable of the defendant's life and habits—regarded as entirely germane such issues as the defendant's age, the number and kind of previous offenses, and the character and reputation of the offender.[48] So important was the latter that "some trials give the appearance of having involved as much a weighing up and balancing of the reputations and social worth of the principals on each side as of the evidence."[49] Therefore, juries were clearly influenced by considerations that went beyond the application of "a narrow and abstract ideal of justice," at least in the sense that we have considered it in the first part of this chapter.[50] Absent in judicial deliberations of the period was the "conviction that what is meted out to one ought in justice be done to all."[51]

Similarly, in the American colonies, juries and magistrates exercised a great deal of discretion and had available to them a wide range of sanctions.[52] The conventionally perceived harshness of punishment during this period was joined by an equally pervasive judicial tendency to exercise some form of mercy. However, it was mercy based upon conspicuously religious, not therapeutic, principles. This is, as we will see, an important distinction. Premodern forms of punishment were certainly harsh and clearly an affront to modern sensibilities. What is sometimes overlooked, however, is that courts often granted pardons or more lenient sanctions to offenders who demonstrated genuine remorse for their illegal deeds. As John Sutton observes, "The severity of punishment was contingent not so much on the severity of the crime as on the degree of repentance shown by the offender."[53] Similarly, Kai Erikson, though he depicts punishment in Puritan New England as fierce and severe, concedes that "throughout the records we find any number of occasions in which the court softened its judgment upon receipt of a touching confession or an earnest promise of reform."[54]

Lawrence Friedman notes that in colonial America the death penalty was actually used "rather sparingly."[55] For example, of those convicted of capital offenses in New York during the eighteenth century, 51.7 percent received some form of pardon. Likewise, in Pennsylvania up until the Revolutionary War, 76 of the 170 capital convictions were "pardoned or reprieved," resulting in an average annual execution rate of only one person per year.[56] Sutton makes much of the stubborn child law in New England—a law that allowed the death penalty as a form of punishment for a perpetually recalcitrant child. He also notes, however, that the law was, "as far as we know, never enforced."[57] Therefore, in colonial America there was extensive judicial discretion, but it was discretion based upon a particular worldview. The law was, in Weberian terms, substantive but as determined by a religiously informed view of the world, a worldview that legitimated harsh punishment as well as generous reprieves.

At the beginning of the nineteenth century the acceptability of these previous penal practices, and the Calvinistic religiosity which informed them, would become increasingly implausible. Growing pluralization and urbanization, fostered by the Industrial Revolution and the expanding influx of European immigrants along with the more culturally palatable influence of Enlightenment philosophies, would have a serious impact on U.S. penal practices. A rather extensive literature has developed on this period of penal reform.[58] Most scholars agree that the period was characterized by the following major changes: the rejection of public shame-based, physical forms of punishment; the rise of the penitentiary as a more "civilized" alternative; greater concern for equality, proportionality, and uniformity in punishment; the privatization, routinization, and professionalization of penal processes; and the wildly optimistic perspective among reformers that, with the appropriate facilities and practices in place, the country could reform the offender and significantly reduce the overall level of crime in society.

The cultural forces behind these changes were multiple. First, the new penitentiaries, like other major structural changes defining the period (i.e., public educational system, military bureaucracies, and the large industrial factories of urban America), reflected the utilitarian qualities of modern industrial capitalism in the United States and Europe. Mirroring these structural developments was the growing cultural salience of Enlightenment philosophies. Scholars point to the important influence of the writings of Kant, Bentham, Beccaria, and Mill on the initiation, design, and functioning of the new penitentiaries.[59] In addition, reformers were also still significantly energized by an evangelical, though less Calvinistic, religious sensibility—a sensibility that influenced overall reform efforts as well as specific programs within the penitentiaries.[60]

The rationalizing processes of the nineteenth century, however, would ultimately undermine the palatability of traditional religious ideals in penal practices, even in their less sectarian form. The story of the American penitentiaries is, in many respects, a classic illustration of Weberian rationalization at work.[61] "Correction" in the United States became a large, bureaucratized, routinized, professionalized, state-funded system. The establishment and growth of this system, in turn, provided a formidable institutionalized defense of a particular ideology of punishment, namely, a very definite preoccupation with notions of utility, efficiency, and cost effectiveness. Just as the rationalizing effects of modern capitalism undermined the religious ethos that had originally contributed to its origin, so the rationalizing influence within the American justice system, and in American culture more broadly, ultimately called into question the religious ideals that once more fully informed and guided punitive practices. By 1900, therefore, as Sutton observes, "the last residue of Protestant spirituality in the refuge ideology gave way to a more professional and scientific discourse of rehabilitation."[62]

The Rehabilitative Era

The beginning of the twentieth century, therefore, marked the onset of a new era in the history of American penalty. With the growing implausibility of Protestant religiosity, the door was opened for the influence of new legitimizing values in criminal justice. It is a process that parallels developments in other major social institutions, most notably America's public education system. Just as John Dewey's experiential, pragmatic, "child-centered" educational philosophies began to take root in American schools at the turn of the century, so too did progressivist ideals begin to deeply influence American penal institutions. As Garland observes, "From the turn of the century onwards this 'progressive' vision of a scientific penology based upon therapy and risk-management—rather than moral censure and punishment—has formed the working ideology of significant sections of the penal professions."[63]

   This period was characterized in part by a rejection of the highly rationalistic policies of the previous century. In place of those policies, progressivists urged greater sensitivity to the individual needs of offenders and the adoption of greater judicial discretion, giving judges the capability to advance a wider spectrum of sanctions beyond or in conjunction with incarceration. Thus began such practices as probation, parole, a separate juvenile justice system, suspended and indeterminate sentences, and the like. In a certain respect the penitentiaries were discredited by the very philosophy that they had helped to advance, namely, the utilitarian ideals of efficacy. This, because the penitentiaries were plagued by the common perception that they simply did not work. Therefore, progressivists advocated adding to the judicial arsenal a greater repertoire of sanctions which could be imposed according to the individual needs of the offender. Developed during this period, which Garland calls "penological modernism," is what is "usually known as the treatment model, correctionalism, or else the rehabilitative ideal."[64] Others see the period as simply the reinvigoration of the same, albeit more secularized, reform impulses of the nineteenth century.[65]

   Important for the purposes of the present analysis is that the progressivist movement represents a step toward the kind of therapeutic jurisprudence that is embodied in the drug court. Its forward-looking perspective and greater practical disregard for the centrality of just desert, in particular, offers a direct, though in some instances unwitting, challenge to classical understandings of justice. As Garland puts it, "Penological modernism took the Enlightenment rationalist framework to its logical conclusion and, in so doing, threw out many of its liberal principles. . . . Punishment in general, and retributive punishment in particular, is viewed by modernists as an irrational disutility, a remnant of premodern traditions based upon emotion, instinct, and superstition. Even the liberal principles of proportionality and uniformity are tainted by archaic thinking."[66]

As is clear in this selection, Garland would go so far as to say that the Progressive era represents the essential onset of therapeutic jurisprudence. Others place its emergence even farther back. Foucault, Rothman, Ignaitieff, and Spierenberg view rehabilitative and therapeutic emphases in penal law as one feature of the nineteenth-century reform efforts. Sutton looks back even farther—to early American colonial practices—for the nascent point of therapeutic justice. Still others, however, see therapeutic justice as a more recent phenomenon. Scull and Cohen, for example, focus on community-based treatment efforts of the late twentieth century. Many of the discrepancies between these views can be explained by differing definitions of therapeutic jurisprudence. Without calling into question the common story of penal change identified by these various scholars, I argue that the kind of jurisprudence represented in the drug court is distinct enough to represent something altogether new. Like Scull and Cohen, I see it as a peculiarly late twentieth-century phenomenon, though clearly one that has its antecedents in the penal practices of the rehabilitative era. An important distinction, therefore, is made here between the "rehabilitative ideal" of the first part of the twentieth century and the "therapeutic ideal" at the very end of the twentieth century.

Three important classificatory issues lead scholars to conclude that therapeutic jurisprudence is something other than a late twentieth-century phenomenon. First, social scientists do not make clear enough a distinction between traditional religious sensibilities and the therapeutic idiom. Consider two examples from the literature. Sutton argues that the "rudiments of a therapeutic model were in place by 1650."[67] He can make this argument only because he conflates traditional religious sensibilities with a therapeutic perspective. For example, Sutton argues that the rise of therapeutic strategies of control in the United States "has been informed in an enduring way by the cultural ethos of American Puritanism" and that "the modern notion of rehabilitation is a secularized version of the Calvinist view of redemption."[68] But this is the important point—it is a *secularized* version and, as such, is something wholly other. Demonstrating remorse is different from growing one's self-esteem.

Pardoning someone of a convicted crime because of perceived repentance is not the same thing as graduating someone to a higher stage of therapy because of compliance with treatment. Even the notion of mercy is only possible when some kind of guilt or wrongdoing is acknowledged. With the absence of both guilt and conviction, pardoning makes no sense. What would be the logic of pardoning a sick person?

Consider another example. Garland similarly acknowledges the enduring presence of non-rational or substantive qualities in American penal law, and even cites Philip Rieff's work as an example.[69] His implicit argument is that certain forms of value-oriented rationality, be they religious or therapeutic, continue to coexist with more highly rationalized penal practices. One would be hard pressed to dispute this point. What Garland fails to note, however, is that therapeutic and religious/moral sensibilities are qualitatively different, an issue about which Rieff is very explicit. Religion and therapy cannot simply be lumped together as non-rational or substantive forces counterposed against legal-rational impulses in American law. They represent very distinct kinds of substantive impulses within the law.

A second classificatory problem is one considered chapter 2. That is, observers of American law often make too wide a distinction between therapeutic and punitive law. Recall, for example, the manner in which Donald Black differentiates between "penal" and "therapeutic" styles of social control. Sutton offers a similar type of distinction.

> The term 'therapeutic justice' is meant to distinguish between the rigid, formalistic, and retributive-oriented strategies of control that are generally associated with premodern and early modern legal systems, and the more fluid repertoire of ameliorative sanctions, oriented toward the moral and psychological transformation of the offender, characteristic of Western penal strategies in the twentieth century.[70]

Such a distinction is problematic for several reasons. First, as we have already seen, therapeutic tendencies in the law can lead to very punitive consequences, something to which Foucault, Rothman, Szasz, and others have given a great deal of attention in the last several decades. Moreover, as we have also seen, premodern legal practices were anything but "rigid" and "formalistic." Magistrates had a great deal of discretion, could appeal to any number of mitigating issues to justify leniency or severity, and could apply a plethora of ameliorative sanctions. Again, the important point is that the mitigating issues were different as were the kind of sanctions they could impose. Sending someone to the stocks is not the same thing as mandating participation in a treatment group; wearing a scarlet letter is different than regulated urine testing; being publicly whipped is other than "motivational jail." In sum, therapy is not the converse of a harsh punitive approach just as traditional religion is not the practical concomitant to highly punitive penal practices.

A final matter that distinguishes therapeutic justice as realized in the drug court from earlier forms of therapeutic jurisprudence is that, in the drug court, unlike in the reform efforts of the Progressive era, the therapeutic idiom actually effects the adjudicative process, the area that the utilitarian J.J.C. Smart maintained was the place of first-order questions. With only limited exceptions (e.g., twentieth-century juvenile courts) therapeutic considerations were not used as a lens for making a decision in the courtroom. Certainly, therapeutic considerations were allowed in determining the form of sanction or length of sentence, but generally speaking they were not matters that shaped the style, philosophy, and structure of the courtroom. Prior to the drug court, therapeutic considerations were primarily applied during the sentencing stage.

Juvenile Justice

An ostensible exception to this last classificatory issue would be the juvenile criminal courts initiated at the beginning of the twentieth century. A brief review of these courts, where the "rehabilitative ideal" arguably found its fullest expression in the courtroom up to that time, will show that the juvenile courts were an important precursor to the drug courts yet were also distinct from them in important ways. Initiated along with such other progressivist movements at the beginning of the century as reform efforts in the public schools and the passage of child labor laws, the juvenile justice system was justified on the grounds that it would provide more individualized and sensitized concern for the child. The first juvenile court was established in Chicago in 1899. Within the next five years, ten other states would initiate juvenile delinquency courts, and by 1920 all but three states had done so.[71] By 1932, over six hundred juvenile courts had spread across the United States.[72]

The juvenile courts have remained an enduring, if not somewhat controversial, feature of the criminal justice system throughout the twentieth century. In the 1970s and 1980s, however, the juvenile courts departed, as we will see, in important ways from the more conspicuous rehabilitative qualities that characterized the juvenile justice system of the first half century. Juvenile courts in the first part of the twentieth century, nonetheless, foreshadowed the drug courts in several respects.

First, as with the drug courts, judges played an important entrepreneurial role in initiating and advancing the juvenile court system. Chicago juvenile court judge, Richard Tuthill, and his chief administrator, Timothy Hurley, for example, "were indefatigable in popularizing the program."[73] Likewise, "Denver's juvenile court judge, Ben Lindsey, was a one-man traveling road show."[74] This level of judicial advocacy was critical in advancing the juvenile court movement. "The juvenile court movement gained momentum from the proselytizing efforts of some of the early judges."[75] Richard Boldt notes the similarities between the strong judicial role in advancing the juvenile courts and "the current drug treatment court movement," which, as we saw in chapter 4, is also "led in important respects by the efforts of charismatic judicial figures."[76]

Also like the drug court movement, juvenile courts were defended on the grounds that they were both humane and tough. As Rothman observes, they "were at once benevolent and tough-minded, helpful and rigorous, protective of the child and altogether mindful of the safety of the community."[77] According to Rothman, the humanitarianism of juvenile court advocates was not just a rhetorical guise masking sinister efforts to seize power and control, as Foucault and others would argue. "The critical point," Rothman argues, "is that reformers saw no conflict here; they did not believe they were in an either/or position. There was nothing hypocritical in their approach, no covert message that had to be sorted out, no code language that had to be cracked."[78] Regardless of the intentions of the reformers, both impulses (punitive and rehabilitative) were advanced to justify the juvenile courts, a rhetorical strategy that, as we have seen, also characterizes defenses of the drug court movement. Such a synthesis is summed up well in a popular Progressive era credo: "Kindliness, common sense, and humane justice can exist side by side with the enforcement of law and order."[79]

Judicial "kindliness," as such, was an intended part of the juvenile courts, where therapeutic forms and symbols were deliberately employed. As Anthony Platt makes clear in his critical assessment of the juvenile courts, "judicial therapists" aimed to achieve a more therapeutic environment. The judge was "expected to establish a one-to-one relationship with 'delinquents' . . . the courtroom was arranged like a clinic and the vocabulary of the participants was largely composed of medical metaphors."[80] Moreover, much as new drug court judges are instructed, the juvenile court judge was advised to assume a personal posture. The juvenile court judge, for example, was told to "evoke" from the juvenile offender "a sympathetic spirit" and, in the words of Cook County juvenile judge Julian Mack, "occasionally put his arm around his shoulder and draw the lad to him." From such behavior the juvenile court judge would "gain immensely in effectiveness, while losing none of his judicial dignity."[81]

As with the drug court, the therapeutic orientation of the juvenile court gave the judge more discretion in sentencing options and greater latitude in determining courtroom procedures. Control over the latter resulted in the unintended consequence of what Rothman calls the "cult of the judicial personality." Denver's Judge Ben Lindsey, known for his flamboyant and domineering personality in the court, was among the more colorful of the early juvenile court judges. "Lindsey's courtroom was his stage, with the youngsters as bit players whose role was to set off Lindsey's charm his intuitive grasp of human nature, and his ingenious solutions to the problems of delinquency."[82] Such a description, of course, could apply just as well to contemporary drug court judges who, as we have seen, deliberately employ theatrical effects.

Again, as with the drug courts, the early twentieth-century juvenile courts opened the door for greater judicial involvement in the personal lives of their clients. No longer were the courts simply concerned with offering a disposition based upon an alleged illegal action committed in the past. Rather, particularly in the context of probation—a defining component of the juvenile courts—the personal lives of the defendants were open territory for judicial exploration. Consider the mandate to probation officers issued at the turn of the century by the Illinois legislature. In Illinois juvenile courts probation officers were, among other things, to "record the history and the circumstances of the child as fully as possible." This comprehensive record was to include information on the child's "character, disposition and tendencies and school record" along with information on "the character of the parents and their capability for governing and supporting the child." To compile this report, probation officers were to interview the child, parents, neighbors, teachers, and so on. And to help make sense of the "peculiarities of each case" judicial officers were to enlist "the services of experts in child psychology and psychiatry."[83]

The lawyer's role was also significantly altered, if not effectively eliminated, in the juvenile court. Again as in drug court, attorneys played a much less active role in juvenile court proceedings. In the words of Minnesota juvenile court judge Grier Orr, "The lawyers do not do very much . . . and I do not believe I can recall an instance where the same attorney came back a second time: he found that it was useless for him to appear . . . for an attorney has not very much standing when it comes to the disposition of children in the juvenile court."[84] According to one report on juvenile courts issued in the 1960s, defendants received attorney representation in less than 10 percent of all cases. A 1964 study of California juvenile courts showed, in fact, that defendants were represented by defense counsel in only 1 percent or less of juvenile cases.[85]

In sum, then, the similarities between the juvenile courts and the drug courts are striking, leading at least one legal scholar to explicate in some detail the related characteristics of both, including the common traits of increased judicial activism and discretion, reliance on informal procedures, and the altered role of lawyers, particularly in the case of defense attorneys.[86] So similar are the two forms of therapeutic jurisprudence that one is tempted to view the juvenile courts as the direct historical antecedent to drug courts. On one level this conclusion has some merit—the parallels between the two courts are pronounced and the fact that the American criminal justice system previously experienced this form of "rehabilitative" justice no doubt makes less alarming and more plausible a program like the drug courts. Left unqualified, however, the apparent historical continuity between juvenile courts and drug courts could lead one wrongly to assume that the kind of therapeutic jurisprudence represented in the drug court is nothing new at all—that it is simply the most recent manifestation of a style of criminal adjudication that has been around for almost a century.

Such a position is problematic for several reasons. First, intriguing parallels notwithstanding, there are important differences between drug courts and early twentieth-century juvenile courts. To begin with, in the juvenile courts the clinics played a much less important role than they do in the drug courts. Not only were clinics available only to juvenile courts in the larger cities, but even these had a relatively limited impact on court decisions and proceedings. As Rothman observes, "The clinics did not exert much influence on the courts. . . . judges were all too often unwilling or unable to follow clinic recommendations." In sum, according to Rothman, the role of the clinics in the juvenile courts were "inconsequential."[87] In the drug courts, as we have seen, treatment providers play a very prominent role where their advice is actively sought and followed.

Traditional juvenile courts also differ from drug courts in that the former had less direct judicial oversight and regular involvement by the judge in the lives of offenders. The overwhelming majority of traditional juvenile court cases resulted in a fine, a dismissal, some form of institutional commitment, or probation.[88] Regular court appearances, therefore, were much less frequent in juvenile courts than they are in drug courts. These differences are made even more clear when one compares the traditional juvenile courts with the new *juvenile drug courts.* Juvenile drug courts have expanded rapidly in recent years. Seven juvenile drug courts were initiated in 1995 and by June of 1998 nearly one hundred juvenile drug courts were either underway or in the planning stages.[89]

Justice Department publications on the new juvenile drug courts readily acknowledge the important differences between the two kinds of juvenile courts. One report notes, for example, that "most juvenile court professionals who are establishing juvenile drug courts are initiating these programs to provide the intensive judicial intervention and supervision of juveniles and families involved in substance abuse *that is not generally available through the traditional juvenile court process.*"[90] Juvenile drug courts differ from juvenile courts in that the former provide "much more active and continuous judicial supervision of the juvenile's case and treatment process" and "much greater focus on the functioning of the juvenile's family, as well as the juvenile throughout the juvenile court process."[91] The Justice Department also identifies "much greater coordination between the court and the treatment community" in the new juvenile drug courts. In contrast to TASC or early twentieth-century juvenile courts, treatment is not supplied primarily or exclusively by a probation officer or treatment provider. In a juvenile drug court "treatment services are not confined to the treatment provider," indeed, "all activity generated by the drug court is designed to have a therapeutic value" and is coordinated by the drug court judge.[92]

The differences between traditional juvenile courts and juvenile drug courts is also reflected in the principal procedural changes made by the earliest juvenile drug courts as reported in a 1997 Justice Department survey. Reflecting the higher level of judicial oversight characteristic to the drug courts, the San Jose, California, juvenile drug court reported implementing "biweekly reviews," and the Las Cruces, New Mexico, juvenile drug court "more frequent appearances and accountability to children." Among the procedural changes necessary to initiate the Lancaster, Ohio, juvenile drug court were "more immediate consequences/ sanctions; increased parent participation," "individual treatment," even "drug testing on parents when substance abuse [is] suspected." Similarly, the Orlando, Florida, juvenile drug court reported the required procedural change of "additional hearings to address clients' needs or problems."[93] Again, this kind of judicial oversight is fully distinguishable from early twentieth-century juvenile courts where, "according to practically every observer, the first recourse of the juvenile court, the preferred sentence, was probation."[94] Moreover, those handling probation often were untrained, maintained heavy case loads, and simply "could not provide significant assistance or even surveillance."[95]

Another reason that it is problematic to place the drug courts in the direct historical lineage of the juvenile courts is that the juvenile courts themselves have undergone significant changes in recent decades. The "rehabilitative ideal" in general, and the juvenile delinquency courts in particular, came under severe criticism from a wide array of political, legal, and scholarly vantage points during the late 1960s and early 1970s. As Francis Allen convincingly demonstrates, "what is most significant about the 1970s . . . is the degree to which the rehabilitative ideal has suffered defections."[96] So substantial were these that Allen arrives at the following "inescapable" conclusion: "The rehabilitative ideal has declined in the United States; the decline has been substantial, and it has been precipitous."[97] Given the reaction against legally mandated forms of rehabilitation, both in juvenile courts and elsewhere, it would be difficult to argue that drug courts are simply the evolutionary extension of a seamless historical process whereby rehabilitation progressively triumphed as a defining theme in the American criminal justice system.

A Return to Just Desert

To the contrary, the rehabilitative ideal was harshly criticized, and notions of just desert were reasserted in the wake of its demise. By the 1970s, as Richard Boldt observes, "utilitarian approaches to punishment in general, and rehabilitation in particular, came under searing attack."[98] Interestingly, and not unrelatedly, this development parallels the evolution in philosophical discussions of justice considered in the first section of this chapter, where ideas of just desert, after falling out of favor, were reasserted in recent decades. As it concerns the juvenile justice system serious concerns were raised about the constitutionality of the process whereby juveniles were essentially denied due process and were not provided adequate legal representation. A significant victory for critics of the juvenile courts was the Supreme Court's 1967 *In Re Gault* decision, which aimed to reestablish greater legal representation for juvenile offenders. Also in 1967, the President's Commission on Law Enforcement and Administration of Justice issued a report encouraging the same.[99]

Two years later, Anthony Platt published a scathing critique of the juvenile courts. In his 1969 book, *Child Savers*, Platt argues that reformers "helped to create a system that subjected more and more juveniles to arbitrary and degrading punishments."[100] Along with challenges to the constitutionality of the juvenile courts, evidence indicated that the system was ineffective in reforming juvenile offenders.[101] In response to these critical assessments and the ideological return of just desert, the focus of the juvenile courts eventually shifted from "assessing the social needs of the offender to assessing the social harm that the offender caused—in short, from rehabilitation to retribution."[102] Mirroring the philosophical return to retribution, the discredited juvenile justice system took several steps back to a "just desert" model of adjudication. As Janet Ainsworth writes of this period, "the proliferation of 'just deserts' juvenile sentencing laws in the 1980s represents telling evidence of the demise of the older court model."[103]

Consideration of one of these state laws reveals the extent to which just desert was reasserted in direct relationship to a classical understanding of justice, a connection, as we have seen, that was prominent in philosophical discussions of the matter. Washington's 1977 Juvenile Justice Act served as a model of reform that legislators in other states would follow.

A central feature of the bill was the retributivist emphasis on just desert. As Washington state representative Kay Becker, a sponsor of the legislation, explained, the "just desert" system enacted by the bill signifies a move "away from the *parens patriae* doctrine of benevolent coercion, and closer to a more classical emphasis on justice."[104] Moreover, according to Becker, the Act makes clear that the juveniles who are being "sentenced— i.e., deprived of liberty—are being punished rather than 'treated.'"[105] Replacing the informal methods of the earlier juvenile courts, the new Washington model required that juveniles be "charged by prosecutorial information" and would be required to "enter a plea of guilty or not guilty."[106] In important respects, then, elements of the retribution approach replaced the imperiled rehabilitation model of the earlier juvenile courts.

Reactions to rehabilitation in criminal law, however, were not limited to critiques of the juvenile courts. As mentioned above, the rehabilitative ideal in general was significantly called into question. Consider the influential report issued by the American Friends Service Committee in 1971, *Struggle for Justice*, that strongly condemned the defining features of the rehabilitative ideal. Among other things, the report denounced the rehabilitative principles of individualized treatment, indeterminate sentences, and unwieldy judicial discretion. Instead, the committee advocated a return to elements of retributivist theory, in particular its limiting qualities. For example, in the place of the "individualized treatment model" the committee urged a return to the principle of fittingness. "We ought to fit the punishment to the crime, not the person."[107] The authors also called for the elimination of indeterminate sentences, the reduction of the discretionary powers of judges and probation officers, and the clear separation of punishment and treatment.[108] The report had a pronounced impact on American criminal adjudication practices. As Francis Allen observes, the report "signaled the wide and precipitous decline of penal rehabilitation that was to characterize the years ahead."[109]

Following publication of *Struggle for Justice*, state and federal legislators introduced bills to reform the criminal justice system. In 1976, for example, the California legislature passed a bill aimed at repealing rehabilitative practices. Consider the new statutory language: "The Legislature finds and declares that the purpose of imprisonment for crime is punishment. This purpose is best served by terms proportionate to the seriousness of the offense with provision for uniformity in the sentences of offenders committing the same offense under similar circumstances."[110]

Two years later the U.S. Congress considered the Federal Criminal Code Reform Act, sponsored by Senator Edward Kennedy of Massachusetts, which proposed similar changes. Citing wide variations in sentences and time served among offenders with similar criminal convictions,

Kennedy endorsed greater uniformity in sentences and less discretion by parole officers for determining release dates. As in the more recent philosophical discussions of punishment, Kennedy's proposal incorporated all four traditional aims of punishment, with the added caveat of downplaying rehabilitation. "The bill on its face does not favor one purpose of sentencing over another, unless the sentence involves a term of imprisonment. In the latter case, the availability of rehabilitation as a rationale is very much discouraged."[111] In addition to downplaying the justificatory role of rehabilitation, Kennedy also discussed the concept of justice in direct relationship to the notion of just desert. Establishing "justice in the federal system," according to the measure, necessarily involves the prescribed assurance of "just punishment" for those convicted of illegal conduct.[112]

The legislation, deliberately "designed to structure judicial sentencing discretion, eliminate indeterminate sentencing, phase out parole release, and make criminal sentencing fairer and more certain," became law in 1984.[113] The reasserted significance of the "just desert" principle was clearly articulated in the bill and was in fact the first of the four stated purposes of sentencing recognized in the legislation. "Title II gives congressional recognition to four purposes of sentencing: (1) the need to reflect the seriousness of the offense, to promote respect for the law, and to provide just punishment. . . ."[114] According to Congress, "this purpose—essentially the 'just deserts' concept—should be reflected clearly in all sentences; it is another way of saying that the sentence should reflect the gravity of the defendant's conduct."[115]

It is therefore apparent that the American criminal justice system has reestablished certain retributivist principles in a manner approximate to philosophical discussions about the purposes of punishment articulated during the same period. In both instances, explicit understandings of the concept of justice focus on the notion of just desert. Again, the other purposes of punishment clearly are regarded as significant, as is illustrated in the 1984 federal legislation and elsewhere. Rarely, if ever, however, are the other three purposes of punishment asserted as matters that constitute the essence of justice. Indeed, rehabilitation in criminal law was discredited for the very reason that it was viewed as having resulted in unjust consequences.

The Therapeutic Ideal

Given the decline of the rehabilitative ideal in criminal law, how does one make sense of the rise of a new form of therapeutic jurisprudence as manifested in the drug court movement? Francis Allen, who offers one of the

most comprehensive and thoughtful accounts of the decline of the rehabilitative ideal in American penology in the 1970s, notes the paradox of
the concomitant rise of a new culturally dominant therapeutic ethos in
American society. In Allen's words, "Accompanying . . . the decline of the
rehabilitative ideal in penal justice has been the rise of a new psychologism, a phenomenon of such magnitude that it can fairly be identified
as one of the principle characteristics of contemporary American
society."[116]

How then do we reconcile the emergence of a therapeutic culture with
the universal discrediting of rehabilitative practices in American criminal
law that began in the late 1960s? While there is not likely to be one simple
explanation for this puzzle, the paradoxical coexistence of these two
trends does suggest that there are qualitative differences between the contemporary therapeutic ethos and the ideological assumptions that informed the rehabilitative ideal. Allen is very clear in his belief that this
"new psychologism" is "sharply distinguishable" from the rehabilitative
ideal. As he puts it, "the dominant assumptions of much of the new psychologism are radically different from those manifested in traditional applications of the rehabilitative ideal."[117]

While Allen does not offer a comprehensive delineation between the
two trends, he does identify one important difference. The rehabilitative
ideal, according to Allen, is, in the final analysis, "dedicated to the
achievement of social purposes." That is, it intends "to bring the offenders' behavior and attitudes into harmony with certain values socially
defined and validated."[118] John Steadman Rice interprets this former type
of therapeutic intervention in a very similar manner. The rehabilitative
ideal is, in his words, a therapy of "adaptation," a form of psychological
discourse which predominated in the United States "up to and through
the 1950s."[119] Rice observes that during this period, "the principal therapeutic impetus was adaptational, aiming to secure the individual's adjustment to the established reality and to instill what can fairly be called 'an
ethic of self-denial,' in which the central principle was that society out-
weighed the individual in judgments about the morality of behavior and
the normality of the self."[120]

In conspicuous contrast, the therapeutic ethos or the new psychologism is what Rice calls a therapy of "liberation," a more recent cultural
disposition informed by "the 'ethic of self-actualization,' which assigns
ultimate moral priority to the self, over and against society."[121] Allen
likewise see the new psychologism as a "movement toward self as the
source, object, and measure of all satisfaction" where "self-realization"
and "personal satisfaction" take priority over "social purposes or the
interests of other individuals."[122] Rice sees this newer view of the self as
propagating a new understanding of sickness. Whereas the emphasis of

rehabilitative or adaptational therapy was to bring the individual into harmony with society, therapies of liberation see society as oppressive and as contributing to a person's illness. Society, as it were, is the cause of a person's sickness.

That the drug court movement is an example of the institutionalization of the new psychologism is certainly evident in the discourse considered in the previous chapter, where we found drug court clients' pathology—particularly the problem of a low self-esteem—to be a common explanation for their criminal behavior.[123] Even the emphasis on individual storytelling, considered in chapter 5, is emblematic of this new form of liberation therapy. Recall, for example, the central place of self-esteem in Valerie's very public story of recovery. Evidence of liberation therapy is also pronounced in the group therapy sessions that function in conjunction with the drug courts.

Much like the discourse of the co-dependency movement—which, as Rice persuasively demonstrates, "articulates perfectly with liberation psychotherapy"—treatment practices in the drug court movement are commensurate with the new psychologism.[124] For example, just as "learning to live life 'on a feeling level'" and conquering the dysfunctional tendency of "being out of touch with emotions" are prominent themes in co-dependency groups, so emotivism is a dominant motif in the therapy sessions of drug court clients.[125] In the Louisville drug court, for example, participating clients are given a thirty-two page handbook that defines the parameters, rules, and phases of the program. In a section on treatment procedures clients are told, "In group therapy, the emphasis is on feelings." Why is this so important? Because, as explained in the handbook, "many of us have ignored our feelings for a long time in an effort to see the facts. In group therapy, **feelings are fact!!!** 'How do you **feel**?' or 'How does that make you **feel**?' are frequently asked questions in group."[126] The self-referential quality of this focus on feelings is evident in the "group process guidelines" listed in the same section. Consider one such guideline.

> Become aware of yourself. During the group process, pay attention to your thoughts and feelings and express them at the appropriate time. Being spontaneous reflects the real you. Speak your honest feelings and thoughts. There are not right and wrong thoughts or feelings. Saying what you think and feel helps the group to get to know the real you better.[127]

Notice the particular understanding of the true self (or the "real you") communicated in this guideline. Authenticity rests not in one's dutiful compliance with external expectations (indeed, there are no right or wrong thoughts or feelings) but in the identification and open expression of one's internal emotional tides.

A program workbook used in the Los Angeles drug court treatment program communicates a similar understanding of the emotivist self. A large section on "Feelings" asserts, "Often patients grew up in emotionally unhealthy families where feelings were not expressed openly. They never learned how to express feelings honestly."[128] In an accompanying section on "Self-Esteem," clients are encouraged to cultivate good feelings about the self. "Self-esteem is your real feelings about yourself. You express your self-esteem by the way you treat yourself, how well you understand yourself, and how you accept your feelings. . . . People with high self-esteem have good feelings about themselves. They value their own opinions and ideas," whereas "people with low self-esteem put little value in their own opinions and ideas." To cultivate self-esteem among program participants, treatment providers in Los Angeles lead drug court clients through such exercises as the following: "Finish this sentence with at least five statements. *I like myself today because* . . ."[129]

The emotional concerns of the actualized self also receive considerable attention in the treatment sessions of the Las Vegas drug court. As in Louisville and Los Angeles, Las Vegas drug court clients are encouraged in therapy groups to value and openly express their feelings. Doing so, again, is understood to help clients get in touch with the real self. "When we bury emotions," a program workbook tells clients, "we lose a part of ourselves. Emotions exist as the light and the shadow of the self; thus we must acknowledge them."[130] In the same workbook, clients are provided a "Bill of Assertive Rights." Here the elevated view of the emotivist self is given rather forceful articulation. There are ten rights listed in all. Consider just four: "I have the right to judge my own behavior, thoughts and emotions, and to take responsibility for them; I have the right not to offer justification for my behavior; I have the right to be illogical in making decisions; and I have the right to say 'no,' without feeling guilty."[131]

Evident in these examples from the different treatment programs are the peculiar qualities of liberation therapy. An important subtheme to the prominent focus on emotions is the essential redefinition of honesty. Freely and openly to express one's emotions, as we have seen, constitutes truthfulness. Clients who do not identify and openly express emotions, on the other hand, come from unhealthy families; are not in touch with their real selves; and are, in essence, dishonest. The understanding of honesty portrayed here corresponds directly with the same view propagated within the co-dependency movement. As Anne Wilson Schaeff, a leading voice in the co-dependency movement, puts it, "To be out of touch with your feelings and unable to articulate what you feel and think is dishonest. To distrust your perceptions and therefore be unable to communicate them is dishonest."[132] Examples from drug court therapy groups also parallel the co-dependency movement's derision of "external referenting," which Schaeff identifies as "the most central characteristic of the . . . disease of co-dependence."[133] Rather, as we have seen, greater attention is paid to the internal impulses of the emotivist self.

Indeed, drug court counselors work to help clients become internally rather than externally focused. As a Broward County, Florida, counselor explained to me of his approach in counseling drug court clients, "We have what I would refer to as a lot of people who are very externally referentiated. They get their sense of self-worth and self-esteem from things outside of the themselves. . . . What I try to do is bring that around to an internal, so that they can begin to have a positive sense of self, regardless of what is going on outside of the themselves." Such an orientation, of course, reflects liberation therapy's view of the onerous and destructive inhibitions of external restraints and the beneficial and liberating qualities of the expressivist self.

The same orientation was evident in a treatment session in the Phoenix, Arizona, drug court program. The theme for this particular weekly therapy group was "communication skills." The counselor introduced the topic with several questions. "First of all, on a therapeutic end, we want to talk about your family growing up. What were the rules around communication? Can you guys think of some rules about communication? How did your family communicate? How did they deal with conflict? How did they deal with resolving issues of conflict?" The clients offered a number of examples, illustrating the nature of communication in their families. The counselor then explained that families generally fall into two different camps, "either an open family system or a closed family system." In a closed system, according to the counselor, "there are a lot of rules." Children who "don't follow the rules will be threatened and intimidated, sometimes beaten, to follow those rules." The basic message in a closed family system is: "We are not open to thinking about other ways of dealing with this. And I don't want to hear what your opinion is. And I don't want to hear what you think will work, because this is the way it is. And if you express an opinion, what are you generally told in a closed family? 'Shut up. You're being disrespectful. Go to your room.' "

As the discussion continued, clients learned that an open family system, on the other hand, is characterized by "open mindedness and open communication." It is "a safe environment to grow and learn and make mistakes and all of that stuff." In an open system there exists a "family spending time together, creating memories." The counselor asked clients, "How many people here don't have a lot of really good memories about their family? When I say 'a lot' I mean more than a dozen really good memories, like memories of trips that were really good times together, nonstressful times, when it was really just fun, and it wasn't stressful. Sometimes vacations are not necessarily fun, right? It isn't being screamed at, the hand coming back to the back [seat of the car] trying to hit you the whole way." The counselor then asked clients to name other qualities which would define an ideal family. Consider the following exchange.

COUNSELOR: What else would be in a perfect family?
FIRST CLIENT: Lots of compliments.
COUNSELOR: Okay, affirmation.
SECOND CLIENT: I think there would be a lot of religion.
COUNSELOR: Okay, good values.

Notice that the counselor adapts the answer in each instance. The latter example is particularly telling: "good values" rather than "religion." Individualized values, of course, are more consistent with a therapy of liberation than are the adaptational demands of religion, particularly as traditionally understood. The same could be said of the two types of family in general. In the closed system, the child is asked to conform. In the open system, there is more room for expression and open-mindedness. It is an environment where one can learn and make mistakes. Though subtle, the distinctions between the two systems are revealing. The conforming, adapting, closed system is disparaged while the expressive, liberating, open system is celebrated.

Certain clients were then asked to sit before the rest of the group and practice "open communication" with each other. One pair was asked to openly communicate about their hypothetical sexual relationship. This was an important exercise, according to the counselor, because "most people feel very uncomfortable talking in a relationship about sex. I don't mean talking about having sex. I mean talking about their sexual relationship, their intimacy, and their relationship. People feel very uncomfortable talking about that. They don't talk about each other's needs in those areas of intimacy." Gaining skills in open communication, as offered in drug court, helps clients of overcome this perceived problem.

This example illustrates the extent to which the expressivist concerns of the esteemed self that characterize the new "therapeutic ideal" may, paradoxically, result in not very liberating consequences. That is, because such themes as open communication, family background, even sexual relationships are part of the discourse of the contemporary therapeutic idiom, legal appropriation of the therapeutic ethos makes these areas of human life open to judicial exploration. Thus, the possibilities for expanded judicial authority in the drug court may extend not only to a growing number of populations in the criminal justice system but to a deeper penetration into the life, mind, psyche, soul of the individual client. The liberated self, ironically, is now open to the therapeutically defined machinations of judicial oversight.

That the new therapeutic ethos would be appropriated in this way is to be expected. Dominant cultural sensibilities eventually and invariably institutionalize themselves into society's major institutional structures, including its legal structures. What we find in the drug courts is a system that relies more heavily on this new psychologism than on the qualities of the rehabilitative ideal. As such, though it is related to the rehabilitative ideal in some respects and may well result in similar unintended consequences, it is distinct enough to represent something fundamentally new. The manner in which the therapeutic paradigm, as such, deliberately reshapes understandings of justice in the context of the drug court movement is the focus of the final chapter.

Eight

Reinventing Justice

> What we are doing here is no less than a complete
> revolution in jurisprudence.
> —Judge Peggy Hora

> The Baltimore court, like other Drug Treatment
> Courts is not a fad. . . . [I]t is a model for a new
> form of justice.
> —William McColl

OFFERING EVEN greater credence to the proposition that drug courts are
a relatively new phenomenon is the uncanny emergence—at precisely the
same historical moment as the drug court movement—of a new theory of
jurisprudence, a theoretical perspective that, much like the drug courts
themselves, reflects the defining features of America's therapeutic culture.
Therapeutic jurisprudence proposes to use a therapeutic interpretive lens
to make sense of and ultimately change a wide range of legal practices,
behaviors, and rules. It was first conceived and articulated in the early
1990s by David Wexler and Bruce Winick, law professors at the University of Arizona and the University of Miami, respectively. Developed initially as a new legal approach to mental health law, therapeutic jurisprudence has since been applied to a growing and diverse scope of legal
fields, including criminal adjudication.[1] Given the increasing scholarly
enthusiasm with the model, David Wexler anticipates that therapeutic
jurisprudence may "grow tremendously in scope to embrace all, or virtually all, legal areas."[2]

Therapeutic Jurisprudence

Generally speaking, therapeutic jurisprudence is an analytical and normative focus on the therapeutic and anti-therapeutic qualities of law. As
Bruce Winick puts it, "Therapeutic jurisprudence is the study of the role
of law as a therapeutic agent. . . . Legal rules, legal procedures, and the
roles of legal actors (such as lawyers and judges) constitute social forces
that, whether intended or not, often produce therapeutic or antitherapeutic consequences."[3] Therapeutic jurisprudence is concerned both with

revealing these consequences and with helping to advance therapeutic and reduce antitherapeutic legal outcomes. The architects of this model are intentionally vague in defining the "therapeutic" of therapeutic jurisprudence, preferring to let scholars "roam within the intuitive and common sense contours of the concept."[4] Broadly speaking, however, by "therapeutic" they mean a focus on the "mental health and psychological aspects of health."[5] Therefore, any consequence of law that is "in at least some sense related to psychological functioning would seem to be within the broad contours of therapeutic jurisprudence."[6]

The following inquiries illustrate the kind of questions asked through a therapeutic jurisprudence lens of interpretation. Does the current law on contracts foster or discourage the self-esteem of disadvantaged consumers?[7] Is a six- or twelve-person jury more stressful for jurors serving on a criminal case?[8] Should jurors be encouraged to express more openly their feelings and "minority viewpoints" to reduce the stress and trauma of jury deliberations?[9] Does termination of welfare benefits without a legal hearing result in psychological harm, lowered self-esteem, and feelings of insecurity among cut-off beneficiaries?[10] Does the application of the "incompetency label" in mental health law result in such antitherapeutic consequences as a diminished "sense of well-being," the perpetration of "learned helplessness," or the production of "law-related psychological dysfunction"?[11] Can judicial proceedings engender higher levels of empathy among delinquent youths by "having those youth serve as attorneys for victims in teen court proceedings"?[12]

Therapeutic jurisprudence scholars do not simply pose and empirically test analytical questions such as these, but ultimately wish to inculcate therapeutic values into the legal system. "Positive therapeutic effects are desirable and should generally be a proper aim of law, and the antitherapeutic effects are undesirable and should be avoided or minimized."[13] One could imagine any number of potential legal changes to which inquiries such as those listed above might lead. David Wexler optimistically anticipates that use of this interpretive lens will uncover the therapeutic undercurrents in many areas of the legal system. As he puts it, "Once one starts approaching legal areas with the use of the therapeutic jurisprudence lens, who can tell what one will find?"[14]

Therapeutic jurisprudence scholars see the model as a distinctively new innovation and as distinguishable from the rehabilitative ideal. For example, in keeping with such conceptions of the therapeutic ethos as Allen's "new psychologism" and Rice's "therapies of liberation," therapeutic jurisprudence is intentionally oriented toward understanding therapeutic or antitherapeutic effects as they are perceived by the individual. In this sense it ostensibly distances itself from the coercive and paternalistic qualities of the rehabilitative ideal that have been so severely criticized since the 1970s. Bruce Winick, for example, asserts that "therapeutic jurisprudence . . . does not embrace a conception of 'therapeutic' that is tied to notions of paternalism. To the contrary, the thrust of much of the existing therapeutic jurisprudence work is that the individual's own views concerning his or her health and how best to achieve it should generally be honored."[15] Advocates also argue that therapeutic jurisprudence seeks neither to establish a "Therapeutic State" nor to give increased power to an expert class of psychologists and psychiatrists.[16]

Not all legal scholars celebrate therapeutic jurisprudence. Critics question for example, whether therapeutic considerations "should play a dominant (or for that matter any) role in judicial decision making."[17] Therapeutic jurisprudence scholars assume, without any straightforward explanation, that therapeutic outcomes in the law are necessarily a desired good. As Wexler and Winick repeatedly assert, "legal rules, legal procedures, and the roles of legal actors . . . constitute forces that, like it or not, often produce therapeutic or antitherapeutic consequences."[18] To which the critic responds, "So what?" One could argue, alternatively, that the law has leisure and antileisure outcomes. A prison sentence, a mandatory court appearance, even compulsory treatment, may directly impact an individual's personal leisure habits. Does the reality of such effects lead one to then conclude that the law should analyze the legal effects on leisure and subsequently advocate reform of the law to enhance leisure outcomes and minimize antileisure outcomes? Obviously not. What does the promotion of leisure or the mitigation of antileisure, one asks, have to do with the law?

Why, then, can therapeutic jurisprudence scholars, employing the same basic logic, so easily assume that therapeutic consequences once identified should necessarily invite legal concern and ultimately judicial reform? Even John Petrila, a critic of the model, concedes that "the popularity of therapeutic jurisprudence among academicians may be attributable in part to its seemingly undeniable logic."[19] I would argue, once again, that an important reason for its indisputable plausibility is the pervasiveness of a dominant therapeutic sensibility in American culture. Therapeutic ideals are so fully taken for granted in American society that therapeutic jurisprudence scholars need not deliberately make the case for the importance of therapeutic ideals. No persuasion is necessary. They need only first assert that the law has therapeutic and antitherapeutic outcomes and then expect people to conclude that the law should be altered in light of these findings. One could imagine the same kind of reasoning offered in support of more traditional legal ideals. The demonstration that a particular law has just or unjust outcomes could naturally lead one to conclude that corresponding legal change is in order. The difference is that "justice," as such, has been a defining feature of criminal law in a way that therapeutic, or for that matter leisure, concerns have not.

Regarding more traditional legal considerations, therapeutic jurisprudence scholars hold that though the therapeutic lens is an important heuristic, it should not be the only one. It should not, they argue, trump fundamental principles of rights and justice. "Therapeutic jurisprudence has always suggested that therapeutic goals should be achieved only within the limits of considerations of justice. . . . Law should be applied fairly, evenhandedly, and non-discriminatorily. Legal actors should seek to apply the law therapeutically but only when consistent with these values."[20] This is, of course, an important qualification. The question remains, however, whether it is really possible to maintain traditional legal principles within a proposed scope of analysis that advances a rather comprehensive and fundamentally new way of looking at and practicing law.[21]

Consider, for example, a therapeutic jurisprudence interpretation of a legal measure relevant to the present analysis, namely, the 1984 Sentencing Reform Act (considered in the previous chapter). Keri Gould acknowledges that the act was passed and the Sentencing Commission established at a time when the rehabilitative ideal had been called into question and a just desert theory of punishment had been reestablished in its place. Without overtly disparaging the just desert model, Gould brings the therapeutic lens to bear on that part of the statute that specifically explicates the retributive perspective, that is, the law's endorsement of "the need to reflect the seriousness of the offense, to promote respect for the law, and to provide just punishment." To Gould the most "intriguing" part of this statutory language is the middle phrase, the stated goal "to promote respect for the law."[22]

While she concedes that this phrase, in the context of the statute, is a retributive goal, she argues that "it makes more sense to extract this goal from its retributive neighbor-phrases and investigate the internalization of a defendant's moral respect and compliance with the legal system."[23] In other words, she wishes to ascertain whether application of the resultant federal sentencing guidelines are "perceived" as fair by individual defendants subjected to them. In her opinion, the manner in which the laws are currently applied "serve to marginalize defendants and inmates" and "ignore differing perceptions of fairness in the law."[24] Guidelines perceived as unfair, according to Gould, can cause "amotivational responses" by defendant-inmates, leading them to feel "helpless, incompetent and 'out-of-control.' "[25]

Gould proposes a therapeutic jurisprudence approach that would investigate this perceived unfairness and subsequent psychological dys-

functioning. If "empirically" demonstrated, Gould's therapeutic jurisprudence would then advocate modifications of "the offending legal
provisions . . . to increase the defendant-inmates' perception of fairness
and promote cooperation and compliance with socially desirable
goals."[26] Such a change is important, from a therapeutic jurisprudence
perspective, because "laws which modify behavior or attitudes in a socially acceptable way should receive greater respect from society than
laws which merely satisfy a sense of retribution without the concomitant
behavioral adaptation."[27] Once having established this more therapeutically acceptable legal condition, according to Gould, the law would then
satisfy its stated goal of promoting respect for the law.

Gould agrees with Wexler and Winick that therapeutic jurisprudential
prescriptions should be limited to "boundaries set by principles of justice."[28] Yet her own analysis essentially redefines the focus, if not the very
meaning, of justice—shifting an understanding of what constitutes fairness to the level of individual subjectivity and encouraging legal actions
aimed at eliciting particular behavioral responses from defendants. Recent and classical articulations of just desert, remember, have nothing to
do with "behavioral adaptation." Indeed, liberal critics of the rehabilitative ideal were strongly opposed to the correctional focus of coercively
modifying behavior. Gould's basic critique of the problematic applications of the sentencing guidelines could alternatively be made according
to traditional legal principles. She concedes as much. One could, for example, question the legitimacy of the federal sentencing guidelines on the
grounds that they are unfair, that the defendant-inmates subjected to
them are not getting their just desert. But this is not how Gould approaches the matter. She focuses on the "offender's emotional and behavioral responses" to the guidelines, on individual perceptions of what is
fair, and on legal prescriptions aimed at achieving "behavioral adaptation." That she can reconfigure the statutory provision of the Act in this
way, while at the same time rhetorically defer to the guiding principles of
"justice," raises questions about just how restricted to traditional legal
concerns advocates of therapeutic jurisprudence actually are (or will be).
The following section explores this question as it relates to the drug court
movement.

Drug Courts: Putting Theory into Practice

Judges Peggy Hora and William Schma were among the first judges to
recognize the theoretical relevance of therapeutic jurisprudence to the
drug court movement.[29] As they observe, the drug court movement and
therapeutic jurisprudence theory had "been growing and evolving on

parallel courses, yet independently of one another."[30] In May 1997, Judges Hora and Schma joined David Wexler and Bruce Winick on a panel at the NADCP's annual training conference in Los Angeles. Then in January 1999, Hora and Schma, along with John Rosenthal, published in the *Notre Dame Law Review* a lengthy article relating therapeutic jurisprudence to the drug court movement. Now, as they claim, "these two powerful concepts have been cast together."[31] One reason this marriage did not occur earlier is that, as we have seen, much of what drives the judge-led drug court movement are not theoretical quandaries but pragmatic concerns with handling the growing number of drug cases. Indeed, very few drug court judges seem much concerned at all about the theoretical underpinnings and implications of the drug court.

This singularly atheoretical orientation among drug court judges has not gone unnoticed, even by some of the judges themselves. Judges Hora and Schma, for example, observe that with court calendars overburdened with "drug cases, few early drug court practitioners worried about the jurisprudential theory behind the drug court movement. Drug courts seemed to work, and the absence of analysis or debate coming from the 'ivory towers' of academia . . . did not much matter."[32] In his assessment of the Baltimore drug court, William McColl notes the same of drug court practitioners. According to McColl, drug court "reform efforts are not guided by theory." Rather, "practitioners in drug courts are guided by what they perceive to be working and they discard what does not work."[33] In spite of the lack of guiding theory among drug court practitioners, McColl does note that there are certain "underlying beliefs" that inform the drug court movement. And these, according to McColl are "primarily therapeutic or medical . . . rather than legal" in focus.[34]

Therefore, though not theoretically informed, drug court judges unwittingly "apply the concepts of therapeutic jurisprudence every day in hundreds of courts across America."[35] Drawing on the very fabric of that which colors the American cultural landscape, they "actively incorporate a therapeutic jurisprudential outlook into their daily routine."[36] In fact, according to Hora and Schma, drug courts "represent the first consistent use of therapeutic jurisprudence in our criminal justice system."[37] As such, the drug courts are a "significant step in the evolution of therapeutic jurisprudence—the evolutionary step from theory to application."[38] McColl, though apparently not aware of therapeutic jurisprudence theory, as such, essentially arrives at the same conclusion. He observes that, "more than any other court, drug courts are the epitome of a therapeutic or medical approach to crime."[39]

Given this archetype of therapeutic jurisprudence, we return to the question of whether the judicial application of a therapeutic perspective can really exist in subjugation to the defining legal principles of rights and justice, or whether, as reflected in Gould's analysis of the federal sentencing guidelines, it ultimately redefines the meaning of justice—rhetorical deferences to traditional ideals notwithstanding. Interestingly, when judges actually discuss the notion of justice as it is applied in the drug courts, they express what is clearly a new understanding of the concept. That is, they seem to suggest that within the ether of therapeutic jurisprudence, at least as it is applied in the drug courts, justice has come to mean something altogether new.

Consider the comments of one judge who, in conversation with a group of other drug court judges, conveyed her thoughts on the defining qualities of the drug court. She believes that in the drug court "justice is being done." For her, however, "justice isn't imposing punishment and increasing sentences, justice is improving the community, and this [the drug court model] is an opportunity to do that." Notice that she doesn't argue that the legal goal of "improving the community" should be pursued only inasmuch as it can be achieved within the confines of traditional legal concerns. Rather, she asserts that improving the community itself constitutes the essence of justice.

In Judge Weber's contribution to the same discussion, he made clear that therapeutic jurisprudence, as realized in the drug court, is not supplemental to the larger concerns of justice. Rather, as he explains, it represents a new focus that, in effect, changes the whole system. "I think one of the things that we are finding both in terms of the drug court and other areas is that the nature of the justice system is changing. We are going less from being in the adversarial process where there is a lawyer on both sides and a judge who arbitrates, and going to more problem resolutions . . . to actually going to the heart of the matter and solving the problem." Judges recognize, indeed celebrate, the novelty of their new healing, problem-solving role in drug court. As Judge Hora put it, "We are the judges that get to color outside the lines. . . . The way that we relate to the people in drug court is totally different than the traditional jurisprudential role." It is important, therefore, according to Hora, that the drug court judge "stay on tract with yourself in this new way of therapeutic jurisprudence" and not revert to traditional practices.

This new way, according to another judge is "justice in its purist sense." Why so? "Because it is taking a case. It is taking an individual. It is looking at that individual case and it is fashioning a disposition in that particular case that is going to benefit not only society, but that particular individual." Recall that individually tailored sanctions were precisely what the liberal critics of the 1970s argued resulted in unjust judicial practices. This judge avoids such a critique not by claiming that individually oriented treatment can coexist with larger considerations of justice but by calling the treatment orientation itself "justice in its purist sense."

The occasional judge who does reflect upon the classical purposes of justice sees the drug courts as outside the boundaries of these traditional goals. Judge Hora puts it this way: "Okay, so traditionally justice is applying the law in an equal and fair manner. Justice is fulfilling sentencing goals such as retribution, rehabilitation, restitution, and so forth. And the way it's redefined [in drug courts] is, the whole idea of this approach, is you have people who have a disease called alcoholism and/or addiction. And *what is just* is getting them well rather than punishing them for their disease." Significantly, not only does she highlight the treatment emphasis of the drug court model, but she argues that the treatment focus itself is what constitutes justice. Healing someone, as it were, is "what is just." Again, earlier critics of the rehabilitative ideal would argue that such a position is logically untenable. Recall Lewis's argument discussed in the last chapter. It is nonsensical, Lewis argues, to talk about a "just cure" because "we demand of a cure not whether it is just but whether it succeeds." Drug court judges, apparently, are not constrained by such logic.

This is certainly clear in Judge Barbara Beck's take on the matter. Beck poses a question about drug courts by first juxtaposing justice and treatment as if in opposition to one another. "Is it justice or is it treatment?" To which she answers, "To me treatment is justice." In the drug courts, then, treatment, healing, problem solving, constitute the meaning of justice. Given such a redefinition, it would not seem that therapeutic jurisprudence, at least as applied in the drug courts, is simply one perspective among others—and one that does not subordinate "due process and other justice values" as therapeutic jurisprudence scholars regularly claim.[40] Instead, it appears comprehensively to reshape the very essence of criminal adjudication and fundamentally to redefine the meaning of justice in the process. In such a context, it is now possible to speak of "just treatment."

This, in fact, is the very language used by judicial activists championing the drug courts and other criminal justice innovations in Massachusetts. In March 1995, the Substance Abuse Project Task Force, chaired by Judge Francis O'Connor, issued a report, the very title of which, "A Matter of Just Treatment: Substance Abuse and the Courts," speaks volumes. In it they argue that the enormous impact of drug crimes on the justice system "challenges our traditional notions of the role of the judiciary." In light of these pressures the judiciary must change to maintain its relevancy and meet "the evolving needs of society."[41] What this means in practice, according to Judge O'Connor, is that judges should use "their unique power to persuade individuals appearing before them to choose the positive benefits of treatment and intensive monitoring over mere punishment."[42] Justice, therefore, in a legal culture of therapeutic jurisprudence, has more to do with "just treatment" than "mere punishment."

The Consequences of Just Treatment

If justice means just treatment then what are the consequences of such a radical judicial reorientation? Of course, previous chapters have considered in some detail the intended and unintended consequences of therapeutic jurisprudence as manifested in the drug courts, though not in direct relationship to this new theory of justice. As we have seen, changes were most often advanced in accordance with pragmatic rather than theoretical concerns. Nevertheless, drug court judges have, if only unwittingly, adopted the central tenets of therapeutic jurisprudence, the defining features of which, at the very least, appear to challenge traditional understandings of justice. In the closing pages of this book, therefore, we will consider defenses of the "therapeutic ideal" offered by drug court judges in response to the more theoretically based criticisms that were similarly leveled against the "rehabilitative ideal." This line of inquiry aims at ascertaining whether drug courts result in similar unintended consequences—evident differences with previous rehabilitative practices notwithstanding—and whether these consequences challenge fundamental principles of justice. If so, how do judges respond to questions about these possible consequences?

To frame this analysis, I draw upon the insights of various critics of the rehabilitative ideal and relate these to the drug court movement. As it concerns contemporary judicial responses to these criticisms, in addition to drawing upon the ruminations of individual drug court judges, I will also rely on the 1999 Hora, Schma, and Rosenthal article in the *Notre Dame Law Review*. This latter source is particularly salient to this exercise for several reasons. First, it is the most comprehensive written articulation of the relationship between the drug courts and therapeutic jurisprudence theory. In explicating this relationship, unlike most other literature on the drug courts, it more directly addresses issues of a theoretical nature. Second, the article is recognized by leaders of the movement as a significant and representative work. It was, for example, purchased by the National Drug Court Institute and sent to all members of the NADCP. The cover letter for this mailing presented the article as a "seminal" work and "an important contribution to the developing drug court literature." Third, the substance of the article anticipates and responds to several of the criticisms previously leveled against the rehabilitative ideal.

One of the more important of these criticisms was the argument that the "helping" emphasis of rehabilitative judicial practices had coercive consequences. That is, though supporters of rehabilitative justice spoke of helping, curing, and reforming, the outcomes of such programs and forms were often more severe and punitive than previous practices. C. S. Lewis, "an early and forceful proponent of the liberal critique" took up this point in his 1953 *Res Judicatae* article.[43] "The things done to the criminal," Lewis writes, "even if they are called cures, will be just as compulsory as they were in the old days when we called them punishments."[44] Various forms of this critique were repeated by other critics of rehabilitative justice. The American Friends Service Committee, for example, held in *Struggle for Justice* that "when we punish a person and simultaneously try to treat him, we hurt the individual more profoundly and more permanently than if we merely imprison him for a specific length of time."[45] Francis Allen likewise noted that in rehabilitative judicial practices the "lines between therapy and repression tend to fade."[46]

Recent critical assessments of the drug courts detect the same tendencies. Richard Boldt, for example, observes that though defendants in drug court "may receive needed rehabilitative services, they still face potential coercive, even punitive, dispositions."[47] Likewise, McColl comments that some drug court clients "experience greater criminal justice system involvement than the ordinary nonviolent offender in a like position."[48] Drug court judges do not object to these characterizations. Indeed, as we saw in chapter 2, judges themselves highlight the punitive features of the court and often warn defendants that noncompliance may result in more serious sanctions than would be experienced in a traditional criminal court. How, then, does the drug court judge respond to the argument that such practices are unjust—which was the basis of earlier critiques of the previously dominant rehabilitative ideal?

Judges Hora and Schma take up this question. They acknowledge that drug court "requirements may prove more onerous than the equivalent traditional court sanctions for the same offenses," and that this particular quality of the drug court "tends to disturb defense attorneys."[49] Moreover, they recognize that drug courts "generally obligate the defendant to make more frequent court appearances and force the defendant to undertake forms of treatment which place more burdens on the defendant than normal probation."[50] In response to the criticism that this may be unjust, they simply assert the preeminence of the therapeutic jurisprudence perspective. For example, according to Hora and Schma, the defense attorney who worries about potentially draconian judicial interventions has "unfounded apprehension" that stems from a "lack of understanding about . . . the concept of therapeutic jurisprudence."[51] From the enlightened therapeutic jurisprudence perspective, on the other hand, one understands that the "significant requirements of the drug court reflect the court's understanding that drug addiction is a disease and that intense court supervision provides the incentive for the defendant to stay in the program."[52] Therefore, the arduous demands of drug court must be interpreted in terms of the therapeutic benefits they offer the defendant.

So complete is this reinterpretation of judicial practices that sanctions themselves get relabeled. As one judge put it, "he did not see himself as imposing punishment but as providing help."[53] Hora and Schma similarly assert, "treatment regimes are not punishment, but the restructuring of the defendant's lifestyle."[54] Notice that these judges do two things. First, they argue that the drug courts are indeed more demanding than the normal court, an argument repeated, as we saw in chapter 2, by a number of judges. Second, they assert that these coercive interventions are not really punishment after all, but only a "restructuring of the defendant's lifestyle." The critical response to this rather remarkable statement is that lifestyle change is not the role of the judiciary. As the American Friends argued, "The whole person is not the concern of law. Whenever the law considers the whole person it is more likely that it will consider factors irrelevant to the purpose of delivering punishment."[55]

Furthermore, simply altering the nomenclature (i.e., "lifestyle restructuring" instead of "punishment") does not make therapeutic legal practices any less punitive. Lewis rather caustically anticipated and denounced these kinds of semantical modifications:

> They are not punishing, not inflicting, only healing. But do not let us be deceived by a name. To be taken without consent from my home and friends; to lose my liberty; to undergo all those assaults on my personality which modern psychotherapy knows how to deliver; to be re-made after some pattern of 'normality' hatched in a Viennese laboratory to which I never professed allegiance; to know that this process will never end until either my captors have succeeded or I grown wise enough to cheat them with apparent success—who cares whether this is called Punishment or not?[56]

Other critics similarly denounced the practice of judicial label changing. Allen, for example, derides the rehabilitative relabeling of solitary confinement as "constructive meditation," of a detention facility as "Cloud Nine," of the disciplinary use of a powerful fire hose on the back of juvenile offenders as "hydrotherapy," of latrine cleaning as "work therapy," and of incarceration as "milieu therapy."[57]

Drug courts, as we have seen, employ similar euphemisms. Short terms of incarceration have been called "shock therapy," "motivational jail," and "my motel." The imposition of a "sanction" is not a form of punishment but a parent-like "response." Indeed, all aspects of drug court are interpreted in terms of their therapeutic effects. Hora and Schma have labeled drug court sanctions "smart punishment," but even this is qualified. "Smart punishment is not really punishment at all, but a thera-peutic response to the realistic behavior of drug offenders in the grip of addiction."[58] Or again, as they put it, sanctions are really just the "re-structuring of a defendant's lifestyle." Drug court judges defend compul-sory "lifestyle change" on the grounds that it is in the best interest of clients, whether or not the client realizes it. "These lifestyle changes pro-vide the defendant with the very best chance of avoiding any further con-tact with the criminal justice system." Therefore, though the drug courts "may appear exhaustive and prohibitive," they "in fact work to ensure that the defendant successfully completes treatment."[59] Because of this benevolent end, defense attorneys should get over their "unfounded ap-prehension" and embrace their new role of assisting in the "total im-provement of the lives of their clients."[60] This, according to Hora and Schma, is defense counsel's "best option," the realization of which simply "requires a therapeutic jurisprudence perspective." Once acquired it will enable defense attorneys "to more completely represent their clients."[61]

A second and related issue for critics of the rehabilitative ideal was the matter of indeterminate sentences, that is, sentences that varied according to one's performance in rehabilitative correctional settings. Ridding the criminal justice system of indeterminate sentences was one the main goals of the 1984 Sentencing Reform Act. Critics of the rehabilitative ideal ar-gued against this practice on several grounds. First, discretion among parole boards, which determined whether and when a prisoner was ade-quately rehabilitated enough for release, resulted in highly disparate outcomes for offenders with similar offenses, a process that was experi-enced as "arbitrary and unjust."[62] Second, higher levels of judicial and parole discretion resulted in sentences for offenders that were on average longer than in previous practices.[63] Third, indeterminacy itself was viewed as a highly punitive and dehumanizing feature of rehabilitative practices. The American Friends Service Committee, for example, de-picted indeterminacy as an "exquisite form of torture." As they stated, "The extension of indefiniteness as the hallmark of sentencing has con-tributed to the dehumanization and personal disintegration of penal ser-vitude."[64] In short, as Norval Morris put it, the indeterminate nature of sentences that resulted from parole discretion was "in all instances an exercise in injustice."[65]

In the drug courts, indeterminacy is also a factor. Most programs are publicly expected to last one year, though they commonly last much longer. A 1999 BBC radio documentary on drug courts discovered a Miami drug court client who had been in the program for seven years.[66] As noted in the documentary, "Some clients take more than a year to work through the stages towards graduation. One person has been at-tending since 1992." Clients are, in fact, sometimes asked to sign waiver

forms permitting the court to keep them in the program for an indeterminate period. Unlike previous rehabilitative practices, indeterminacy in the
case of the drug courts relates not to the length of a prison sentence but to
the amount of time a client spends under the authority of the judge-led
drug court program. Therefore, the issue of indeterminacy plays itself out
in the adjudicative rather than the correctional setting. This structural
relocation may make less apparent and less glaring the issue of indeterminacy in the drug court. Still, recent critics have made the comparison to
previous rehabilitative judicial practices.[67]

The drug court response to accusations regarding the injustice of indeterminacy are several. First, as McColl summarizes, "In relationship to
the disease theory of addiction, such measures are necessary to break
through the mechanism of denial and to institute a feeling of responsibility in otherwise unresponsive defendants."[68] Thus, the therapeutic jurisprudence perspective argues that the length of one's participation in drug
court should be evaluated in therapeutic rather than legal terms. Does it
break down denial? Does it contribute toward recovery? These are the
questions one must ask. Additionally, applying the treatment perspective,
as we have seen, means being patient with relapse. Relapses typically
translate into extended periods of program participation. Allowing for
relapse, as Hora and Schma argue, represents the "application of therapeutic jurisprudence in the drug court setting."[69]

The indeterminate nature of the drug courts is also curiously defended
on the grounds that it reflects the drug court's tough and rigorous qualities. In fact, judges argue that indeterminacy, and concomitant lengthy
periods of participation, are evidence that the drug courts are tough
rather than soft on crime, data that can be used to assuage the concerns
of "tough on crime" oriented prosecutors.

> Some prosecutors worry that drug court sentencing of a defendant to a treat-
> ment program lets the defendant "get away" without accounting for his of her
> crime. This derivative of the soft on crime idea appears groundless when one
> compares the length and rigor of traditional incarceration and probation sen-
> tences and the length and requirements of drug court mandated treatment pro-
> grams. Recent statistics show that a person convicted of a drug possession
> offense is just as likely to get probation as jail time and that median length of
> jail sentence for a drug possession offense is three months, while probation
> time is twenty-four months. Considering the fact that most drug court treat-
> ment programs last at least one year, not including recycle periods for relapse,
> the time commitment for treatment may not be much less than probation and
> probably will be greater than that of incarceration.[70]

Drug court judges, therefore, defend indeterminacy, conceding that
participation in the program rarely lasts the anticipated one year and
may well last as long as a two-year probation term, if not longer, which

they assert to fend off potential criticisms that drug courts coddle criminals.

William McColl likewise notes that, as with indeterminacy in previous judicial practices, indeterminacy in the drug courts typically leads to longer sentences. Like the drug court judges, he notes that indeterminacy and longer sentences actually provide a defense for drug court activists against the accusation that the drug courts are too easy on drug offenders. "The probability of receiving jail time and years of court-enforced treatment could serve to mollify those who favor punishment over other competing goals."[71] While it may assuage the concerns of the "tough on crime" crowd, however, it also makes the drug court more vulnerable to criticism from the left regarding the unjust nature of indeterminacy, a criticism that plagued previous advocates of the rehabilitative ideal.

In this regard, one issue that was taken up by liberal critics of the rehabilitative ideal is that indeterminacy and other features of rehabilitative justice can lead to serious violations of individual rights. Chapter 3 presented this issue in the discussion of the defense attorney's redefined role in the drug court. Recall the finding that the defense attorney—whose conventional role is to defend and guard the constitutional rights of his or her client—is compelled, in the context of the drug court's team approach, to put aside some traditional predilections. The forfeiting of such rights was precisely what bothered earlier critics of rehabilitative justice.

These same concerns were among the first expressed in opposition to the juvenile courts of the first part of the twentieth century. The lawyers of families involved with the early juvenile courts "questioned the court's right to deprive a child of liberty without due process, to forego trial by jury, to deny the right to appeal, to impose unequal penalties, and to disregard provisions for the equal protection of the law."[72] With respect to the rehabilitative ideal more generally, the American Friends noted "a growing tendency among prisoners to view procedures based on the rehabilitative ideal as clever strategies for stripping them of constitutional rights."[73] Lewis likewise argued that the rehabilitative ideal, "merciful though it appears, really means that each one of us, from the moment he breaks the law, is deprived of the rights of a human being. . . . Instead of a person, a subject of rights, we now have a mere object, a patient, a 'case.' "[74]

Recent critiques of the drug court have likewise raised questions about possible violations of individual constitutional rights. Boldt, for example, argues that for many drug court defendants, "the decision to participate in the treatment court process means that they effectively forego the presumption of innocence and the panoply of trial rights guaranteed by the Constitution."[75] In fact, as discussed previously, drug court clients typically sign forms waiving a host of constitutional rights to participate in drug court. Consider several examples of the language found in these waiver forms:

I . . . by signing this document, give up my right to have a Preliminary Hearing and Jury Trial in this case.[76]

I understand that these waivers of preliminary hearing and speedy jury trial are FINAL. If I change my mind at a later time or date, or if a judge later decides not to follow any plea bargained recommendation, or if I am terminated from the Drug Court, I cannot automatically regain the right to have a preliminary hearing or complain that my jury trial was not timely held pursuant to my right to speedy trial.[77]

I hereby waive any and all claims I may have under the New Mexico or United States Constitution Double Jeopardy Clauses that participation in the Drug Court bars prosecution if I fail to successfully complete the Drug Court Program or am terminated from the Drug Court Program.[78]

I understand and agree that the treatment program is projected to be completed within a six (6) month period, however, I further understand and agree that the Court may extend the treatment program to allow me to successfully complete my requirements.[79]

I understand and agree that if I fail any part of the treatment program, as ordered by the Court, such as testing positive for drug or alcohol use, missing treatment appointments, or any failure to abide by the terms of this agreement or orders of the Court, I will be subject to sanctions, including program set backs, jail time and ultimately dismissal from the Program.[80]

I agree that I may be subject to search and seizure without the requirement of probable cause or a search warrant during the time I am a participant in the drug court program.[81]

Hora and Schma acknowledge the waiving of "certain legal rights in order to gain entrance into the treatment program" is "chief among defense attorneys' concerns" with the drug court program.[82] They assert, however, that the "preadjudicative model appears most consistent with the therapeutic orientation of the drug court concept," because it facilitates the therapeutic goal of getting a client immediately into treatment, even if the client must waive fundamental rights to do so.[83] They argue further that the Supreme Court and other levels of the judiciary have "dealt with these issues and found that preadjudicative detention regimes do not necessarily infringe upon an individual's rights."[84]

Another common defense for the drug court's provisional denial of constitutional rights is that participation in the drug courts, at least in preadjudicative programs, is entirely voluntary.[85] In postadjudicative courts, where drug courts can be in essence a rather intensive condition of probation, they are clearly not voluntary. But even in preadjudicative courts, where clients more commonly sign waiver forms, some evidence suggests that client participation is not always purely a voluntary decision. Consider one example a drug court judge provided during an interview.

> Now this morning, for instance, there is this guy who is eligible. I tell him about the program. He says, "Well I'm about to get a job. I'm not interested in that." I said, "Okay, if you want to see a lawyer, that's fine." I said, "If you are going to have a job, you say you want to go through the public defender, well the public defender, unless you are very low income, won't be able to represent you. So do you want to hire a private attorney? Is that what you think you would like to do and then have about 15 pre-trials before this finally gets resolved? Or would it be more convenient for you if you are already working and then have to go to jail? Or would you like to come hear about the [drug court] program?"

The judge admitted to having pushed this client too hard. "Now I probably pushed too hard on that one. That probably I shouldn't have done, but I felt like doing that this morning. So I did." A comment like this suggests that clients may not always have the kind of choice that is commonly asserted by drug court officials. But that the judge would push the client in this manner is actually consistent with the overall therapeutic jurisprudence philosophy and the conviction that treatment is best for the client, even if the client does not initially realize it. In fact, drug court advocates now have data pointing to the ostensible efficacy of coerced treatment.[86] As reported in one drug court document, "Research indicates that a person coerced to enter treatment by the criminal justice system is likely to do as well as one who volunteers."[87]

Coerced treatment, as such, is most apparent in postadjudicative assignments to the drug court. Recall that in approximately 16 percent of the drug court programs, all participating clients are post-plea, that is, they enter drug courts before trial, but after a plea of guilty. In another 12 percent, drug court clients participate post-conviction but with deferred sentencing. In the second case, they are simply assigned participation in drug court with virtually no choice in the matter. Drug court judges admit that "the postadjudicative model does present some problems," and that in it a client "may risk waiving certain defenses to charges, as well as the right to a trial."[88] While Hora and Schma see the preadjudicative model as more in keeping with therapeutic jurisprudence theory, they also believe that the postadjudicative model "may have great therapeutic impact."[89] They believe this because having to admit publicly to drug use can force a client out of denial. As they put it, "The court proceedings may force the offender to accept her addiction and may help her overcome denial, one of the hallmarks of drug abuse and addiction."[90] Notice that it is admitting to drug use not guilt that they view as therapeutically beneficial. In fact, inasmuch as the postadjudicative model forces the client to admit guilt, this may be "antitherapeutic because postadjudication drug courts which require guilty pleas often meet with resistance."[91]

As can be seen in these discussions, the just desert model is not so much resisted as it is replaced. The judges do not really debate whether certain legal sanctions or methods of adjudication are fair or unfair, too harsh or too lenient, proportional or excessive. Rather, practices are interpreted according to the extent to which they promote or discourage therapeutic outcomes. Inasmuch as therapeutic jurisprudence becomes an increasingly dominant paradigm, debate over the traditional goals of punishment will not so much be resolved as made irrelevant. But will the therapeutic jurisprudence model ever become that dominant? This question relates to another concern expressed by the earlier critics of the rehabilitative ideal, namely, the net-widening tendencies of rehabilitative programs in the judicial system.

Lewis was among the first to anticipate this tendency. "For if crime and disease are to be regarded as the same thing, it follows that any state of mind which our masters choose to call 'disease' can be treated as crime; and compulsorily cured."[92] David Rothman likewise noted, in his critique of the juvenile delinquency courts, that the use of probation did not so much provide an alternative to incarceration as it did a substitute for dismissing a case.[93] Therefore, more rather than fewer juveniles were brought into the criminal justice system by this rehabilitative practice. Rothman provides evidence, moreover, demonstrating the differences in defendant dismissal rates for juveniles in juvenile courts as compared to regular courts of the period and concludes that "the regular courts moved in and out of their cases quickly, while juvenile courts exercised more supervision and retained longer jurisdiction."[94] Recall, similarly, that in the TASC diversion programs—the most direct historical antecedent to the drug courts—observers noted a "net-widening" effect, where over time more individuals with varying criminal offenses became eligible for the program.[95]

The net-widening effect, in a very similar if not more pronounced manner, has been a defining feature of the drug court movement. Contrary to the typical claims of drug court advocates, drug courts can actually increase rather than relieve the burden of an individual court's caseload. In Denver, Colorado, for example, the number of drug cases grew dramatically *after* the initiation of drug courts, from 1,135 filed cases in 1993 (the last full year before the implementation of drug court) to 3,017 in 1996 (the second full year of drug court).[96] According to Judge Morris

Hoffman of the Denver criminal court, "The very presence of drug court, with its significantly increased capacity for processing cases, has caused police to make arrests in, and prosecutors to file, the kinds of ten- and twenty-dollar hand-to-hand drug cases which the system simply would not have bothered with before."[97] The expansion of cases in the Miami drug court led to one of the few critical media accounts of the movement. Reacting to reports on the Miami drug court's inclusion of serious offenders with long criminal histories, Seminole County Circuit Judge O. H. Eaton, Jr., worried that the program was becoming a "dumping ground," and a Miami drug court prosecutor compared the expansion of the Miami drug court to a "rubber band that is being stretched and stretched and stretched . . . and very soon it may snap."[98]

In chapter 6 we saw not only that eligibility criteria have expanded within the drug court, but that the drug court model has been increasingly applied to other populations within the criminal justice system.[99] Like previous rehabilitative practices, then, a definite net-widening effect is evident in the drug courts. Therapeutic jurisprudence scholars do not necessarily see this as a problem. Indeed, they welcome it as a desired good. The expansion of a therapeutic program such as the drug court, from a therapeutic jurisprudence perspective, is a desirable application of the normative dimension of the theoretical model.

Drug court practitioners share this view. Jeffrey Tauber, for example, enthusiastically anticipates the drug court movement's continued expansion. "I think clearly there is a larger movement of programs that address rehabilitation issues, and drug courts are the initial wave. I have every expectation that the drug court model will be duplicated and is being duplicated in domestic violence court, in juvenile drug court, in family drug courts and other courts that share using comprehensive treatment, supervision, and judicial monitoring."[100] Tauber welcomes these developments and encourages drug court practitioners to help push them forward. Recall Tauber's statement at the 1998 drug court conference that "this organization is ready to take center stage, is ready to move it's own agenda forward on both the local, state, and national levels." Elsewhere Tauber has written that "what is needed is a way to augment existing programs, creating drug court systems that can deal with a greatly expanded population base and ultimately all drug-using offenders living in our communities."[101]

As discussed in the previous chapter, the net-widening qualities of the drug court involve more than programmatic expansion. Therapeutic jurisprudence also allows the court to extend its authority into the lives of drug court clients in unprecedented ways. Consider a discussion among California drug court judges who sought to amend the California penal code so that drug courts might have authority randomly to search drug court clients and their homes. The proposed amendment called for a "requirement that the defendant submit to a search by a probation officer or peace officer of his or her person, personal effects, automobile or home, any time of the day or night, with or without probable cause." Most judges supported the measure. In fact, several admitted to already using the practice. The one judge who did object to the amendment was offered the following defense of the practice by another drug court judge.

> I support a search clause for drug treatment court clients because I think a search clause is therapeutic. . . . Random [urine] testing keep clients clean and so will a search clause. It also enables us to do other interventions such as getting a using partner into couples counseling, anger management, etc., and provide parenting classes if the home situation is not good. It helps keep participants from associating with the "wrong people" and with being in the "wrong place at the wrong time." . . . I don't see a search clause as a sanction so much as an additional therapeutic intervention that will help them succeed.

Notice that the therapeutic perspective not only justifies random searches of the drug court client's person and home without probable cause but allows the court to make judgments regarding persons associated with the drug court client, the result of which may be further judicially sanctioned therapeutic intervention (e.g., parenting and anger management classes). Consider a related example from the state of New York. Judge Judith Kaye celebrates not only the continued expansion of drug courts in New York but the application of the model to new "Family Courts" in the state, "where the courts' coercive power is not incarceration but removal of children from parents whose substance abuse causes neglect."[102]

Drug court judges do not always discuss the net-widening tendencies of the drug court in such sanguine terms. Hora and Schma, for example, in discussing the altered role of prosecuting attorneys in drug court, acknowledge that net-widening tendencies can be problematic for prosecutors. They even suggest that "to combat the problem of net-widening, all the members of the drug court team must remain vigilant." In the next paragraph of the same article, however, they argue that most of the problems prosecutors have with the drug courts simply have to do with their ignorance of and inexperience with a therapeutic perspective. "Due to the questions and concerns pointed out here, prosecutors, schooled in the traditional jurisprudential theories of retribution, deterrence, rehabilitation, and incapacitation may have grave misgivings about the philosophical and moral underpinnings of drug courts. Since therapeutic jurisprudence is a relatively new theory of jurisprudence and has not been rigorously applied to the drug court concept prior to this Article, most prosecutors have viewed drug courts through the lenses of inappropriate jurisprudential theories." Therefore, prosecutorial concerns based on these traditional theories of justice are, in the context of the drug court, somehow "inappropriate."[103]

Hora and Schma drive this point home several lines later. "What prosecutors should realize is that in a drug court setting, therapeutic jurisprudence helps to ensure that drug court actors recognize that the orientation, structure, and procedures of a court can negatively or positively affect how an individual responds to court-sanctioned treatment." Instead of "inappropriate" theories, according to Hora and Schma, prosecutors should be cognizant of a therapeutic jurisprudence perspective and participate in advancing a therapeutic perspective in the court.

The Fate of Justice

In sum, previous critiques of the rehabilitative ideal are relevant to the drug courts in several respects. As with the formerly dominant rehabilitative ideal in criminal law, the distinction between punishment and treatment "withers away"[104]; participation in the program is of an indeterminate length; individual constitutional rights are waived, albeit "voluntarily," to participate in the program; and the applicability of the model both within and outside of the drug court movement continues to expand. The difficulties associated with these consequences are often addressed by sidestepping the legal issues and asserting the preeminence of a therapeutic jurisprudence perspective. Though therapeutic jurisprudence scholars and drug court judges contend that therapeutic jurisprudence, as applied in the drug court setting, does not trump traditional goals of criminal justice, traditional views of justice recede in importance. Thus, though the previous critiques are still logically salient, they are artfully handled not so much through forceful refutation as through a culturally inspired altering of the terms of debate, a process that portends the eventual dissolution of traditional conceptions of justice.

In closing I wish to take up one final critique of the rehabilitative ideal that, unlike those reviewed above, may not so fully apply to the drug court model. Consider a final issue raised by Lewis.

> Only the psychotherapist can tell us what is likely to cure. It will be in vain for the rest of us, speaking simply as men, to say, "but this punishment is hideously unjust, hideously disproportionate to the criminal's deserts." The experts with perfect logic will reply, "but nobody was talking about deserts. No one was talking about punishment in your archaic vindictive sense of the word. Here

are the statistics proving that this treatment deters. Here are the statistics proving that this other treatment cures. What is your trouble?"[105]

Lewis raises two important points. First, he notes the manner in which
rehabilitative justice is defended on the grounds of program efficacy.
Allen similarly identified this tendency as one of the most corrosive features of rehabilitative practices in criminal law. He wrote of the "devas-
tating . . . practice of rehabilitationists to seek public support of their
agenda by promising savings to taxpayers."[106] Utilitarian concerns have
likewise been a consistent justificatory theme legitimizing various forms
of drug social control throughout the twentieth century, including most
recently the drug court movement. Indeed, drug courts are regularly defended on the grounds of program efficacy and fiscal utility.[107] While the
claims of efficacy have proven somewhat dubious, to enter into a debate
about whether drug courts are or are not efficacious is to miss the larger
point. The more important question is what effect does a preoccupation
with efficacy have on the meaning of justice.

Few, if any, would support a policy of capital punishment for drug
offenders. Yet such a policy could conceivably be justified on utilitarian
grounds. Such a policy would eliminate all rehabilitation and correctional costs to the taxpayer and would produce a zero percent recidivism
rate. In spite of these utilitarian outcomes, such a policy, of course, would
be highly problematic. But it would be so on the grounds of just desert.
The death penalty is not proportional to the offense. Defenders of classical conceptions of justice, therefore, might worry that the continued
spread of utilitarian and therapeutic legitimizing values in criminal law
would make more difficult arguments against certain practices that,
though less egregious than the example provided here, might be similarly
unjust.

Arguably, the drug legalization debate is best framed according to a
just desert understanding of the purpose for punishment. From this vantage point, those in favor of legalization view the harsh sentences as dis-
proportional to the offense of drug use. Those opposed to the legalization
of drugs argue that involvement with drugs deserves some form of criminal sanction. Those in the middle view certain drug offenses (e.g., selling
narcotics to minors) as deserving strict sentences and others (e.g., recrea-
tional use of marijuana) as perhaps warranting no penalty at all. Regardless of one's position, the questions are still the same. Are the laws just?
Are the sentences proportional to the offense? The contours of the drug
legalization debate, as such, rely on a just desert notion of justice. But the
drug court circumvents the legalization debate altogether. It does not
make drug use a wholly medical matter, because it does not remove the
social control of drugs from the legal world. Rather the therapeutic and

legal views are intertwined. The drug courts employ the knowledge and expertise of the therapeutic worldview, but in the very center of the criminal adjudication process.

This brings us to the second point raised by Lewis, namely, the presence, authority, and expertise in the legal setting of those who represent the psychological paradigm. Lewis criticized a legal situation where "only the psychotherapists can tell us what is likely to cure." He anticipated difficulties with objecting to therapeutically justified sanctions because they are classified as "'treatment,' not punishment" and can therefore "be criticized only by fellow experts on technical grounds, never by men as men and on grounds of justice."[108] This was a major concern of other critics of the rehabilitative ideal, who saw previous forms of rehabilitative justice as providing therapeutic experts greater authority based on their possession of a particular form of knowledge-power.

Certainly, as we have seen, treatment providers play a vital role in the drug court program. Judges regularly take their advice in determining how to handle drug court clients. This is an important feature of the drug court and an unprecedented development for any judicial setting. However, it is only a small part of a much larger story. More significant than the new role of the therapeutic practitioners in the courtroom is the overall transformation of the adjudicative setting according to the therapeutic paradigm. The role of each actor in the courtroom drama is reshaped in accordance with therapeutic themes. Therefore, the exercising of power according to this knowledge system is not limited to the counselor but is available to all actors in the drug court, including the clients.

A parallel process has taken place in America's schools. While counselors do play a more central role in America's public schools, both with respect to the time they spend with children and in the role they play in shaping classroom curricula, the more important and more profound development in American education has been the fundamental transformation of the entire educational process according to a therapeutic paradigm. As with the judges in the drug court, the teachers themselves have been, in many instances, trained to behave as therapists in the classroom. The entire pedagogical experience becomes a therapeutic enterprise. Even parental opposition to counseling intervention in the lives of school children has been advanced according to therapeutic categories, as these represent the most plausible cultural reference points to either object or accept therapeutic pedagogy.[109]

The same could be said of the drug courts. A therapeutic interpretive lens has already been employed to critique drug court and highlight the potential dangers of the judge's unique authority in the drug court. The perceived dangers, however, have to do with negative therapeutic rather than harmful legal outcomes.[110] What evidence that does exist, moreover, suggests that resistance from drug court participants is rather minimal and that treatment, in particular, is viewed favorably by clients.[111] Any objections that are put forth are offered within a therapeutic rather than a traditional legal perspective. Recall the objections from drug court clients in the Washington, D.C., drug court considered in chapter 5. These clients were frustrated not on the grounds of injustice. Rather, they felt counselors could do a better job helping them to help themselves and that the drug court could do more in providing them with educational and vocational opportunities.

In the 1997 Justice Department survey of drug court participants, many of the suggestions for changing the program were of a similar self-referential quality, where, if anything, clients desired more judicial oversight. For example, a Bakersfield, California, drug court client recommended "more one-on-one sessions to help know [the] client better."[112] A Washington, D.C., client wanted "individualized treatment planning."[113] A Santa Barbara client suggested that "smaller groups would be nice" because it would give "more individual counciling to those who want it [sic]."[114] As in the Washington, D.C., example, several Chicago drug court clients recommended more job placement opportunities.[115] A Klamath Falls, Oregon, client was grateful that most of the counselors had "had previous drug problems themselves," because it made them "easier to relate to and understand. They know where we have been."[116] One client even expressed appreciation for the indeterminate nature of the drug court program and was grateful "that you kept it open ended" so that "everyone progresses at their own pace [sic]."[117]

Reflected in these comments are the self-referential qualities of the "therapeutic ideal" rather than the adaptive orientation of the "rehabilitative ideal." Therefore, though new experts may be one part of the story, they are not the experts with exclusive access to therapeutically defined knowledge-power. Therapeutic knowledge is more widely disseminated and available to all the actors in the courtroom drama, as is evident in the viewpoints of drug court participants, in the practical outworkings of the drug court, and in the normative focus of therapeutic jurisprudence legal theory. Therefore, while Lewis's emphasis on the exclusive and power-granting expertise of the psychotherapist may not be applicable to the contemporary drug court model, concerns about the declining salience of protests based on the grounds of justice is still a crucial point. Indeed, in the context of therapeutic jurisprudence, such objections may be even more difficult to make.

Given the cultural dominance of the therapeutic idiom and its widespread accessibility, objections based on classical conceptions of justice become less tenable. Put another way, it is not that arguments based upon justice are refused and ignored by the "experts." Rather, increasingly, no one thinks to offer protests on these grounds. They make no sense in a culture and legal world influenced by a therapeutic perspective. Once justice can be plausibly spoken of as "just treatment," any objections based on "just desert" become meaningless. Justice in such a context has been reinvented and the revolution in therapeutic jurisprudence made more complete.

Notes

Introduction

1. Abram Kanof, "Uriah Levy: The Story of a Pugnacious Commodore," *Publications of the American Jewish Historical Society*, 39 (September 1949–June 1950): 1–66. Kanof provides other details of Levy's life and Naval career, including that Levy sailed as a cabin boy when he was only ten years old. He was also the victim of a mutiny, the miscreants of which he later captured and had prosecuted. And he once rescued a South Carolinian family from death during a tornado on Dubardieus Island. Fiercely patriotic, Levy while in Paris once hit a French officer in the face for hissing at and refusing to toast President Andrew Jackson. At the outset of the Civil War Levy reportedly offered Abraham Lincoln his entire fortune of some three million dollars to help finance the Union Army, an offer that Lincoln apparently declined.

2. Levy's admiration was due in part to his gratitude for the third president's strong commitment to religious freedom.

3. Simon Wolf, "Biographical Sketch of Commodore Uriah P. Levy," *The American Jewish Year Book 5663* (October 2, 1902–September 21, 1903): 42.

4. For an account of these various forms of discipline employed by Levy, see Kanof, 48–49.

5. Kanof, 49 and Myre C. Glenn, *Campaigns Against Corporal Punishment: Prisoners, Sailors, Women, and Children in Antebellum America* (Albany: SUNY Press, 1984), 143.

6. Glenn, *Campaigns Against Corporal Punishment*, 144.

7. The story has a happy ending. Levy was eventually reinstated into the Navy after a review of his case in 1855. Some have speculated that his court martials (of which there were six in all) were caused, at least in part, by his Jewish heritage, though there is some debate on this topic. Myre C. Glenn, for example, writes, "Although personal animosities and anti-Semitism played a role in these proceedings, Levy's harsh sentence also indicated officers' belief that ridicule was indeed a cruel and humiliating punishment. In their 1850 Reports on Corporal Punishment most naval officers denounced badges of disgrace in these terms" (144). See also an article by Herman F. Krafft, reported in the "Secretary's Notes" section of the *United States Naval Institute Proceedings*, 55, nos. 311–322 (1929); 270–3.

8. For an excellent statement of the important influence of culture on penal change, see David Garland *Punishment and Modern Society: A Study in Social Theory* (Chicago: University of Chicago Press, 1990). In it Garland writes, "My concern has been to show how society's cultural patterns come to be imprinted upon its penal institutions, so that punishment becomes a practical embodiment of some of the symbolic themes, constellations of meaning, and particular ways of feeling which constitute the wider culture. Much of my argument has been cast in historical terms, seeking to show that the sources of penal change and the determinants of penal form are to be located not just in penological reasoning, or economic interest, or strategies of power, but also in the configurations of value,

meaning, and emotion which we call 'culture'" (p. 149). Mary Ann Glendon, Michael W. Gordon, and Christopher Osakwe similarly write, "Law is a concentrated expression of the history, culture, social values and the general consciousness and perceptions of a given people" (*Comparative Legal Traditions* [St. Paul: West Publishing Company, 1982], 10).

9. For a theoretical overview of the impact of the American therapeutic culture on its legal institutions, see James L. Nolan, Jr., *The Therapeutic State* (New York: New York University Press, 1998), especially 1–45, and, as it directly relates to the drug courts, 77–112.

10. In the material sent to the author from the Drug Court Clearinghouse and Technical Assistance Project, Office of Justice Programs, Department of Justice, it was reported that as of July 31, 2000, 263 drug courts had been operational for at least two years, 262 had been recently implemented, and 295 were in the planning stages, for a total of 820 drug courts.

11. I also collected materials from other national conferences that I did not personally attend.

12. All unfootnoted quotes in this book have been taken from the statements made at local drug court sites (i.e., either in interviews with the author or in statements made during court sessions) or from national or regional conferences (i.e., either in interviews with the author or in statements made during various panel discussions).

Chapter One
Drugs and the Law

1. The first phrase comes from John M. Johnson and Linda Waletzko, "Drugs and Crime: A Study of the Medicalization of Crime Control," in *Perspectives on Social Problems*, vol. 3, ed. James A. Holstein and Gale Miller (Greenwich, CT: JAI Press, 1992), 199; the second from Howard Becker, *Outsiders* (New York: The Free Press, 1963), 142.

2. William Butler Eldridge, *Narcotics and the Law: A Critique of the American Experiment in Narcotic Drug Control* (Chicago: University of Chicago Press, 1967), 13. Consider also Becker's description of the religious cultural disposition in America: "One legitimizing value, a component of what has been called the Protestant Ethic, holds that the individual should exercise complete responsibility for what he does and what happens to him; he should never do anything that might cause loss of self-control. Alcohol and the opiate drugs, in varying degrees and ways, cause people to lose control of themselves; their use, therefore, is evil" (Becker, *Outsiders*, 136).

3. Eldridge, *Narcotics and the Law*, 14. Also Charles Terry and Mildred Pellens, in one of the most comprehensive studies ever conducted on the use opium in the United States, observe that the American public regards opium use in any form as "a habit, vice, sign of weak will or dissipation" (*The Opium Problem* [New York: The Committee on Drug Addiction in collaboration with The Bureau of Social Hygiene, 1928], 1).

4. Wayne H. Morgan, *Drugs in America: A Social History, 1800–1980* (Syracuse, N.Y.: Syracuse University Press, 1981), 37.

5. Ibid., 9.

6. Becker, *Outsiders*, 139.

7. John C. Burnham, *Bad Habits: Drinking, Smoking, Taking Drugs, Gambling, Sexual Misbehavior, and Swearing in American History* (New York: New York University Press, 1993), 116.

8. James B. Bakalar and Lester Grinspoon, *Drug Control in a Free Society* (Cambridge: Cambridge University Press, 1984), 77.

9. Morgan, for example, observes, "Many . . . began to use drugs at the hands of a careless and ignorant physician" (*Drugs in America*, 53). Similarly Sally Satel argues that "the first wave of cocaine, heroin, and morphine addicts was inadvertently created from the 1880s to the early 1900s, originally by well-meaning physicians" *Drug Treatment: The Case for Coercion* (Washington D.C., AEI Press, 1999), 3. John C. Burnham likewise notes that "in the late nineteenth century, a large number of Americans—frequently of the middle or upper class—developed addictions, primarily through the intervention of well-meaning physicians" (*Bad Habits*, 113).

10. Morgan, *Drugs in America*, 2–3. See also David F. Musto, *The American Disease: Origins of Narcotics Control* (New Haven: Yale University Press, 1973), 42; Edwin Schur, *Narcotic Addiction in Britain and America: The Impact of Public Policy* (Bloomington: Indiana University Press, 1962), 18; and "Importation and Use of Opium," Hearings before the Committee on Ways and Means of the House of Representatives, 61st Cong., 3rd sess., 14 December 1910 and 11 January 1911, 144.

11. Musto, *The American Disease*, 4.

12. Eldridge, *Narcotics and the Law*, 44.

13. Burnham, *Bad Habits*, 114.

14. Terry and Pellen, *The Opium Problem*, 141.

15. Ibid., 145.

16. Morgan, *Drugs in America*, 44.

17. Terry and Pellens, *The Opium Problem*, 142.

18. As Foster Kennedy put it in a 1914 issue of the *New York Medical Journal*, "morphinism is not an unmoral or a demented, but a physical condition, a diseased state, of the inception of which the sufferer is usually innocent" (quoted in Terry and Pellens, *The Opium Problem*, 147). In 1876, a *New York Times* article put it this way: "It is not a vice which afflicts them [addicts], but a disease, which presents as marked and as specific a symptomatology as do many of the better known diseases, and requiring, as they do, proper medical aid and systematic treatment to effect a cure" (quoted in Morgan, *Drugs in America*, 67).

19. Terry and Pellens, *The Opium Problem*, 139–140.

20. Troy Duster, *The Legislation of Morality: Law, Drugs, and Moral Judgment* (New York: Free Press, 1970), 8; Morgan, *Drugs in America*, 71.

21. Morgan, *Drugs in America*, 76.

22. Ibid.

23. Ibid., 71.

24. Musto, *The American Disease*, 83. Similarly, Morgan asserts, "The disease concept now widened to include the mind as well as the body" (*Drugs in America*, 87).

25. "Report on the Committee on the Narcotic Drug Situation in the United States," *Journal of the American Medical Association*, 74 (8 May 1920): 1327–8.

26. Ibid., 1326

27. Musto, *The American Disease*, 96

28. Patricia Tice, *Altered States: Alcohol and Drugs in America* (Rochester, N.Y.: The Strong Museum, 1992), 76.

29. Morgan, *Drugs in America*, 98

30. Musto, *The American Disease*, 31–2.

31. In the months preceding the Shanghai conference, reformers grew concerned that the absence of restrictive federal narcotics laws in the United States would be an embarrassment to American delegates seeking to advance international restrictions. Because of this, reformers lobbied Congress to prohibit legislatively the importation of opium for non-medicinal purposes, in particular, opium prepared for smoking. That a section of the 1906 Pure Food and Drug Act already banned the importation of any drug that was "dangerous to the health of the people in the United States" (Musto, *The American Disease*, 34–5), suggests that this effort was largely symbolic. That is, passage of the measure would serve the purpose of demonstrating that the United States was serious about restricting the use of opium within its own borders, thus making credible its efforts to restrict opium trafficking at the international level. Therefore, the bill, though narrow in scope and limited in effect, had symbolic significance and was approved by Congress on February 9, 1909, approximately one week after the Shanghai conference finally began.

32. The other countries present at the Shanghai conference were China, France, Germany, Great Britain, Japan, the Netherlands, Portugal, Russia, Austria-Hungary, Italy, Siam, and Persia.

33. See, for example, Lawrence Friedman, *Crime and Punishment in American History* (New York: Basic Books, 1992), 138. Musto argues, "By 1914 prominent newspapers, physicians, pharmacists, and congressmen believed opiates and cocaine predisposed habitués toward insanity and crime. They were widely seen as substances associated with foreigners or alien subgroups. Cocaine raised the specter of the wild Negro, opium the devious Chinese, morphine the tramps in the slums; it was feared that use of all these drugs was spreading into the 'higher classes'" (*The American Disease*, 65).

34. Morgan, *Drugs in America*, 47.

35. Burnham, *Bad Habits*, 115.

36. Duster, *The Legislation of Morality*, 9.

37. Ibid., 23.

38. David Garland gives attention to this same oversight as it has played itself out in more general theories of punishment. Garland concedes that "cultural forms are 'bound up with' or 'supported by' material practices," but this does not "imply that they are merely a reflection of something else, or that their intrinsic characteristics are fully determined elsewhere." Rather, "the discourses, symbolic forms, and mental representations of the cultural sphere have their own *sui generis* reality and their own internal dynamics" (*Punishment and Modern Society*, 211).

39. Duster, *The Legislation of Morality*, 3.

40. "Importation and Use of Opium," Hearings, 72.

41. "Opium Problem," Sen. Doc. 377, 21 February 1910, 49.

42. "Importation and Use of Opium," Hearings, 82–3.

43. "Opium Problem," Sen. Doc. 377, 49.

44. "Importation and Use of Opium," Hearings, 82–3.

45. Ibid., 71.

46. Ibid., 82–3.

47. "Opium Problem," Sen. Doc. 377, 49.

48. "Importation and Use of Opium," Hearings, 86.

49. "Opium Problem," Sen. Doc. 377, 51.

50. Ibid., 48.

51. John Burnham observes a diversity in class use of drugs throughout the first part of the twentieth century: "User groups therefore often included not only the customary prostitutes, sporting figures, and criminals but also people from the arts and theater and 'fast' society groups who had money and wanted to be trend-setters—the continuing reality behind the traditional stereotype of the degeneracy of the very lowest classes united with the decadence of parts of the upper classes" (*Bad Habits*, 119).

52. "Importation and Use of Opium," Hearings, 107.

53. Ibid., 139

54. House, William Jennings Bryan, in letter to Congress, *Cong. Rec.*, 63rd Cong, 1st sess., 12 April 1913, 284.

55. *Cong. Rec.*, 63rd Cong. 3rd sess., Ch. 1 (Public Act No. 223), 785–90.

56. Eldridge, *Narcotics and the Law*, 9

57. As Duster argues, *The Legislation of Morality*, 23.

58. Morgan, *Drugs in America*, 107. Also evident in this selection is the persisting influence of utilitarian concerns.

59. Ibid., 110.

60. House, Congressman Henry T. Rainey in an exchange with William L. Crounse, a representative of the National Wholesale Druggists' Association testifying before the Subcommittee of the Committee on Ways and Means on H.R. 14500, "The Exportation of Opium," 8 December 1920, 47.

61. *United States v. Doremus*, 249 US 88 (1919).

62. *Webb et al. v. United States*, 249 US 99–100 (1919).

63. House, Congressman John Miller, statement introducing hearing on H.R. 14500, "Exportation of Opium," before Subcommittee of the Committee on Ways and Means, 8 December 1920, 6.

64. House, Dr. Howard A. Kelly, in testimony before Subcommittee of the Committee on Ways and Means on H.R. 14500, "Exportation of Opium," 8 December 1920, 22.

65. Ibid.

66. Ibid., 23.

67. House, Mr. J. Frank Chase of Boston, MA, in testimony before Subcommittee of the Committee on Ways and Means on H.R. 14500, "Exportation of Opium," 8 December 1920, 24.

68. Dr. J. W. Schereschewsky, Assistant Surgeon General, Chief of Division of Scientific Research, Treasury Department, in testimony before the Subcommittee

of the Committee of Ways and Means, House of Representatives, Washington, D.C., January 4, 1921, 135.

69. Charles E. Terry, in testimony before Subcommittee of the Committee on Ways and Means on H.R. 14500, U.S. House of Representatives, December 8, 1920, 103.

70. Ibid., 104.

71. Ibid., 105.

72. Musto, *The American Disease*, 57.

73. Morgan, *Drugs in America*, 137.

74. Musto, *The American Disease*, 206. James A. Inciardi, Duane C. McBride, and James E. Rivers note that the hospitals actually became prisons in 1974 (*Drug Control and the Courts* (London: Sage, 1996), 30).

75. Musto, *The American Disease*, 212.

76. Becker, *Outsiders*, 135.

77. Morgan, *Drugs in America*, 141.

78. Thomas Szasz, *Ceremonial Chemistry: The Ritual Persecution of Drugs, Addicts, and Pushers* (Holmes Beach, Fla.: Learning Publications, 1985), 201.

79. Schur, *Narcotic Addiction in Britain and America*, 197.

80. Ibid., 192.

81. As cited in Schur, *Narcotic Addiction in Britain and America*, 191.

82. Morgan, *Drugs in America*, 143

83. Ibid., 147.

84. *Robinson v. California*, 370 US 674 (1962).

85. *Robinson v. California*, 370 US 660 (1962).

86. See, for example, Duster's ethnographic analysis of the California Rehabilitation Center, analyzed in *The Legislation of Morality*, 133–213. For discussions of civil commitment programs see also, Satel, *Drug Treatment*, 12–14; Inciardi, et al., *Drug Control and the Courts*, 28–33; and Schur, *Narcotic Addiction in Britain and America*, 217–19.

87. See Duster, *The Legislation of Morality*, 142 and 212–13. In describing the problem of evaluating failure in the program, Duster notes, "In an ordinary hospital when a physician sends the patient away from the hospital on an outpatient basis, he does so because he believes that the patient can manage outside of the complete dependency of the hospital. If the ailment flares up again, he is called back, examined, and perhaps retained for more treatment. The original treatment is not called a failure" (212). On the issue of indeterminacy, Morgan observes of the civil commitment programs: "Therapies based on psychology seemed interminable and often unproductive, another kind of life sentence whose costs the public thought onerous" (*Drugs in America*, 153).

88. Duster, *The Legislation of Morality*, 147–8.

89. Ibid., 142.

90. Ibid., 138. A 1967 report by the Presidential Commission on Law Enforcement and Administration also raised concerns about violations of civil liberties in civil commitment programs. As Musto notes, "the 1967 Commission criticized civil commitment as denying freedom to an individual who was convicted of no crime but was merely suffering a diseased state—addiction" (*The American Disease*, 240).

91. Bakalar and Grinspoon, *Drug Control in a Free Society*, 49. See also Inciardi, et al., *Drug Control and the Courts*, 32; Musto, *The American Disease*, 239–40; and Satel, *Drug Treatment*, 14.

92. As stated in a Justice Department publication on TASC: "A 1962 landmark Supreme Court decision, *Robinson v. California*, stipulated that because chemical addiction is an illness rather than a crime, the State may force an addict to submit to treatment and may impose criminal sanctions for failure to comply with that treatment program. In the developing attitude of the times, penal coercion was being rejected as an effective rehabilitation incentive and community-based treatment for substance abuse was slowly gaining credibility. Alternatives to routine criminal justice system processing for drug-dependent offenders seemed worthy of serious consideration" ("Treatment Alternatives to Street Crime: TASC Programs," April, 1992, Bureau of Justice Assistance, U.S. Dept. of Justice, Washington, D.C., 5).

93. Beth Weinman, "A Coordinated Approach for Drug-Abusing Offenders," in *Drug Abuse Treatment in Prisons and Jails*, eds. Carl G. Leukefeld and Frank M. Tims, *NIDA Research Monograph one hundred eighteen* (1992): 234.

94. Matthew Cassidy in testimony presented to the U.S. House of Representatives Select Committee on Narcotics Abuse and Control, 28 October 1991.

95. Johnson and Waletzko, "Drugs and Crime," 201.

96. Ibid., 205.

97. Ibid., 206.

98. John Steadman Rice, *A Disease of One's Own: Psychotherapy, Addiction, and the Emergence of Co-Dependency* (New Brunswick, N.J.: Transaction, 1998), 28–34.

99. Francis Allen, *The Decline of the Rehabilitative Ideal: Penal Policy and Social Purpose* (New Haven: Yale University Press, 1981), 28.

Chapter Two
The Drug Court Movement

1. The Dade County model is distinguishable from other programs also called "drug courts," namely fast-track courts or Expedited Drug Case Management Courts (EDCM). The focus of EDCMs is on expediting drug cases, rather than on providing treatment. Some drug court professionals prefer the term "drug treatment courts" (DTC) to distinguish the treatment model from fast-track drug courts. Hereafter, when referring to drug courts, I have DTCs, as such, rather than EDCMs in mind. Consider the following fundamental difference between the two: "EDCMs do not emphasize treatment and recovery and do not try to solve the underlying problem of many, if not all, drug cases—the drug addiction of the accused. Unlike the philosophy of EDCMs, the DTC concept focuses not only on fixing the immediate concern of court congestion; it also attempts to ascertain and attack the real foundation of the drug offender's problem—drug addiction" (Peggy Fulton Hora, William G. Schma, and John T. A. Rosenthal. "Therapeutic Jurisprudence and the Drug Treatment Court Movement: Revolutionizing the Criminal Justice System's Response to Drug Abuse and Crime in America," *Notre Dame Law Review* 74 [January 1999]: 452).

2. Ibid., 504. Also see, "Over 3,000 Professionals to Attend NADCP 5th Annual Training Conference in Miami," *NADCP News* 6 (Spring 1999): 1.

3. See for example, *Drug Courts: A Revolution in Criminal Justice* (Washington, D.C.: Drug Strategies, 1999). In the preface to this document, Jeffrey Tauber begins: "A Revolution has been going on in the criminal justice system over the past ten years" (2). Later it is argued: "In the decade since the first drug courts opened, this entirely new approach has revolutionized traditional attitudes toward criminal justice" (5).

4. Philip Bean, "America's Drug Courts: A New Development in Criminal Justice," *Criminal Law Review* (October 1996): 720.

5. Caroline S. Cooper, "1997 Drug Court Survey Report: Executive Summary," Drug Court Clearinghouse and Technical Assistance Project: A Project of the Drug Courts Program Office, Office of Justice Programs, U.S. Department of Justice (October 1997), 18.

6. Ibid., 17.

7. Caroline S. Cooper, Shanie R. Bartlett, Michelle A. Shaw, and Kayla K. Yang, "Drug Courts: 1997 Overview of Operational Characteristics and Implementation Issues," Drug Court Clearinghouse and Technical Assistance Project, Office of Justice Programs, U.S. Department of Justice, Volume Six: *Drug Court Treatment Services* (May 1997), 81, and Volume One: *General Program Information*, 72.

8. The following are identified by the authors as the common "essential elements" of all drug courts: "(1) intervention is immediate; (2) the adjudication process is nonadversarial in nature; (3) the judge takes a hands-on approach to the defendant's treatment program; (4) the treatment program contains clearly defined rules and structured goals for the participants; and (5) the concept of the DTC [drug treatment court] team—that is judge, prosecutor, defense counsel, treatment provider, and corrections personnel—is important" (Hora et al., "Therapeutic Jurisprudence," 453).

9. Barry McCaffrey has addressed several national drug court conferences and has said that "the establishment of drugs courts, coupled with [their] judicial leadership, constitutes one of the most monumental changes in social justice in this country since World War II" (*Drug Courts: A Revolution in Criminal Justice*, 5). At the 1999 drug court conference in Miami, Governor Jeb Bush asserted, "Drug courts are successful because they break the nexus between drugs and crime through coerced abstinence." He thanked the large audience of drug court practitioners for their work: "Your efforts are to be commended and replicated all across the country." Bill Clinton, at a roundtable discussion at a 1996 White House Leadership Conference on Youth, Drug Use and Violence, stated, "But I think the question of the aggregate impact on this country would be if every community of any size had a [drug] court like this—which requires a community support system because you've got to show up on a regular basis and all that—is quite significant. And the one I watched in Miami for long periods of time on two separate occasions, the whole atmosphere was different, the chemistry of the court was different, the way that the defense lawyer and the prosecutor and the judge related to each others was different, because they knew what they were trying to do was to save the defendant and, in the process, get the law observed

and make the community safer. It's a very exciting thing. I would like to see it done everywhere. And I think what you are doing is very important" ("Remarks by the President in Roundtable Discussion at The White House Leadership Conference on Youth, Drug Use and Violence," Eleanor Roosevelt High School, Greenbelt, Maryland, 7 March 1996).

10. Cooper, "1997 Drug Court Survey Report: Executive Summary," 24.

11. *Cutting Crime: Drug Courts in Action* (Washington, D.C.: Drug Strategies, 1997), 21. See also, *Drug Courts: A Revolution in Criminal Justice*, which calls drug courts "a truly grassroots phenomenon" (11).

12. Bean, "America's Drug Courts," 718–21.

13. For discussion of the expansion of drug courts to other types of crime see John Goldkamp, "Justice and Treatment Innovation: The Drug Court Movement" (Washington, D.C.: National Institute of Justice, 1993), 35; and *Cutting Crime: Drug Courts in Action* (Washington, D.C.: Drug Strategies, 1997), 30.

14. See "Defining Drug Courts: The Key Components," Drug Courts Program Office, Office of Justice Programs, U.S. Department of Justice (January 1997), 6; and *Drug Courts: A Revolution in Criminal Justice*, 31–7.

15. *Cutting Crime: Drug Courts in Action*, 30.

16. Ibid.

17. For a discussion of these measures see Hora et al., "Therapeutic Jurisprudence," 457–9; and William McColl, "Baltimore City's Drug Treatment Court: Theory and Practice in an Emerging Field," *Maryland Law Review* 55 (1996): 475. As is considered later in this chapter, the strengthening of drug laws, as such, does not necessarily indicate a development incongruent with the kind of treatment orientation evident in programs like TASC. As will become clear, a strong treatment orientation is not at all incompatible with a strong punitive approach.

18. Sally Satel explains the attractiveness of the drug court alternative in a very similar manner: "The revolving door to the justice system seemed to be spinning out of control. Drug courts promised a way to break the cycle of 'reserving' jail and prison beds for dangerous offenders while sending criminally involved addicts to treatment" (*Drug Treatment: The Case for Coercion*, 22).

19. *Drug Courts: A Revolution in Criminal Justice*, 14.

20. Ibid., 15.

21. See Hank Johnston and Bert Klandermans, *Social Movements and Culture* (Minneapolis: University of Minnesota Press, 1995); Enrique Larana, Hank Johnston, and Joseph R. Gusfield, eds., *New Social Movements: From Ideology to Identity* (Philadelphia: Temple University Press, 1994); and Joel Best, *Random Violence: How We Talk About New Crimes and New Victims* (Berkeley: University of California Press, 1999), especially 86–91.

22. Doug McAdam, "Culture and Social Movement," in *New Social Movements*, 39.

23. Ibid.

24. Ibid.

25. Best, *Random Violence*, 87.

26. For a fuller delineation of the defining themes of the therapeutic ethos see Nolan, *The Therapeutic State*, 1–21. For a recent discussion of the rise of self-esteem and other defining features of the therapeutic culture see also John P.

Hewitt, *The Myth of Self-Esteem: Finding Happiness and Solving Problems in America* (New York: St. Martin's Press, 1998). Hewitt, for example, observes that "in the last fifty years—roughly since the end of World War II—psychology in one form or another has become a major presence in our culture" (137). In addition to highlighting the significant place of self-esteem in American culture Hewitt discusses the role of a new priestly class of therapists, the pathological reinterpretation of behavior, and the central cultural focus on feelings and victimization (xii, 138, 93, 102–3, 96). Hewitt specifically observes that as it concerns the issue of drug abuse, "Americans are apt to look to psychological theories in their search for solutions to the problem" (21). For a discussion of the impact of therapeutic cultural resources on crime and new social movements, see also Best, *Random Violence*. Best, for example, argues that "during the course of the twentieth century . . . the influence of physicians, psychiatrists, and the medical model rose while religious ideologies seemed to lose much of their clout" (176). He also discusses the role of therapists in medicalizing "family dynamics and other aspects of their patients' lives" and in contributing to the widespread acceptance of new categories of victimization (101–2, 95–96). As he sees it, "the medical model's authority, and its natural focus on the afflictions experienced by patients, made it easy to describe individual's' troubled behaviors as 'disorders' or 'syndromes' that, often, were products of victimization" (101).

27. *Defining Drug Courts: The Key Components*, 15.
28. Ibid., 6.
29. Garland, *Punishment and Modern Society*, 210.
30. Ibid.
31. McColl, "Baltimore City's Drug Treatment Court," 500.
32. Ibid.
33. *Defining Drug Courts: The Key Components*, 6.
34. Hora et al., "Therapeutic Jurisprudence," 463.
35. Ibid.
36. Ibid., 463–64.
37. Ibid., 468.
38. Peggy Fulton Hora and William G. Schma, "Drug Treatment Courts: Therapeutic Jurisprudence in Practice," *Judicature* 82 (July–August 1998): 1–4.
39. Sally Satel, for example, in a study of fifteen drug courts reports that "judges sometimes hug participants after graduation" (69). In fact, in fourteen of the fifteen courts Satel observed, she noted some form of physical contact between judge and client (Sally Satel, "Observational Study of Courtroom Dynamics in Selected Drug Courts," *National Drug Court Institute Review* 1 [Summer 1998]: 63–64).
40. Donald Black, *The Behavior of Law* (New York: Academic Press, 1976), 4–5.
41. Erich Goode, *Between Politics and Reason: The Drug Legalization Debate* (New York: St. Martin's Press, 1997), 55.
42. Ibid., 56.
43. Ibid., 55–72.
44. "Survey of American Political Culture" (The Post-Modernity Project, University of Virginia, 1996). Percentages represent those who answered "important" or "very important" to the question.

45. Garland, *Punishment and Modern Society*, 245.

46. S. M. Lipset, *Political Man: The Social Bases of Politics* (New York: Anchor Books, 1960), 86–87.

47. Judith S. Kaye, "Lawyering for a New Age," *Fordham Law Review* 67 (October 1998): 3.

48. Ibid., 6.

49. Judge Jeffrey Tauber, "Preface," in *Drug Courts: A Revolution in Criminal Justice*, 3.

50. Garland, *Punishment and Modern Society*, 21.

51. See Nolan, *The Therapeutic State*, 101–2, for examples of drug court defenses based on program efficacy.

Chapter Three
Therapeutic Theater

1. Erving Goffman, *The Presentation of Self in Everyday Life* (New York: Anchor Books, 1959).

2. Robert D. Benford and Scott A. Hunt, "Dramaturgy and Social Movements: The Social Construction and Communication of Power," in *Social Movements: Critiques, Concepts, Case-Studies*, ed. Stanford M. Lyman (New York: New York University Press, 1995), 84–109.

3. Ibid., 87.

4. Jeffrey S. Tauber, "A Judicial Primer on Drug Courts and Court-Oriented Drug Rehabilitation Programs" (presented at the California continuing Judicial Studies Program, Dana Point, Cal., August 20, 1993, 5).

5. "The NADCP/COPS Mentor Court Network Working Together Within a Unified System," presented in partnership with The National Association of Drug Court Professionals and The Office of Community Oriented Policing Services, U.S. Dept. of Justice, 12.

6. See Benford and Hunt, "Dramaturgy and Social Movements," 94.

7. Tauber, "A Judicial Primer," 8.

8. Ibid.

9. Ibid., 9.

10. Ibid.

11. Satel, "Observational Study of Courtroom Dynamics," 61. Satel also notes the manner in which the drug court judge deliberately puts on a show to produce a certain effect. "The drug court judge has the latitude to shape a courtroom drama. He or she can orchestrate the timing and sequencing of cases heard and perhaps most dramatic, can arrange for these dynamics to have an impact on participants seated in the courtroom and—more important—on those defendants who are sitting in the jury box as a sanction" (48).

12. Satel, "Observational Study of Courtroom Dynamics," 51.

13. Jamey Weitzman, *Drug Courts: A Manual for Planning and Implementation* (a manual published with support from the American Bar Association), 9.

14. Jeffrey Tauber, "A Judicial Primer," 8.

15. *Treatment Drug Courts: Integrating Substance Abuse Treatment with Legal Case Processing*, Treatment Improvement Protocol (TIP) Series 23. (Washington, D.C.: U.S. Department of Health and Human Services, Substance Abuse

and Mental Health Services Administration, Center for Substance Abuse Treatment), 7–8.

16. As asserted in a *Harvard Law Review* note, "Perhaps the most serious challenge to traditional adversarial principles [in drug courts] is the change in the role of the defense attorney" ("Alternatives to Incarceration for Drug-Abusing Offenders," *Harvard Law Review* 111 [May 1998]: 1918).

17. American Bar Association Standards for Criminal Justice, Standard 4–1.2.b, The Function of Defense Counsel.

18. John Goldkamp, "Justice and Treatment Innovation: The Drug Court Movement: A Working Paper of the First National Drug Court Conference" (National Institute of Justice, Office of Justice Programs, U.S. Department of Justice, December 1993), 14.

19. Ibid.

20. Michael Judge, "Critical Issues in the Design and Operation of a Drug Court Program: Current and Emerging" (supporting material presented at the 1995 National Symposium on the Implementation and Operation of Drug Courts, Portland, Oregon, 4 December 1995).

21. Goldkamp, "Justice and Treatment Innovation," 15.

22. "Defining Drug Courts: The Key Components" (Drug Courts Program Office, Office of Justice Programs, U.S. Department of Justice, January 1997), 12.

23. As summarized in the *Harvard Law Review* note on drug courts: "Thus, drug courts create potentially serious conflicts of interest for defense attorneys. As part of the treatment 'team,' the defense attorney is supposed to act in accordance with his client's best interests, even when those interests involve sanctions. This change in perspective subverts the traditional role of defense counsel as zealous advocates for their clients' legal rights, which requires counsel to argue in accordance with their clients' wishes, not necessarily their best interests" (1918).

24. That is, it is feared that the absence of the traditional defense role "may imperil defendants' individual rights and put them at a disadvantage in future cases" ("Alternatives to Incarceration," 1918).

25. As Satel notes, "This conforms to what behaviorists have long appreciated, that behavior is shaped most effectively when punishments are swift and sure but not necessarily severe" (Satel, "Observational Study of Courtroom Dynamics," 46).

26. Cooper et al., "Drug Courts: 1997 Overview," 71–74.

27. Ibid.

28. Goldkamp, "Justice and Treatment Innovation," 16.

29. Cooper et al., "Drug Courts: 1997 Overview," 231.

30. Ibid., 232.

31. Ibid., 231.

32. Trevor Jensen, "Departing Drug Judge Too Lenient, Critics Say," *Sun-Sentinel*, 2 April 1995, B1.

33. *Defining Drug Courts: The Key Components*, 11, emphasis added.

34. Tauber, "A Judicial Primer," 9.

35. Jane Gross, "Probation and Therapy Help Some Drug Users," *New York Times*, 21 June 1991, B, 6:3. The full attitudinal adjustment of probation officers to their new roles was confirmed in my visit to the cite in 1995.

36. Ibid.

37. *Drug Courts: A Revolution in Criminal Justice*, 19.

38. Satel, "Observational Study of Courtroom Dynamics," 68.

39. Cooper et al., "Drug Courts: 1997 Participants Perspectives," 80.

40. Ibid., 56.

41. Adele Harrell and Barbara Smith also report in their study of the Washington, D.C., drug court that one participant was not an addict but a dealer. As they report, "One long-term seller, with four felony convictions, was a relatively light user. He used the treatment offer as an opportunity to avoid an almost certain long prison term. He attended a treatment program . . . for a period of time, tested clean consistently, then got a job, and reduced participation in treatment. After getting probation, he quit work but is completing his required community service. He is sure he will not have to serve time as long as he avoids rearrest. He says continuing to stay clean is not a problem because he was never addicted" ("Evaluation of the District of Columbia Superior Court Drug Intervention Program: Focus Group Interviews" [January 1996], 12–13). Research was supported by the National Institute of Justice and funds provided by the Center on Substance Abuse Treatment and Mental Health Services Administration. Likewise, treatment providers in Mobile, Alabama, where two clients were "shot and killed," identified the admittance of drug dealers and gang members as one of the program's "most serious problems" (Cooper et al., "Drug Courts: 1997 Overview," 229).

42. *Federal Confidentiality Laws and How They Effect Drug Court Practitioners* (Washington, D.C.: National Drug Court Institute, 1999), 1.

43. Ibid., 2.

Chapter Four
The Un-Common Law

1. Roscoe Pound, "What is the Common Law?" in *The Future of the Common Law* (Cambridge: Harvard University Press, 1937), 7–8, 11.

2. Ibid., 11.

3. Karl Llewellyn, *The Common Law Tradition: Deciding Appeals* (Boston: Little, Brown, 1960), 36–37.

4. Karl Llewellyn, *Jurisprudence: Realism in Theory and Practice* (Chicago: University of Chicago Press, 1962), 302.

5. Llewellyn, *The Common Law Tradition*, 36.

6. Mary Ann Glendon, *A Nation Under Lawyers: How the Crisis in the Legal Profession is Transforming American Society* (New York: Farrar, Straus and Giroux), 118.

7. Lawrence Friedman, *Crime and Punishment in American History* (New York: Basic Books, 1993), 20–21.

8. "During the trial [in a civil law proceeding], the presiding judge takes the lead in examining the witnesses and the defendant. Two major differences from the common law adversary model are that the judge is less a passive arbiter between the parties, while the prosecutor is less partisan" (Glendon et al., *Comparative Legal Traditions*, 95). Thus, the drug court model approximates the civil

law tradition both as it concerns the more activist role of the judge as well as the less partisan role of the prosecutor.

9. Alexis de Tocqueville, *Democracy in America*, vol. 1 (New York, Vintage Books, 1945), 102–3.

10. Abraham Lincoln, "The Perpetuation of Our Political Institutions: Address Before the Young Men's Lyceum of Springfield, Illinois, January 27, 1838," in *Abraham Lincoln: His Speeches and Writings*, ed. Roy P. Basler (New York: World Publishing Company, 1946), 77, 84–85. While the desire for "celebrity and fame" played a role in the work of America's founders (as Lincoln essentially acknowledged), even from the beginning notions of judicial duty required the judge to shun (or at least control) such considerations, a position demonstrated in John Marshall's judicial philosophy. See, for example, Robert F. Faulkner "John Marshall and the 'False Glare' of Fame," in *The Noblest Minds: Fame, Honor, and the American Founding*, ed. by Peter McNamara (New York: Rowman and Littlefield, 1999), 163–84.

11. Lincoln, "The Perpetuation of Our Political Institutions," 83.

12. Ibid., 82.

13. Nathan Glazer, "Towards and Imperial Judiciary?" *Public Interest* 41 (1975), 106.

14. Glendon, *A Nation Under Lawyers*, 117.

15. Ibid., 118, 152.

16. Ibid., 111.

17. Ibid., 112.

18. Charles E. Wyzanski, Jr., Letter to Senator Leverett Saltonstall, 12 January 1959, reprinted in Walter F. Murphy and C. Herman Pritchett, *Courts, Judges, and Politics: An Introduction to the Judicial Process* (New York: Random House, 1986), 108.

19. Ibid., 109.

20. Judicial Oath, Judiciary Act of 1789, 28 U.S. Codes. 453 (1992).

21. Glendon, *A Nation Under Lawyers*, 151.

22. These illustrations reveal that William McColl does not overstate matters when he concludes that judicial discretion in the drug court is "exceedingly high" ("Baltimore City's Drug Treatment Court," 514).

23. Caroline S. Cooper, "Report of Symposium Proceedings," 1995 SJI National Symposium on the Implementation and Operation of Drug Courts, 25–6. Jeffrey Tauber likewise observes that the new role of the drug court judge "was to be more than simply dealing with the offender from the bench, but also to become a community leader responsible for the court and its programs" (*Drug Courts: A Revolution in Criminal Justice*, 3).

24. John Goldkamp, *Justice and Treatment Innovation: The Drug Court Movement* (Washington D.C.: National Institute of Justice, U.S. Department of Justice), 6.

25. Judge Jeffrey S. Tauber, "A Judicial Primer on Drug Courts and Court-Ordered Drug Rehabilitation Programs," paper presented at the California Continuing Judicial Studies Program, Dana Point, California, 20 August 1993, 4.

26. *Drug Courts: A Revolution in Criminal Justice*, 24.

27. Cooper et al., "Drug Courts: 1997 Overview," 120–7.

28. Tauber, "A Judicial Primer," 8.

29. Glendon, *A Nation Under Lawyers*, 162.

30. Sally Satel, "Observational Study of Courtroom Dynamics," 51.

31. Ibid.

32. Weitzman's description of her court is consistent with McColl's observations of the Baltimore drug court: "Judge Weitzman, the first Baltimore city DTC judge, inquired into many facets of offenders' lives, including employment, health and family life. In fact, as shown, the judge is familiar with each defendant in an almost parental role" (McColl, "Baltimore City's Drug Treatment Court," 517).

33. Judicial Oath, Judiciary Act of 1789, 28 U.S. Codes. 453 (1992).

34. Glendon, *A Nation Under Lawyers*, citing Geertz, 128.

35. Ibid., 117.

36. Glazer, "An Imperial Judiciary?" 118.

37. Gary Craig, "50 Former Addicts Graduate from Rochester Rehabilitation Program," *Democrat and Chronicle*, 18 January 1997, 1A.

38. *Drug Courts: A Revolution in Criminal Justice*, 27.

39. Hora and Schma, "Drug Treatment Courts," 5. See also Deborah J. Chase and Peggy Fulton Hora, "The Implications of Therapeutic Jurisprudence for Judicial Satisfaction," *Court Review* 37 (Spring 2000): 12–20.

Chapter Five
Drug Court Storytelling

1. Nolan, *The Therapeutic State*, 235–79.

2. See Richard Delgado, "Storytelling for Oppositionists and Others: A Plea for Narrative," *Michigan Law Review* 87 (1989): 2411–41; Harlon L. Dalton, "Storytelling on its Own Terms," in *Law's Stories: Narrative and Rhetoric in Law*, ed. Peter Brooks and Paul Gewirtz (New Haven: Yale University Press, 1996); and Paul Gewirtz, "Narrative and Rhetoric in Law," in *Law's Stories: Narrative and Rhetoric in Law*.

3. Peter Brooks, "The Law as Narrative and Rhetoric," in *Law's Stories: Narrative and Rhetoric in Law*, 16.

4. Daniel Farber and Suzanna Sherry, "Legal Storytelling and Constitutional Law: The Medium and the Message," in *Law's Stories: Narrative and Rhetoric in Law*, 43.

5. Toni M. Massaro, "Empathy, Legal Storytelling, and the Rule of Law: New Words, Old Wounds?," *Michigan Law Review* 87 (1989): 2108.

6. See, for example, Joseph E. Davis, ed., *Stories of Change: Narrative and Social Movements* (New York: SUNY Press, 2001).

7. Gary Fine, "Public Narration and Group Culture: Discerning Discourse in Social Movements," in *Social Movements and Culture*, ed. Hank Johnston and Bert Klandermans (Minneapolis: University of Minnesota Press, 1995), 135–6.

8. Fine, "Public Narration and Group Culture," 136.

9. Ibid., 136.

10. John Goldkamp and Doris Weiland. "Assessing the Impact of Dade County's Felony Drug Court—Final Report" (National Institute of Justice Research Report, August 1993), 52–62.

11. Ibid., 53.

12. This study was published by the Drug Court Clearinghouse and Technical Assistance Project sponsored by the U.S. Department of Justice and located at American University.

13. Harrell and Smith, "Evaluation of the District of Columbia Superior Court Drug Intervention Program."

14. Adele Harrell and Shannon Cavanagh, "Drug Test Results during the Month Before Sentencing: Preliminary Results from the Evaluation of the D.C. Superior Court Drug Intervention Program for Drug Felony Defendants" (Presented at the National Association of Drug Court Professionals Conference, Washington, D.C., 10 May 1996).

15. W. Clinton Terry, "Broward County Drug Court: A Preliminary Report" (November 1993), 26, emphasis added.

16. Ibid.

17. Mara E. Camposeco, "Drug Court Offers Treatment, Second Chance," *Sacramento Bee*, 16 May 1995, B1.

18. Michael Higgins, "Drug War on the Cheap: Studies Tout Savings, Other Benefits of Treatment for Addicts," *American Bar Association Journal* 83 (August 1997): 24.

19. Mark Curriden, "Drug Courts Gain Popularity: Studies Show Rearrests Lower for Defendant Treated for Addiction," *American Bar Association Journal* 80 (May 1994): 16.

20. Consella A. Lee, "First Graduates Finish Drug Court Program in Anne Arundel County to Treat Users: Probation Before Judgment Granted for Completion," *The Baltimore Sun*, 18 September 1990, 8B.

21. Michael Higgins, "Drug War on the Cheap," 24.

22. Mireya Navarro, "Experimental Courts Are Using New Strategies to Blunt the Lure of Drugs," *New York Times* (17 October 1996): A25.

23. Christopher Johns, "This is Your Court on Drugs—And it Works," *The Arizona Republic*, 19 February 1995, C3.

24. Jennifer L. Stevenson, "Drug Court Pushes Treatment Over Jail," *St. Petersburg Times*, 28 June 1990, 1B.

25. David Barstown, "In this Drug Court They Seal Records for Most Everyone," *St. Petersburg Times*, 27 March 1991, 9a.

26. Tracey Kaplan, "Supervisor Donates $40,000 Needed to Start Drug Court Program," *Los Angeles Times*, 18 March 1994, B6.

27. Goldkamp and Weiland, "Assessing the Impact," 95.

28. Michael Isikoff, "Miami 'Drug Court' Demonstrates Reno's Unorthodox Approach," *The Washington Post*, 20 February 1993, A1.

29. For a more detailed discussion of findings in the Goldkamp and Weiland report see Nolan, *The Therapeutic State*, 103–11.

30. Morris B. Hoffman, "The Drug Court Scandal," *North Carolina Law Review*, 78 (June 2000): 1490.

31. "Drug Courts: Overview of Growth, Characteristics, and Results" (report to the Committee on the Judiciary, House of Representatives, United States General Accounting Office, July 1997), 13.

32. Ibid.

33. Ibid., 113.

34. Ibid., 102.

35. Hoffman, "The Drug Court Scandal," 1491.

36. Steven Belenko, "Research on Drug Courts: A Critical Review," *National Drug Court Institute Review* 1 (Summer 1998): 1–42.

37. As Hoffman writes, "The Belenko study is by far the most optimistic meta-study done to date. But even Belenko concedes that most drug court evaluators continue to target drug court graduates instead of all drug court participants, that only a 'few' studies have tracked recidivism for more than a one year follow-up period, and that only two of the studies used a random method of identifying target drug court defendants" ("The Drug Court Scandal," 1497).

38. Belenko, "Research on Drug Courts: A Critical Review," 17.

39. Ibid., 27.

40. "Drug Courts: Overview," 117.

41. Belenko, "Research on Drug Courts: A Critical Review," 36.

42. Ibid., 33–37.

43. Hora et al., "Therapeutic Jurisprudence," 529.

44. Ibid., 529–30.

45. Jeffrey Tauber, "The 1997 GAO Report: Déjà Vu All Over Again," *NADCP News* 4 (Summer 1997):16.

46. Ibid.

47. Mark Curriden, "Drug Courts Gain Popularity: Studies Show Rearrests Lower for Defendant Treated for Addiction," *American Bar Association Journal* 80 (May 1994): 16.

48. Goldkamp and Weiland, "Assessing the Impact of Dade County's Felony Drug Court," 16.

49. Ibid., 12.

50. Which may help to explain why, as Morris Hoffman puts it, "the drug court train rolls on, undeterred by the utter lack of evidence of its effectiveness" (1497–8).

Chapter Six
The Pathological Shift

1. Hora et al., "Therapeutic Jurisprudence," 463.

2. Garland, *Punishment and Society*, 247.

3. In addition to previous arguments by Rieff, Lasch, Berger, and the like, documenting this broader shift, Joel Best has recently written that "during the course of the 20th century . . . the influence of physicians, psychiatrists, and the medical model rose while religious ideologies seemed to lose much of their clout" (*Random Violence*, 176).

4. For a recent critical examination of this debate see Hoffman, "The Drug Court Scandal," 1469–73. Hoffman concludes, in this regard, that "It is

important for all of us to recognize that the twin pillars upon which the popular rush to drug courts rests—the alleged drug epidemic and our alleged ability to treat drug addiction—have beguiled the experts for decades. They are hardly as unassailably sturdy as conventional political and judicial wisdom would have us believe" (1473).

5. Recent studies not only reveal that self-esteem isn't positively correlated with healthy social behavior (see, for example, Andrew Mecca, Neil Smelser, and John Vasconcellos, eds., *The Social Importance of Self-Esteem* [Berkeley: University of California Press, 1989]), but that high self-esteem may in fact be positively related to violent behavior (see Roy F. Baumeister, Laura Smart, and Joseph M. Boden, "Relation of Threatened Egotism to Violence and Aggression: The Dark Side of High Self-Esteem," *Psychological Review* 101 [1995]: 5–33). For discussions about the specific link between self-esteem and drug use, see Hewitt, *The Myth of Self-Esteem*, 6–7; Rodney Skager and Elizabeth Kerst, "Alcohol and Drug Use and Self-Esteem: A Psychological Perspective," in *The Social Importance of Self-Esteem*, 248–93; and Harry H. L. Kitano, "Alcohol and Drug Use and Self-Esteem: A Sociocultural Perspective," in *The Social Importance of Self-Esteem*, 294–326. Kitano notes that in spite of the claims that "alcoholics or drug addicts behave as they do because of low self-esteem," there is actually "a paucity of good research, especially studies that could link the abuse of alcohol and drugs with self esteem" (319–20).

6. Hewitt, *The Myth of Self-Esteem*, observes the same basic understandings advanced in contemporary discourse about self-esteem. "I think both public and private uses of the word self-esteem are moving in a medical direction. Increasingly, I suspect, high self-esteem is becoming thought of as an indicator of psychological or mental health, and low self-esteem as a form of illness" (138).

7. See, for example, Rita Kramer, *Ed School Follies* (New York: The Free Press, 1991); Christopher Lasch, "For Shame: Why Americans Should be Wary of Self-Esteem," *The New Republic*, 10 August 1992, 29–34; Christopher Lasch, "The Narcissist Society," *The New York Review*, 30 September 1976, 5–13; James L. Nolan, Jr., "Acquiescence or Consensus: Consenting to Therapeutic Pedagogy," in *Counseling and the Therapeutic State*, ed. James J. Chriss (New York: Aldine de Gruyter, 1999), 107–129; and Hewitt, *The Myth of Self-Esteem*, 73–96.

8. Philip Rieff, *Fellow Teachers: Of Culture and its Second Death* (Chicago: University of Chicago Press, 1972), 47.

9. Ibid., 55–6.

10. Cooper et al., "Drug Courts: 1997 Overview," 9–13.

11. William McColl essentially concludes the same in his critical assessment of the Baltimore City drug court. As he puts it, "Although the concept of guilt has not vanished, the DTCs attempt to sidestep the problem of determining blame or fault through a plea-bargaining process. Thus in Baltimore City, the question of guilt is resolved or becomes irrelevant. The question then is no longer whether the crime happened, but rather, what is compelling the crime and how do we stop it? As Barbara Wootton imagined, this question is resolved by treatment personnel" ("Baltimore City's Drug Treatment Court," 501–2).

12. "Justice and Treatment Innovation: The Drug Court Movement" (a Working Paper of the First National Drug Court Conference, December 1993, U.S. Department of Justice, National Institute of Justice, State Justice Institute), 35.

13. Ibid.

14. "Looking at a Decade of Drug Courts" (prepared by the Drug Court Clearinghouse and Technical Assistance Project, U.S. Department of Justice, Office of Justice Programs, American University, Washington, D.C., June 1998), 14.

15. Cooper et al., "Drug Courts: 1997 Overview," 13–17.

16. Ibid.

17. For an insightful discussion of the therapeutic legal defense forced on Ted Kaczynski, see William Finnegan, "Defending the Unabomber," *The New Yorker*, 16 March 1998, 53–63.

18. Cooper, "1997 Drug Court Survey Report: Executive Summary," 16.

19. As already noted, treatment providers play an important role in the drug court program. "Since drug treatment drives DTCs, however, treatment providers play an integral role in the DTC process" (Hora et al., "Therapeutic Jurisprudence," 480).

20. Others have concluded the same. Hora et al., for example, observe that "Some [, if not all,] drug courts give great weight to the recommendations of the treatment program representative when making case decisions" ("Therapeutic Jurisprudence," 480, brackets included in original). These authors were only strengthening a statement made in a BJA document: "Some drug courts give great weight to the recommendations of the treatment program representative when making case decisions" (Bureau of Justice Assistance, U.S. Dept. of Justice, Pub. No. NJC-144531 *Program Brief: Special Drug Courts* 1 [1993], 10). McColl similarly observes that "although not required to do so, the [drug court] judge almost always follows the recommendations of treatment providers" (McColl, "Baltimore City's Drug Treatment Court," 497).

21. "NADCP News," V (Winter 1998): 3.

22. Best, *Random Violence*, 124.

23. Cooper et al., "Drug Courts: 1997 Overview," 162.

24. Ibid., 164.

25. Ibid., 162.

26. Ibid., 159–61.

27. Best, *Random Violence*, 125.

Chapter Seven
The Meaning of Justice

1. Immanuel Kant, *The Metaphysical Elements of Justice*, trans. John Ladd (London: Macmillan, 1965), 100.

2. Ibid., 101.

3. Hegel, *Philosophy of Right*, trans. T. M. Knox (Oxford: Clarendon Press, 1942). Here Hegel writes, "But the determinate character given by the concept to

punishment is just that necessary connexion between crime an punishment already mentioned; crime, as the will which is implicitly null, *eo ipso* contains its negation in itself and this negation is manifested as punishment" (72).

4. Ibid., 71.

5. Ibid., 70.

6. Eng. Magna Carta §20 as cited in Robert Blecker, "Haven or Hell? Inside Lorton Central Prison: Experiences of Punishment Justified," *Stanford Law Review* 42 (May 1990): 1170. Blecker also points to the Biblical foundation for the retributivist perspective in Leviticus 24:19: "As he has done, it shall be done to him" (1164, fn 27), and specifically on the matter of proportionality in Deuteronomy 24:16: "The fathers shall not be put to death for the children, nor shall the children be put to death for the fathers; every man shall be put to death for his own sin" (1170, fn 45). Blecker also finds evidence of the retributivist perspective in the ancient Code of Hammurabi §196, "If a man has put out the eye of a free man, they shall put out his eye" (1164, fn 27).

7. H.L.A. Hart, *Punishment and Responsibility: Essays in the Philosophy of Law* (Oxford: Oxford University Press, 1958), 158–9.

8. Jeremy Bentham, *The Rationale of Punishment* (1830, 19–41) as cited in Peter W. Low, John Calvin Jeffries, Jr., and Richard J. Bonnie, *Criminal Law: Cases and Material*, 2nd ed. (New York: The Foundation Press, 1986), 8.

9. Ibid.

10. Oliver Wendell Holmes, Jr., *The Common Law* (Boston: Little, Brown and Company, 1881), 46.

11. Ibid., 45.

12. Ibid., 47.

13. Ibid., 42.

14. Lloyd L. Weinreb, "Desert, Punishment, and Criminal Responsibility, *Law and Contemporary Problems* 49 (Summer 1986): 47–80. Among the composite theories that, according to Weinreb "comes closest to the reflective judgment of most people is that utilitarian considerations ought to determine what conduct is criminal but that considerations of desert restrict the imposition and extent of punishment in a particular case" (49).

15. A. C. Ewing, *The Morality of Punishment* (London: Kegan Paul, Trench, Trubner & Co., 1929), 44.

16. Ibid., 44–45.

17. Francis Allen similarly writes, "Ideas of desert supply what Norval Morris calls limiting principles, not defining principles" (*The Decline of the Rehabilitative Ideal*, 72).

18. Ewing, *The Morality of Punishment*, 15.

19. Ibid., 20.

20. Hart, *Punishment and Responsibility*, 182.

21. Ibid., 185.

22. For a critique of Hart's argument on this issue, see J. L. Mackie, "The Grounds of Responsibility," in *Law, Morality, and Society*, ed. P.M.S. Hacker and J. Raz (Oxford: Clarendon Press, 1977).

23. As cited in Low, Jeffries, and Bonnie, *Criminal Law*, 3 fn. c.

24. Hart, *Punishment and Responsibility*, 173.

25. The notion of distribution, as such, conceptually links the ideals of criminal justice with social justice. That is, one could argue justice is meaningful in both cases because it is fair, has been earned, and is proportional to actions that were committed in the past. Thus, it is the retributivist concern with fairness or proportionality that makes the broader concept of justice intelligible. As T. M. Scanlon summarizes such a position: "Certain acts deserve punishment, certain contributions merit rewards, and institutions are just if they distribute benefits and burdens in accord with these forms of desert" ("The Significance of Choice," in *The Tanner Lectures on Human Values*, vol. 8 [Salt Lake City: University of Utah Press, 1988] delivered at Brasenose College, Oxford University, May 23, 1986, 188). There are some who would dispute this analogy on the grounds that social justice cannot be practically or theoretically conceived in terms of desert. Foremost among those holding this position is John Rawls, who forcefully debunks the notion of desert as it relates to social justice. Interestingly, however, in discussing penal justice, Rawls essentially accepts the notion of distribution but claims there is no comparison between social justice and criminal justice. "It is clear that the distribution of economic and social advantages is entirely different. These arrangements are not the converse, so to speak, of the criminal law, so that just as the one punishes certain offenses, the other rewards moral worth" (*A Theory of Justice* [Cambridge, Mass.: Belknap, 1971], 315). However, as Michael Sandel convincingly demonstrates, Rawls's argument does not hold up here. "[T]he more basic question is how Rawls can admit desert in retributive justice without contradicting the theory of the self and related assumptions that ruled it out for purposes of distributive justice. If such notions as pre-institutional moral claims and intrinsic moral worth are excluded from a theory of distributive justice in virtue of an essentially unencumbered self too slender to support them, it is difficult to see how retributive justice could differ in any relevant way" (*Liberalism and the Limits of Justice* [Cambridge: Cambridge University Press, 1982], 90). Others who support the notion of desert in theories of social justice, however, are more inclined to see this conceptual linkage between the two kinds of justice. See, for example, George Sher, *Desert* (Princeton: Princeton University Press, 1987), especially chapters 5 and 6. In fact, Sher sees these two areas as those where the claims of desert are most salient (p. 209–10). See, also, Geoffrey Cupit, *Justice as Fittingness* (Oxford: Clarendon, 1996); and Russell Muirhead, *Just Work* (Cambridge: Harvard University Press, forthcoming).

26. In a recent review of various theories of punishment, Martin David Matravers comes to the same conclusion on Hart's work. As Matravers puts it, "In the end, however, one surely has to take Hart's model as expressing the conditions of deserved punishment" ("Justice and Punishment: The Rationale of Coercion," Thesis submitted for the degree of Doctor of Philosophy, London School of Economics and Political Science, 1994, p. 24).

27. C. S. Lewis, "The Humanitarian Theory of Punishment," *Res Judicatae*, VI (June 1953): 225.

28. J.J.C. Smart, "Comment: The Humanitarian View of Punishment," *Res Judicatae*, VI (February 1954): 368.

29. Ibid., 370.

30. Ibid.

31. Ibid.

32. Norval Morris and Donald Buckle, "The Humanitarian Theory of Punishment: A Reply to C. S. Lewis," *Res Judicatae* VI (June 1953): 232.

33. Ibid.

34. Ibid., 236.

35. Ibid.

36. Norval Morris, *The Future of Imprisonment* (Chicago: Chicago University Press, 1974), 76.

37. Norval Morris and Gordon Hawkins, *Letter to the President on Crime Control* (Chicago: Chicago University Press, 1977), 68.

38. Low et al., *Criminal Law*, 4.

39. Ibid., 13.

40. Ibid., 7.

41. Ibid., 28.

42. Ibid.

43. Ibid.

44. Nolan, *The Therapeutic State*, chapter 2.

45. Garland, *Punishment and Modern Society*, 209.

46. Garland writes, "One important example of a cultural form which has changed over time and has influenced penal practice accordingly is the concept of justice" (*Punishment and Modern Society*, 205).

47. J. M. Beattie, *Crime and the Courts in England, 1660–1800* (Princeton: Princeton University Press, 1986), 403.

48. Ibid., 440.

49. Ibid., 442.

50. Ibid., 403.

51. Ibid., 439.

52. Sutton writes, "There was a wide spectrum of penalties available in criminal cases, from referral for ministerial counseling, to wearing a visible symbol of guilt, on up to the more severe and stigmatizing stocks, brandings, and mutilations" ("Therapeutic Justice: The Legal Construction of Deviant Persons," in *Social Structures and Human Lives*, ed. Matilda White Riley [Newbury Park, CA: Sage, 1988], 70). See also David J. Rothman, *The Discovery of the Asylum: Social Order and Disorder in the New Republic* (Boston: Little, Brown and Company, 1971), 49–50.

53. Sutton, "Therapeutic Justice," 70.

54. Kai Erikson, *Wayward Puritans: A Study in the Sociology of Deviance* (New York: Macmillan, 1966), 194.

55. Friedman, *Crime and Punishment in American History*, 42.

56. Ibid., 42.

57. Sutton, "Therapeutic Justice," 70.

58. See, for example, Rothman, *The Discovery of the Asylum*; Rothman, *Conscience and Convenience: The Asylum and its Alternatives in Progressive America* (Boston: Little, Brown and Company, 1980), especially chapter 1; Michel Foucault, *Discipline and Punish: The Birth of the Prison* (New York: Vintage Books, 1979); Myra C. Glenn, *Campaigns Against Corporal Punishment: Prisoners, Sail-*

ors, Women, and Children in Antebellum America (Albany: State University of New York Press, 1984).

59. Garland, for example, writes of this period: "Against the 'harsh' methods and 'terroristic' objectives of absolutist penal regimes, this liberal reforming movement counterposed utility, rationality, the rights of man, and the rule of law. Punishments were to be regulated by law and by reason, carefully calibrated to ensure the maximum effect from the minimum of pain, put to good use rather than striking out destructively and at random. From Montesquieu, Voltaire, and Beccaria to Howard, Betham, and Mill, punishments were to rationally administered and made positive in their results" ("Penal Modernism and Postmodernism," in *Punishment and Social Control: Essays in Honor of Sheldon L. Messinger*, ed. Thomas G. Blomberg and Stanley Cohen [New York: Aldine de Gruyter, 1995], 186). Similarly, Rothman writes, "Beccaria's summary advice was succinct and his program straightforward: 'Do you want to prevent crimes? See to it that the laws are clear and simple and that the entire force of a nation is united in their defense. The young republic quickly took this message to heart, for it fit well with its own history and revolutionary ideas" (*The Discovery of the Asylum*, 60).

60. As Rothman notes, "The arrangements at the Philadelphia prison, as partisans described them, guaranteed that convicts would avoid all contamination and follow a path to reform. Inmates remained in solitary cells for eating, sleeping, and working, and entered private yards for exercise; they saw and spoke with only carefully selected visitors, and read only morally uplifting literature—the Bible" (*The Discovery of the Asylum*, 85). See also Peter Spierenburg, who writes, "Apart from labor, religious exercises and instruction originally had a prominent place in the projected daily programs" ("From Amsterdam to Auburn: An Explanation for the Rise of the Prison in Seventeenth-Century Holland and Nineteenth-Century America," *Journal of Social History* 20 [Fall 1986]: 445); and Michael Ignatieff, who observes, "Its penitential regime of solitude, hard labor and religious instruction became the model for all national penal servitude prisons and most country prisons besides" ("State, Civil Society and Total Institutions: A Critique of Recent Social Histories of Punishment," in *Social Control and the State*, ed. Stanley Cohen and Andrew Scull [New York: St. Martin's Press, 1983], 80).

61. "As Raymond Saleilles put it, this new criminology attempted to replace the value rationality of traditional penal morality with a new purposive-rationality, which would adopt whatever technical methods were best suited for the control of crime" (Garland, *Punishment and Modern Society*, 185).

62. See Sutton, "Therapeutic Justice," 74. Garland makes a similar observation: "In certain aspects of punishment, as elsewhere in modern society, technical relations have tended to displace moral ones, therapies have replaced judgments, and the social sciences have occupied a space that used to be definitively moral and religious" (*Punishment and Modern Society*, 189).

63. Garland, *Punishment and Modern Society*, 185.

64. Garland, "Penal Modernism and Postmodernism," 186.

65. Sutton, "Therapeutic Justice," 63–82.

66. Garland, "Penal Modernism and Postmodernism," 187.

67. Sutton, "Therapeutic Justice," 67.

68. Ibid., 64.

69. Garland, "Penal Modernism and Postmodernism," 189.

70. Sutton, "Therapeutic Justice," 65.

71. Rothman, *Conscience and Convenience*, 215.

72. Anthony M. Platt, *The Child Savers: The Invention of Delinquency* (Chicago: University of Chicago Press, 1977), 10.

73. Rothman, *Conscience and Convenience*, 214.

74. Ibid., 215.

75. Janet E. Ainsworth, "Re-Imagining Childhood and Reconstructing the Legal Order: The Case for Abolishing the Juvenile Court," *North Carolina Law Review* 69 (1991): 1097.

76. Boldt, "Rehabilitative Punishment and the Drug Treatment Court Movement," 1272.

77. Rothman, *Conscience and Convenience*, 224.

78. Ibid.

79. Ibid., 225.

80. Platt, *The Child Savers*, 142.

81. Ibid., 144.

82. Rothman, *Conscience and Convenience*, 240.

83. Ibid., 218.

84. Ibid., 216.

85. Platt, *The Child Savers*, 164

86. Richard Boldt, "Rehabilitative Punishment and the Drug Treatment Court Movement," *Washington University Law Quarterly* 76 (1998): 1269–77.

87. Rothman, *Conscience and Convenience*, 245.

88. Approximately 30 percent of the cases resulted in a fine or dismissal, 28 percent in some form of incarceration, and 28 percent in a probation term (Rothman, *Conscience and Convenience*, 256). Also, Richard Boldt notes that in juvenile courts there was a "heavy reliance on probation" ("Rehabilitative Punishment and the Drug Treatment Court Movement," 1272).

89. "Juvenile and Family Drug Court Activity: Summary Information" (prepared by the Drug Court Clearinghouse and Technical Assistance Project, Drug Courts Program Office, Office of Justice Programs, U.S. Department of Justice, 1998).

90. "Juvenile and Family Drug Courts: An Overview" (prepared by the Drug Court Clearinghouse and Technical Assistance Project, Drug Courts Program Office, Office of Justice Programs, U.S. Department of Justice, 1998) 7, emphasis added.

91. "Juvenile Drug Courts: Preliminary Report" (prepared by the Drug Court Clearinghouse and Technical Assistance Project, Drug Courts Program Office, Office of Justice Programs, U.S. Department of Justice, 1997), 1.

92. Ibid., 3.

93. "Juvenile and Family Drug Courts: Profile of Program Characteristics and Implementation Issues" (prepared by the Drug Court Clearinghouse and Technical Assistance Project, Drug Courts Program Office, Office of Justice Programs, U.S. Department of Justice, 1998), 129–30.

94. Rothman, *Conscience and Convenience*, 254.

95. Ibid.

96. Allen, *The Decline of the Rehabilitative Ideal*, 8–9.

97. Ibid., 10.

98. Boldt, "Rehabilitative Punishment and the Drug Treatment Court Movement," 1221.

99. "Counsel must be appointed where it can be shown that failure to do so would prejudice the rights of the person involved. . . . Wherever coercive action is a possibility, the presence of counsel is imperative" (Platt, *Child Savers*, 162).

100. Ibid., xvii.

101. As Janet E. Ainsworth observes, "Despite several decades of experience with rehabilitative penology in the adult and juvenile systems, however, criminal recidivism stubbornly refused to wither away" ("Re-Imagining Childhood," 1104).

102. Ibid., 1105.

103. Ibid., 1106.

104. Ibid.

105. Ibid., 1106–7.

106. Ibid., 1108.

107. *Struggle for Justice. A Report on Crime and Punishment in America.* Prepared for the American Friends Service Committee (New York: Hill & Wang, 1971), 147.

108. The authors regarded the combination of treatment and punishment as highly problematic. "When we punish the person and simultaneously try to treat him, we hurt the individual more profoundly and more permanently than if we merely imprison him for a specific length of time" (*Struggle for Justice*, 148).

109. Allen, *The Decline of the Rehabilitative Ideal*, 7.

110. Ibid., 8

111. Edward M. Kennedy, "Toward a New System of Criminal Sentencing: Law with Order," *The American Criminal Law Review* 16 (September 1979): 371.

112. Ibid.

113. Senate Committee on the Judiciary, Continuing Appropriations, Comprehensive Crime Control Act of 1983, S. Rep. No. 225, 98th Cong. 2d Sess. 65, reprinted in U.S. Code Cong. & Admin. News 3250. Considered here is the Sentencing Reform Act—one part of Title II of the Comprehensive Crime Control Act, which became law in 1984.

114. Senate Committee on the Judiciary, Continuing Appropriations, Comprehensive Crime Control Act of 1983, S. Rep. No. 225, 98th Cong., 2d Sess. 50, reprinted in U.S. Code Cong. & Admin. News 3233.

115. Senate Committee on the Judiciary, Continuing Appropriations, Comprehensive Crime Control Act of 1983, S. Rep. No. 225, 98th Cong., 2d Sess. 75, reprinted in U.S. Code Cong. & Admin. News 3258.

116. Allen even concedes that this "new psychologism" has "gone far to transform issues formerly defined as problems of education, morals, and politics into occasions for therapeutic diagnosis and manipulation." In short, according to

Allen, our society has become "psychocivilized" (*The Decline of the Rehabilitative Ideal*, 25–26).

117. Allen argues further that this new psychologism was in fact an "important factor" in the decline of the rehabilitative ideal: "The reliances on human malleability in the new psychologism are sharply distinguishable from those expressed in the rehabilitative ideal, and this fact explains not only why the rise of the new psychologism is compatible with the decline of penal rehabilitationism, but also why it has been an important factor in that decline" (*The Decline of the Rehabilitative Ideal*, 28).

118. Allen, *The Decline of the Rehabilitative Ideal*, 27–28.

119. Rice, *A Disease of One's Own*, 28.

120. Ibid.

121. Ibid., 29.

122. Allen, *The Decline of the Rehabilitative Ideal*, 27–28.

123. John P. Hewitt, in *The Myth of Self-Esteem*, discusses the concept of self-esteem in close association with Rice's notion of liberation therapy. In one usage of the concept, for example, Hewitt observes that "self-esteem seems to be based not merely or even primarily on socially acceptable behavior or the approval of others, but on following one's inner wishes or allowing oneself to flower in one's own way and not along the lines dictated by society. Each person has an essence, perhaps an inherently good self . . . and self-esteem consists of living up to that essence. This usage of self-esteem makes the word a synonym for self-actualization, for the pursuit of a self unfettered by the false expectations and judgments of others" (8). Drawing on the work of Ralph Turner, Hewitt also makes the distinction between "institutional and impulsive self-anchorage," a distinction that corresponds closely with Rice's distinction between adaptation and liberation therapies. Hewitt notes, for example, that a century ago, "people defined themselves in terms of societal standards and felt true to themselves when they could take pride in meeting them. Now, the argument runs, people look within themselves for self-definition and feel true to themselves—or feel happy—by following their own inclinations, not doing what others expect or demand. The institutionally anchored person experienced self through an emotional vocabulary that heavily emphasized pride, self-respect, humility, and shame. The impulsively anchored person experiences an emotional self through such contemporary words as happiness, self-esteem, joy and depression" (131–2).

124. Rice, *A Disease of One's Own*, 76.

125. Ibid., 77. For discussions of the critical place of emotions, see also 83, 112, and 208.

126. Program Handbook, Jefferson County Drug Court Diversion Program (November 1994), 19 (emphasis in original).

127. Ibid., 20.

128. "Program Workbook" (Impact Drug and Alcohol Treatment Center, Los Angeles, CA), 54.

129. Ibid., 70.

130. "A Wellness Model for the Healing of Addictions" (Choices Unlimited, Las Vegas, "Session 10—Feelings: Positive").

131. Ibid.

132. As cited in Rice, *A Disease of One's Own*, 83.

133. Ibid.

Chapter Eight
Reinventing Justice

1. As Keri Gould notes, "Therapeutic jurisprudence was originally envisioned as an alternative to traditional constitutional doctrinal analysis of mental health law. Increasingly, however, there has been significant 'spill-over' into other substantive fields including tort law, attorney-client relationships, criminal law, criminal procedure law, and juvenile law" ("Turning Rat and Doing Time for Uncharged, Dismissed or Acquitted Crimes," in *Law in a Therapeutic Key: Developments in Therapeutic Jurisprudence*, ed. David B. Wexler and Bruce Winick [Durham, NC: Carolina Academic Press, 1996], 179).

2. David B. Wexler, "Reflections on the Scope of Therapeutic Jurisprudence," in *Law in a Therapeutic Key*, 820.

3. Bruce J. Winick, "The Jurisprudence of Therapeutic Jurisprudence," in *Law in a Therapeutic Key*, 646.

4. Ibid., 653.

5. Ibid.

6. Ibid., 655.

7. Jeffrey L. Harrison, "Class, Personality, Contract, and Unconscionability," in *Law in a Therapeutic Key*, 525–67.

8. Wexler, "Reflections," 814.

9. Daniel W. Shuman, Jean A. Hamilton, and Cynthia E. Daley, "The Health Effect of Jury Service," in *Law in a Therapeutic Key*, 949–77. The authors offer the following as one solution to reduce the stress of serving on a jury: "A post-trial instruction encouraging jurors to share their feelings during deliberations and discuss the case fully to encourage those with minority viewpoints to make their views known, and to respect the views of all members of the jury might be reasonable. This approach is an example of therapeutic jurisprudence" (976).

10. Tom Tyler, "The Psychological Consequences of Judicial Procedure," in *Law in a Therapeutic Key*, 3–15. Tyler notes that the Supreme Court, in *Goldberg v. Kelley*, recognized that "termination [of welfare benefits] without a hearing could be psychologically harmful, potentially damaging feelings of security, dignity, and self-worth" (4).

11. Bruce Winick, "The Side Effects of Incompetency Labeling and the Implications for Mental Health Law," in *Law in a Therapeutic Key*, 17–58.

12. Winick, "The Jurisprudence of Therapeutic Jurisprudence," 650. Also as judges Hora and Schma note of the therapeutic qualities of teen courts, "To obtain the maximum empathetical benefit, a teen former offender could be appointed the victim's attorney to provide a personal experience of a victim's trauma. Such empathy produces a positive psychological impact on that offender's own rehabilitation" ("Drug Treatment Courts," 2).

13. Winick, "The Jurisprudence of Therapeutic Jurisprudence," 649.

14. Wexler, "Reflections," 820.

15. Winick, "The Jurisprudence of Therapeutic Jurisprudence," 653.

16. Winick specifically argues that therapeutic jurisprudence is not "a servant of the professions of psychiatry and psychology, and is by no means a device to reinforce or rationalize existing power imbalances between clinicians and their patients" ("The Jurisprudence of Therapeutic Jurisprudence," 657).

17. John Petrila, "Paternalism and the Unrealized Promise of Essays in Therapeutic Jurisprudence," in *Law in a Therapeutic Key*, 686.

18. Winick, "The Jurisprudence of Therapeutic Jurisprudence," 646.

19. Petrila, "Paternalism and the Unrealized Promise," 686.

20. Winick, "The Jurisprudence of Therapeutic Jurisprudence," 665.

21. C. S. Lewis asked a very similar question in his 1954 *Res Judicatae* article: "Can the Law assume one philosophy in practice and continue to enjoy the safeguards of a different philosophy?" (522).

22. Gould, "Turning Rat," 189–90.

23. Ibid., 190.

24. Ibid., 181.

25. Ibid., 200.

26. Ibid., 197.

27. Ibid., 190.

28. Ibid., 178.

29. See also Sheila Murphy, "Therapeutic Jurisprudence: Its Time Has Come," *Trial Judges News* (Winter 1997/1998): 3.

30. Hora et al., "Therapeutic Jurisprudence," 441. Elsewhere, Hora and Schma write that after developing "simultaneously yet independently" it was eventually discovered that "they were not only compatible but natural companions" ("Drug Treatment Courts," 3).

31. Hora et al., "Therapeutic Jurisprudence," 537.

32. Ibid., 449.

33. McColl, "Baltimore City's Drug Treatment Court," 500.

34. Ibid., 469, 500.

35. Hora et al., "Therapeutic Jurisprudence," 448.

36. Ibid., 536.

37. Ibid. Hora and Schma similarly argue that drug courts "are the most recent and widespread example of the application of therapeutic jurisprudence principles in the criminal justice system" ("Drug Treatment Courts," 3).

38. Hora et al., "Therapeutic Jurisprudence," 448.

39. McColl, "Baltimore City's Drug Treatment Court," 501. Judge Schma describes well the salience of therapeutic jurisprudence theory to the drug court. First he summarizes therapeutic jurisprudence:

> To me therapeutic jurisprudence is the structuring of the law and the structuring of the roles of the people who participate in the practice of the law and the execution of the law in such a way that you accomplish a therapeutic outcome, particularly as opposed to an anti-therapeutic outcome. . . . By changing attitudes, structures, and laws and roles you can dramatically alter the therapeutic effect on the people that come into contact with the system.

His understanding of therapeutic jurisprudence is fully in keeping with that of the therapeutic jurisprudence theorists, though it clearly emphasizes the norma-

NOTES TO CHAPTER 8

tive rather than the analytic feature of therapeutic jurisprudence. How, practically, does this theoretical model work itself out in drug court? Judge Schma posits,

> When you are dealing with nothing but an addict, instead of throwing him into the criminal system, throw him into a therapeutic system, for example, a drug court. And deal with him therapeutically. And of course the outcome is totally different. You have the chance to cure an addict. You also have the chance to save society a ton of money. . . . The anti-therapeutic way, even if he is found guilty, and even if he is punished, as soon as he can get out he's back on the street because he is not cured. That's stupid, we're not structuring our system properly when we allow that to happen.

40. David Wexler and Bruce Winick, "Introduction" in *Law in a Therapeutic Key*, xvii.

41. "A Matter of Just Treatment: Substance Abuse and the Courts" (Final Report, Supreme Judicial Court Substance Abuse Project Task Force, State Justice Institute, March 1995), 7.

42. Ibid. 10.

43. Boldt, "Rehabilitative Punishment," 1241.

44. Lewis, "The Humanitarian Theory of Punishment," 224.

45. *Struggle for Justice*, 148.

46. Allen, *The Decline of the Rehabilitative Ideal*, 46.

47. Boldt, "Rehabilitative Punishment," 1216.

48. McColl, "Baltimore City's Drug Treatment Court," 503.

49. Hora et al., "Therapeutic Jurisprudence," 522.

50. Ibid., 523.

51. Ibid., 522.

52. Ibid., 523.

53. Satel, "Observational Study of Courtroom Dynamics," 52.

54. Hora et al., "Therapeutic Jurisprudence," 523. Earlier in the same article, the authors describe sanctions imposed in drug court as "smart punishment" but then argue that "smart punishment is not really punishment at all, but a therapeutic response to the realistic behavior of drug offenders in the grip of addiction" (470).

55. *Struggle for Justice*, 147.

56. Lewis, "The Humanitarian Theory of Punishment," 227.

57. Allen, *The Decline of the Rehabilitative Ideal*, 51.

58. Hora et al., "Therapeutic Jurisprudence," 470.

59. Ibid., 523.

60. Ibid.

61. Hora et al. state, "The defense counsel should view the DTC process as the best method for 'ending the cycle of drugs and crime [which] is in the best interest[s] of the client' " (Hora et al., "Therapeutic Jurisprudence," 523).

62. Kennedy, "Toward a New System of Criminal Sentencing," 360; and *Struggle for Justice*, 93.

63. Boldt, "Rehabilitative Punishment," 1230.

64. *Struggle for Justice*, 29.

65. Morris, *The Future of Imprisonment*, 34.

66. "Drug Court USA," pres. David Jessel, prod. Susan Marling (BBC Radio 4, 1999).

67. Boldt, for example, observes that "variation in outcomes is entirely consistent with the design of modern drug treatment courts, which tends to link decisions regarding the imposition of incarcerative sentences and length of supervision to the performance of offender in treatment" ("Rehabilitative Punishment," 1232).

68. McColl, "Baltimore City's Drug Treatment Court," 497.

69. Hora et al., "Therapeutic Jurisprudence," 469.

70. Ibid., 518.

71. "As in other indeterminate sentencing situations, it is a peculiar phenomenon that the time for treatment can be far longer than the jail sentence normally given" (McColl, "Baltimore City's Drug Treatment Court," 503).

72. Rothman, *Conscience and Convenience*, 232.

73. *Struggle for Justice*, 95. Francis Allen similarly notes that "the assumption of benevolent purpose in penal regimes with strong rehabilitative bents sometimes undermines systems of criminal procedure based on the conception of individual rights" (*The Decline of the Rehabilitative Ideal*, 48).

74. Lewis, "The Humanitarian Theory of Punishment," 225.

75. Boldt, "Rehabilitative Punishment," 1255.

76. "Waiver and Preliminary Hearing and Speedy Trial" (The Twenty-Second Judicial District, State of Oklahoma, Drug Court Division), 1.

77. Ibid., 2.

78. "Drug Court Agreement and Waiver: Diversion & Probation" (Second Judicial District County of Bernalillo, State of New Mexico), 1.

79. Ibid., 3.

80. Ibid., 3.

81. "Placer County Drug Court Participant Agreement" (Placer County, California Drug Court, 15 September 1995), A9.

82. Hora et al., "Therapeutic Jurisprudence," 521.

83. Ibid., 513.

84. Ibid., 514; see also 512.

85. Ibid., 512.

86. For perhaps the most comprehensive discussion of the efficacy of coerced treatment, see Satel, *Drug Treatment*. For other discussions of the issue, see Satel, "Observational Study of Courtroom Dynamics," 53; and McColl, "Baltimore City's Drug Treatment Court," 476.

87. "Defining Drug Courts: The Key Components" (Drug Courts Program Office, Office of Justice Programs, U.S. Dept. of Justice, January 1997), 9, citing R. Hubbard, M. Marsden, J. Rachal, H. Harwood, E. Cavanaugh, and H. Ginzburg, *Drug Abuse Treatment: A National Study of Effectiveness* (Chapel Hill: University of North Carolina Press, 1989).

88. Hora et al., "Therapeutic Jurisprudence," 516.

89. Ibid., 515.

90. Ibid., 515–16.

91. Ibid., 516.

92. Lewis, "The Humanitarian Theory of Punishment," 229.

93. Rothman, *Conscience and Convenience*, 254.

94. Ibid., 256.

95. Johnson and Waletzko, "Drugs and Crime," 206.

96. Hoffman, "The Drug Court Scandal," 1502.

97. Ibid., 1503.

98. Jeff Leen and Don Van Natta, Jr., "Drug Court: Favored by Felons," *The Miami Herald*, 29 August 1994, 1A, 6–7A. For a discussion of this report in relation to the net-widening effect, see also Hora et al., 519–20.

99. Others have observed this quality as well. See, for example, McColl, "Baltimore City's Drug Treatment Court," 503.

100. As cited in Boldt, "Rehabilitative Punishment and the Drug Treatment Court Movement," 1213, fn39.

101. Tauber, "The Future of Drug Courts," 90.

102. Judith S. Kaye, "Lawyering for a New Age," *Fordham Law Review* 67 (October 1998): 5. Coercive measures such as these are common in new "Family Drug Courts," which have been established not only in New York but also in Michigan, Nevada, Missouri, and Florida. As Sally Satel observes, "These new institutions are notable because they are determined to use incentives such as child custody, visitation privileges, and the removal of children from homes as leverage to compel parents to comply with drug treatment and remain drug-free" (*Drug Treatment: The Case for Coercion*, 37).

103. Hora et al., "Therapeutic Jurisprudence," 520.

104. This terminology is from Barbara Wootton, *Crime, Responsibility, and Prevention* (1963), 169, as quoted in McColl: "Wootton thus recommended that the distinction between criminal justice and the medical system must 'wither away'" (McColl, "Baltimore City's Drug Treatment Court," 493).

105. Lewis, "The Humanitarian Theory of Punishment," 226.

106. Allen, *The Decline of the Rehabilitative Ideal*, 55.

107. Nolan, *The Therapeutic State*, 101–3. Richard Boldt likewise observes: "Indeed prominent in all the public efforts to establish and fund [drug courts] has been the rhetoric of utility and savings promised by an approach designed to clear court dockets and relieve prison overcrowding" (Boldt, "Rehabilitative Punishment," 1244).

108. Lewis, "The Humanitarian Theory of Punishment," 229.

109. See Nolan, "Acquiescence or Consensus," 107–29. Consider also that counter movements against therapeutic efforts to recover false memories likewise resorted to therapeutic categories. "Thus, the leading social-movement organization challenging recovered-memory therapies, the False Memory Syndrome Foundation (FMSF), argues that patients who recover memories have been victimized by their therapists, and suffer from 'false memory syndrome.' This term enrages victim advocates, who charge that the FMSF has illegitimately seized medical language to make a political argument" (Best, *Random Violence*, 116).

110. Satel, "Observational Study of Courtroom Dynamics in Selected Drug Courts," 55.

111. See Susan Turner, Peter Greenwood, Terry Fain, and Elizabeth Deschenes, "Perceptions of Drug Court: How Offenders View Ease of Program Completion, Strengths and Weaknesses, and the Impact on Their Lives," *Na-*

tional Drug Court Institute Review 2 (Summer 1999): 61–86; and Cooper et al.,
"Drug Courts: 1997 Overview."

112. Cooper et al., "Drug Courts: 1997 Participant Perspectives," 92.
113. Ibid., 96.
114. Ibid., 93.
115. Ibid., 97–8.
116. Ibid., 99.
117. Ibid., 100.

Selected References

Ainsworth, Janet E. "Re-Imagining Childhood and Reconstructing the Legal Order: The Case for Abolishing the Juvenile Court." *North Carolina Law Review* 69 (1991): 1083–1133.

Allen, Francis. *The Decline of the Rehabilitative Ideal: Penal Policy and Social Purpose.* New Haven: Yale University Press, 1981.

Allison, J.W.F. *A Continental Distinction in the Common Law: A Historical and Comparative Perspective on English Public Law.* Oxford: Clarendon Press, 1996.

"Alternatives to Incarceration for Drug-Abusing Offenders." Developments in the Law. *Harvard Law Review* 111 (May 1998): 1898–1921.

Bakalar, James B., and Lester Grinspoon. *Drug Control in a Free Society.* Cambridge: Cambridge University Press, 1984.

Baumeister, Roy F., Laura Smart, and Joseph M. Boden, "Relation of Threatened Egotism to Violence and Aggression: The Dark Side of High Self-Esteem." *Psychological Review* 101, no. 1 (1995): 5–33.

Bean, Philip. *The Social Control of Drugs.* London: Martin Robertson, 1974.

———. *Punishment: A Philosophical and Criminological Commentary.* Oxford: Martin Robertson, 1981.

———. "New Developments in the US Drug Courts." *Drugs: Education, Prevention and Policy* 3, no. 2 (1996): 211–13.

———. "America's Drug Courts: A New Development in Criminal Justice." *Criminal Law Review* (October 1996): 718–21.

———. "Transplanting the USA's Drug Courts to Britain." *Drugs: Education, Prevention and Policy* 5, no. 1 (1998): 101–4.

Beattie, J. M. *Crime and the Courts in England, 1660–1800.* Princeton: Princeton University Press, 1986.

Becker, Howard. *Outsiders.* New York: The Free Press, 1963.

Belenko, Steven. "Research on Drug Courts: A Critical Review." *National Drug Court Institute Review* 1 (Summer 1998): 1–42.

Benford, Robert D., and Scott A. Hunt. "Dramaturgy and Social Movements: The Social Construction and Communication of Power." In *Social Movements: Critiques, Concepts, Case-Studies.* Edited by Stanford M. Lyman, 84–109. New York: New York University Press, 1995.

Best, Joel. *Random Violence: How We Talk About New Crimes and New Victims.* Berkeley: University of California Press, 1999.

Black, Donald. *The Behavior of Law.* New York: Academic Press, 1976.

Blecker, Robert. "Haven of Hell? Inside Lorton Central Prison." *Stanford Law Review* 42 (1990): 1149–1218.

Blomberg, Thomas G., and Stanley Cohen, editors. *Punishment and Social Control: Essays in Honor of Sheldon L. Messinger.* New York: Aldine de Gruyter, 1995.

Boldt, Richard. "Rehabilitative Punishment and the Drug Treatment Court Movement." *Washington University Law Quarterly* 76 (1998): 1205–1306.

Brooks, Peter, and Paul Gewirtz, editors. *Law's Stories: Narrative and Rhetoric in Law*. New Haven: Yale University Press, 1996.

Burnham, John C. *Bad Habits: Drinking, Smoking, Taking Drugs, Gambling, Sexual Misbehavior, and Swearing in American History*. New York: New York University Press, 1993.

Chriss, James J., editor. *Counseling and the Therapeutic State*. New York: Aldine de Gruyter, 1999.

Cohen, Stanley. "The Punitive City: Notes on the Dispersal of Social Control," *Contemporary Crises* 3 (1979): 339–63.

Cohen, Stanley, and Andrew Scull. *Social Control and the State*. New York: St. Martin's Press, 1983.

Cooper, Caroline, Shanie R. Bartlett, Michelle A. Shaw, and Kayla K. Yang. "Drug Courts: 1997 Overview of Operational Characteristics and Implementation Issues." Drug Court Clearinghouse and Technical Assistance Project, Office of Justice Programs, U.S. Department of Justice, 1997.

Courtwright, David Todd. "Opiate Addiction in America, 1800–1940." Dissertation presented at Rice University, 1979.

Cupit, Geoffrey. *Justice as Fittingness*. Oxford: Clarendon Press, 1996.

Davis, Joseph E., editor. *Stories of Change: Narrative and Social Movements*. New York: SUNY Press, 2001.

"Defining Drug Courts: The Key Components." U.S. Department of Justice, Office of Justice Programs, Drug Courts Program Office, 1997.

Delgado, Richard. "Storytelling for Oppositionists and Others: A Plea for Narrative." *Michigan Law Review* 87 (1989): 2411–41.

Dostoyevsky, Fyodor. *Crime and Punishment*. Translated by Sidney Monas. New York: New American Library, 1968.

Drug Addiction: Crime or Disease? Interim and Final Reports of the Joint Committee of the American Bar Association and the American Medical Association on Narcotic Drugs. Introduction by Alfred R. Lindesmith. Bloomington: Indiana University Press, 1969.

"Drug Courts: Overview of Growth, Characteristics, and Results." Report to the Committee on the Judiciary, House of Representatives. United States General Accounting Office, July 1997.

Duster, Troy. *The Legislation of Morality: Law, Drugs, and Moral Judgment*. New York: Free Press, 1970.

Eldridge, William Butler. *Narcotics and the Law: A Critique of the American Experiment in Narcotic Drug Control*. Chicago: University of Chicago Press, 1967.

Erikson, Kai T. *Wayward Puritans: A Study in the Sociology of Deviance*. New York: Macmillan, 1966.

Ewing, A. C. *The Morality of Punishment*. London: Kegan Paul, Trench, Trubner & Co., 1929.

Eyerman, Ron, and Andrew Jamison. *Social Movements: A Cognitive Approach*. University Park: Pennsylvania State University Press, 1991.

Feinberg, Joel. *Doing and Deserving: Essays in the Theory of Responsibility.* Princeton: Princeton University Press, 1970.

Fine, Gary. "Public Narration and Group Culture: Discerning Discourse in Social Movements." In *Social Movements and Culture.* Edited by Hank Johnston and Bert Klandermans. Minneapolis: University of Minnesota Press, 1995.

Fisher, Seymour, and Alfred M. Freedman, editors. *Opiate Addiction: Origins and Treatment.* New York: John Wiley & Sons, 1973.

Foucault, Michel. *Discipline and Punish: The Birth of the Prison.* New York: Vintage Books, 1979.

Friedman, Lawrence. *A History of American Law.* New York: Simon and Schuster, 1973.

———. *Crime and Punishment in American History.* New York: Basic Books, 1992.

Friedman, Milton, and Thomas Szasz. *On Liberty and Drugs: Essays on the Free Market and Prohibition.* Washington, D.C.: The Drug Policy Foundation Press, 1992.

Garland, David. *Punishment and Modern Society: A Study in Social Theory.* Chicago: University of Chicago Press, 1990.

———. "Penal Modernism and Postmodernism." In *Punishment and Society Control: Essays in Honor of Sheldon L. Messinger.* Edited by Thomas G. Blomberg and Stanley Cohen, 181–210. New York: Aldine de Gruyter, 1995.

Genders, E., and E. Player. *Grendon: A Study of a Therapeutic Prison.* Oxford: Oxford University Press, 1995.

Glazer, Nathan. "Towards and Imperial Judiciary?" *Public Interest* 41 (1975): 104–23.

Glendon, Mary Ann. *State, Law and Family: Family Law in Transition in the United States and Western Europe.* New York: North-Holland, 1977.

———. *Abortion and Divorce in Western Law: American Failures, European Challenges.* Cambridge: Harvard University Press, 1990.

———. *A Nation Under Lawyers: How the Crisis in the Legal Profession is Transforming American Society.* New York: Farrar, Straus and Giroux, 1994.

———, Michael W. Gordon, and Christopher Osakwe. *Comparative Legal Traditions.* St. Paul: West Publishing Company, 1982.

Glenn, Myra C. *Campaigns Against Corporal Punishment: Prisoners, Sailors, Women, and Children in Antebellum America.* Albany: State University of New York Press, 1984.

Goffman, Erving. *The Presentation of Self in Everyday Life.* New York: Anchor Books, 1959.

Goldkamp, John. "Justice and Treatment Innovation: The Drug Court Movement: A Working Paper of the First National Drug Court Conference." National Institute of Justice, Office of Justice Programs, U.S. Department of Justice, December 1993.

———, and Doris Weiland. "Assessing the Impact of Dade County's Felony Drug Court—Final Report." National Institute of Justice Research Report, August 1993.

Goode, Erich. *Between Politics and Reason: The Drug Legalization Debate*. New York: St. Martin's Press, 1997.

Gusfield, Joseph. *Symbolic Crusade: Status Politics and the American Temperance Movement*. 2nd Edition. Urbana: University of Illinois, 1986.

Hacker, P.M.S., and J. Raz. *Law, Morality, and Society: Essays in Honour of H.L.A. Hart*. Oxford: Clarendon Press, 1977.

Halleck, Seymour. "Responsibility and Excuse in Medicine and Law: A Utilitarian Perspective." *Law and Contemporary Problems* 49 (Summer 1986): 127–46.

Harrell, Adele, and Shannon Cavanagh. "Drug Test Results during the Month Before Sentencing: Preliminary Results from the Evaluation of the D.C .Superior Court Drug Intervention Program for Drug Felony Defendants." Presented at the National Association of Drug Court Professionals Conference, Washington, D.C. 10 May 1996.

Harrell, Adele, and Barbara Smith. "Evaluation of the District of Columbia Superior Court Drug Intervention Program: Focus Group Interviews." Research supported by the National Institute of Justice, January, 1996.

Hart, H.L.A. *Punishment and Responsibility: Essays in the Philosophy of Law*. Oxford: Oxford University Press, 1968.

Hart, Henry M. "The Aims of Criminal Law," *Law and Contemporary Problems* 23 (1958): 401–41.

Hegel, Georg Wilhelm Friedrich. *Philosophy of Right*. Translated by T. M. Knox. Oxford: Clarendon Press, 1942.

Herman, Ellen. *The Romance of American Psychology: Political Culture in the Age of Experts*. Berkeley: University of California Press, 1995.

Hewitt, John P. *The Myth of Self-Esteem: Finding Happiness and Solving Problems in America*. New York: St. Martin's Press, 1998.

Hoffman, Morris. "The Drug Court Scandal." *North Carolina Law Review* 78 (June 2000): 1437–1534.

Holmes, Oliver Wendall, Jr. *The Common Law*. Boston: Little, Brown, and Company, 1881.

Hora, Peggy Fulton, William G. Schma, and John T. A. Rosenthal. "Therapeutic Jurisprudence and the Drug Treatment Court Movement: Revolutionizing the Criminal Justice System's Response to Drug Abuse and Crime in America." *Notre Dame Law Review* 74 (January 1999): 439–538.

Hora, Peggy Fulton, and William G. Schma. "Drug Treatment Courts: Therapeutic Jurisprudence in Practice." *Judicature* 82 (July–August 1998): 1–6.

Horwitz, Allan. "Therapy and Social Solidarity." *Toward a General Theory of Social Control*. Vol. 1. Edited by Donald Black. New York: Academic Press.

Ignatieff, Michael. "State, Civil Society and Total Institutions: A Critique of Recent Social Histories of Punishment." In *Social Control and the State*. Edited by Stanley Cohen and Andrew Scull, 75–105. New York: St. Martin's Press, 1983.

Inciardi, James A., and Carl D. Chambers, editors. *Drugs and the Criminal Justice System*. London: Sage, 1984.

Inciardi, James A., editor. *The Drug Legalization Debate*. London: Sage, 1991.

Inglis, Brian. *The Forbidden Game: A Social History of Drugs*. London: Hodder and Stoughton, 1975.

Jackson, Kathryn N. "Punishment as Therapy: A Reply to Halleck." *Law and Contemporary Problems* 49 (Summer 1986): 147–59.

Johnston, Hank, and Bert Klandermans. *Social Movements and Culture*. Minneapolis: University of Minnesota Press, 1995.

Johnson, John M., and Linda Waletzko. "Drugs and Crime: A Study of the Medicalization of Crime Control." In *Perspectives on Social Problems*, volume 3, 197–219, edited by James A. Holstein and Gale Miller. Greenwich, CT: JAI Press, 1992.

Kaminer, Wendy. *Its all the Rage: Crime and Culture*. New York: Addison-Wesley, 1995.

Kanof, Abram. "Uriah Levy: The Story of a Pugnacious Commodore." *Publications of the American Jewish Historical Society* 39 (Sept. 1949–June 1950): 1–66.

Kant, Immanuel. *The Metaphysical Elements of Justice*. Translated by John Ladd. New York: Macmillan, 1965.

Kennedy, Edward M. "Toward a New System of Criminal Sentencing: Law with Order." *The American Criminal Law Review* 16 (September 1979): 353–82.

Kittrie, Nicholas N. *The Right to be Different: Deviance and Enforced Therapy*. Baltimore, MD: Penguin Books, 1971.

Krafft, Herman F. "Secretary's Notes: The Navy and Flogging." *United States Naval Institute Proceedings*, 55, nos. 311–322 (1929): 270–73.

Kramer, Rita. *Ed School Follies*. New York: The Free Press, 1991.

Larana, Enrique, Hank Johnston, and Joseph R. Gusfield. *New Social Movements: From Ideology to Identity*. Philadelphia: Temple University Press, 1994.

Larimore, Granville W., and Brill, Henry. "The British Narcotic System, Report of Study." *New York State Journal of Medicine* 60 (January 1960): 107.

Lewis, C. S. "The Humanitarian Theory of Punishment." *Res Judicatae* VI (June 1953): 224–30.

———. "On Punishment: A Reply." *Res Judicatae* VI (February 1954): 368–71.

Lipset, S. M. *Political Man: The Social Bases of Politics*. New York: Anchor Books, 1960.

Llewellyn, Karl. *The Common Law Tradition: Deciding Appeals*. Boston: Little, Brown, 1960.

———. *Jurisprudence: Realism in Theory and Practice*. Chicago: University of Chicago Press, 1962.

Low, Peter W., John Calvin Jeffries, Jr., and Richard Bonnie. *Criminal Law: Cases and Material*. 2nd Edition. New York: The Foundation Press, 1986.

Lyman, Stanford M., editor. *Social Movements: Critiques, Concepts, Case-Studies*. New York: New York University Press, 1995.

Massaro, Toni M. "Empathy, Legal Storytelling, and the Rule of Law: New Words, Old Wounds?" *Michigan Law Review* 87 (1989): 2099–127.

McAdams, Doug. "Culture and Social Movements." In *New Social Movements: From Ideology to Identity*. Edited by Enrique Larana, Hank Johnston, and Joseph R. Gusfield, 36–57. Philadelphia: Temple University Press, 1994.

McColl, William D. "Baltimore City's Drug Treatment Court: Theory and Practice in an Emerging Field." *Maryland Law Review* 55 (1996): 467–518.

McNamara, Peter. *The Noblest Minds: Fame, Honor, and the American Founding.* New York: Rowman and Littlefield, 1999.

Mecca, Andrew, Neil Smelser, and John Vasconcellos. *The Social Importance of Self-Esteem.* Berkeley: University of California Press, 1989.

Morgan, Wayne H. *Drugs in America: A Social History, 1800–1980.* Syracuse, N.Y.: Syracuse University Press, 1981.

Morris, Norval. *The Future of Imprisonment.* Chicago: University of Chicago Press, 1974.

———, and Donald Buckle. "The Humanitarian Theory of Punishment: A Reply to C. S. Lewis," *Res Judicatae* VI (June 1953): 231–37.

———, and Gordon Hawkins. *Letter to the President on Crime Control.* Chicago: University of Chicago Press, 1977.

Murphy, Sheila M. "Therapeutic Jurisprudence: Its Time Has Come." *Trial Judges News* (Winter 1997/1998): 3.

Murphy, Walter F., and C. Herman Pritchett. *Courts, Judges, and Politics: An Introduction to the Judicial Process.* New York: Random House, 1986.

Musto, David F. *The American Disease: Origins of Narcotics Control.* New Haven: Yale University Press, 1973.

Nolan, James L., Jr. *The Therapeutic State: Justifying Government at Century's End.* New York: New York University Press, 1998.

———. "Acquiescence or Consensus: Consenting to Therapeutic Pedagogy." In *Counseling and the Therapeutic State.* Edited by James J. Chriss, 107–29. New York: Aldine de Gruyter (1999).

Peele, Stanton. *Diseasing of America: Addiction Treatment Out of Control.* Lexington, Mass.: Lexington Books, 1989.

Platt, Anthony M. *The Child Savers: The Invention of Delinquency.* Chicago: University of Chicago Press, 1977.

Plucknett, Theodore F. T. *A Concise History of the Common Law.* Rochester, N.Y.: The Lawyers Cooperative Publishing Company, 1929.

Polsky, Andrew J. *The Rise of the Therapeutic State.* Princeton: Princeton University Press, 1991 .

Pound, Roscoe. "What is the Common Law?" In *The Future of the Common Law*, 3–23. Cambridge: Harvard University Press, 1937.

Rawls, John. *A Theory of Justice.* Cambridge, Mass.: Belknap Press.

"Report on the Committee on the Narcotic Drug Situation in the United States." *Journal of the American Medical Association* 74 (8 May 1920): 1324–28.

Rheinstein, Max. *Max Weber on Law in Economy and Society.* Cambridge: Harvard University Press, 1954.

Rice, John Steadman. *A Disease of One's Own: Psychotherapy, Addiction, and the Emergence of Co-Dependency.* New Brunswick, N.J.: Transaction, 1998.

Rieff, Philip. *The Triumph of the Therapeutic.* Chicago: University of Chicago Press, 1966.

———. *Fellow Teachers: of Culture and Its Second Death.* Chicago: University of Chicago Press, 1972.

Rothman, David J. *The Discovery of the Asylum: Social Order and Disorder in the New Republic.* Boston: Little, Brown and Company, 1971.

———. *Conscience and Convenience: The Asylum and its Alternatives in Progressive America.* Boston: Little, Brown and Company, 1980.

Rublowsky, John. *The Stoned Age: A History of Drugs in America.* New York: G.P. Putnam's Sons, 1974.

Sandel, Michael. *Liberalism and the Limits of Justice.* 2nd edition. Cambridge: Cambridge University Press, 1998.

Satel, Sally. *Drug Treatment: The Case for Coercion.* Washington, D.C.: AEI Press, 1999.

———. "Observational Study of Courtroom Dynamics in Selected Drug Courts." *National Drug Court Institute Review* 1 (Summer 1998): 43–72.

Schur, Edwin M. "Drug Addiction in America and England." *Commentary* 30 September (1960): 241–48.

———. *Narcotic Addiction in Britain and America: The Impact of Public Policy.* Bloomington: Indiana University Press, 1962.

Sher, George. *Desert.* Princeton: Princeton University Press, 1987.

Smart, J.J.C. "Comment: The Humanitarian Theory of Punishment." *Res Judicatae* VI (February 1954): 368–71.

Smelser, Neil. *Theory of Collective Behavior.* New York: Free Press, 1962.

Spierenburg, Peter. "From Amsterdam to Auburn: An Explanation for the Rise of the Prison in Seventeenth-Century Holland and Nineteenth-Century America." *Journal of Social History* 20 (Fall 1986): 439–61.

Struggle for Justice. A Report on Crime and Punishment in America. Prepared for the American Friends Service Committee. New York: Hill & Wang, 1971.

Sutton, John R. "Therapeutic Justice: The Legal Construction of Deviant Persons." In *Social Structures and Human Lives.* Edited by Matilda White Riley, 63–82. Newbury Park, Cal.: Sage, 1988.

Sutton, John R. *Stubborn Children: Controlling Delinquency in the United States, 1640–1981.* Berkeley: University of California Press, 1988.

Szasz, Thomas. *Ceremonial Chemistry: The Ritual Persecution of Drugs, Addicts, and Pushers.* Holmes Beach, Fla.: Learning Publications, 1985.

Tauber, Jeffrey S. "A Judicial Primer on Drug Courts and Court-Oriented Drug Rehabilitation Programs." Presented at the California Continuing Judicial Studies Program. Dana Point, California, 20 August 1993.

Terry, Charles E., and Mildred Pellens. *The Opium Problem.* New York: The Committee on Drug Addiction in collaboration with The Bureau of Social Hygiene, 1928.

Terry, W. Clinton. "Broward County Drug Court: A Preliminary Report." November 1993.

Tice, Patricia. *Altered States: Alcohol and Drugs in America.* Rochester, N.Y.: The Strong Museum, 1992.

Tocqueville, Alexis de. *Democracy in America.* Vol. 1. New York: Vintage Books, 1945.

Von Hirsch, Andrew. *Doing Justice: The Choice of Punishments.* Boston: Northeastern University Press, 1986.

Weber, Max. *Economy and Society*. Vols. 1 and 2. Edited by Guenther Roth and Claus Wittich. Berkeley: University of California Press, 1978.

Weinreb, Lloyd L. "Desert, Punishment, and Criminal Responsibility." *Law and Contemporary Problems* 49 (Summer 1986): 47–80.

Weitzman, Jamey. "Drug Courts: A Manual for Planning and Implementation." A manual published with support from the American Bar Association.

Wexler, David B., and Bruce Winick. *Essays in Therapeutic Jurisprudence*. Durham: Carolina Academic Press, 1991.

———, editors. *Law in a Therapeutic Key: Developments in Therapeutic Jurisprudence*. Durham: Carolina Academic Press, 1996.

Wolf, Simon. "Biographical Sketch of Commodore Uriah P. Levy." *The American Jewish Year Book* 5663 (October 2, 1902–September 21, 1903): 42–45.

Index